Phenomena

Phenomenal Reading

Essays on Modern and Contemporary Poetics

Brian M. Reed

THE UNIVERSITY OF ALABAMA PRESS
Tuscaloosa

Typeface: Minion & Stone Sans
Cover design by Burt&Burt

∞

The paper on which this book is printed meets the minimum requirements of American National Standard for Information Sciences—Permanence of Paper for Printed Library Materials, ANSI Z39.48-1984.

Library of Congress Cataloging-in-Publication Data

Reed, Brian M.
Phenomenal reading : essays on modern and contemporary poetics / Brian M. Reed.
p. cm. — (Modern & contemporary poetics)
Includes bibliographical references and index.
ISBN 978-0-8173-5694-1 (pbk. : alk. paper) — ISBN 978-0-8173-8601-6 (electronic)
1. Poetics. 2. Literature, Modern—20th century—History and criticism. 3. Literature, Modern—21st century—History and criticism. I. Title.
PN1042.R39 2012
808.1—dc23

2011034717

I would like to thank all of the editors, journals, and presses involved in the publication of earlier versions of chapters 1 to 11. "Carl Sandburg's The People, Yes, Thirties Modernism, and the Problem of Bad Political Poetry," *Texas Studies in Language and Literature* 46.2 (Summer 2004): 181–212. "Carry on England: Tom Raworth's 'West Wind,' Intuition, and Neo-Avant-Garde Poetics," *Contemporary Literature* 47.2 (Summer 2006): 170–206. "Ezra Pound's Utopia of the Eye: The Chinese Characters in the Rock-Drill Cantos," *Paideuma* 26 (Fall-Winter 1997): 111–21. "Now Not Now: Gertrude Stein Speaks," *English Studies in Canada* 33.4 (Dec. 2007): 103–13. "The Baseness of Robert Grenier's Visual Poetics," *Verdure* no. 3–4 (Winter-Spring 2001): 67–70. "'Lost Already Walking': Caroline Bergvall's 'Via,'" *Jacket* no.34 (Oct. 2007): n.p. "Modernist Ohio: Hart Crane and the Challenge of Akron," *Hiram Poetry Review* no. 69 (Spring 2008): 47–62. "Robert Duncan and Gertrude Stein from *Writing Writing* to *Ground Work II*," *(Re:)Working the Ground: Essays on the Late Writings of Robert Duncan*, ed. James Maynard (New York: Palgrave, 2011) "Reginald Shepherd at Hart Crane's Grave," *Callaloo* 32.4 (Fall 2009): 1274–92. "Splice of Life: Rosmarie Waldrop Renews Collage," *How2* no. 8 (Fall 2002): n.p. "The Time Has Come to Talk of Queens: John Ashbery's 'Coma Berenices,'" *Seattle Review* 1.1 (Summer 2007): 159–77.

To Jody, Laura, Rebecca, and Nick.
Primite s ulybkoiu, moi druz'ia,
svobodnoi muzy prinoshen'e.

Contents

Preface

How Reed Wrote Certain of His Essays

Beginning Again

This book gathers twelve essays written over a twelve-year span. Eleven of them were published previously in a range of different venues, from ezines to refereed journals. Each essay focuses on one or more twentieth- or twenty-first-century poets known for formal and linguistic experiment. Together, they offer a discontinuous partial overview of several storylines: modernism's unpredictable shifts and self-reinventions, the links between the historical and neo-avant-gardes, and collaboration between poets and artists working in other media. The account might be slightly off-center—gay men and women predominate—but the goal is less revisionism than affirmation. Here are writers worth reading. "Taste them and try . . . Sweet to tongue and sound to eye" (Rossetti 2).

A Body Does Get Around

The oldest essay in this book dates back to my time as a graduate student at Stanford University during the height of the dotcom boom. I had the opportunity to study with such eminent scholars as Terry Castle, George Dekker, Albert Gelpi, Robert Harrison, Seth Lerer, Diane Middlebrook, Stephen Orgel, and Jeffrey Schnapp. Above all, I had the chance to work with Marjorie Perloff. From "Introduction to Graduate Studies" to my dissertation defense, she was my mentor; she taught me to write and think as a literary critic. Over the last decade, she has remained an adviser, an interlocutor, and a constant inspiration. Her imprint will be obvious throughout *Phenomenal Reading*.

Less obvious might be the rhetorical agenda that unites these essays, which can in fact be traced back to a moment of insight that predates my arrival in the Bay Area. It happened in November 1992, just before Thanksgiving. I had just begun a two-year stint at Oxford University, and I was on a mission to see everything included in the *Lonely Planet* guide. Near the top of the list was the Tate Gallery, at the time still a one-stop pilgrimage site for aspiring art snobs. (The Tate Modern did not open until 2000.) Here is how I described my first visit to my parents in a letter:

> Saturday I (big surprise) went into London (for the fifth time). I saw the Tate Gallery, a big art museum with lots of British paintings from Q Liz I's day to 1992. . . . I wanted to see Francis Bacon's stuff (20th century Brit painter), almost all of which is owned by the Tate, but they had all but one painting in storage, to make way for temporary exhibits like *The Nude in Art* (ranging from pasty women to abstract blobs, very dull) and *British Art During World War II* (looked like a high school show). The best thing by far was a special installation piece by Richard Serra. The middle of the Tate is a long series of three galleries, two elongated rectangular ones connected by an octagonal, column-bedecked one. They had emptied the whole space of paintings, and Serra had put two forty-ton iron shoebox shapes in each of the rectangular galleries. The iron was roughly wrought, nice to the touch and pleasingly irregular, with glorious red/black rust patterns, and the boxes were about six foot tall, so standing on tiptoe I could just barely see over them. The blocks really made you feel the space of the galleries themselves—large, solid presences announced themselves loudly but kind of almost got drowned out by the gulfs around them. They were also the same size as the gap between the columns that led into the octagonal gallery, so the whole thing felt spatially unified, though tension filled at the same time. Cool. (personal correspondence, 26 Nov. 1992)

Everything said here is accurate. I did marvel over Serra's *Weight and Measure* installation, and I was surprised that any single artwork could so decisively transform a person's experience of a remarkably busy architectural space.

I entirely leave out, however, the most important occurrence that day. You see, I wasn't alone. I was exploring the Tate with a new friend, a Rhodes Scholar from Minneapolis. As I scooted from gallery to gallery, she trailed behind me, suspended between bemusement and irritation. By the time we reached the Serra sculptures, she had had enough. I began to praise rust patterns and sight lines. She interrupted me. "They're big slabs of iron. They just sit there. They mean nothing to me." I tried to explain that minimalist sculpture wasn't obscure, that no one needed a degree in art history to appreciate its invitation to attend to space and spatial relations as tangible, physical facts. She interrupted again.

"Brian, you've studied modern art. You know it's okay to behave like some kid discovering the world for the first time. I studied international politics. I have no clue what I'm supposed to think or feel when looking at tons of rusting metal. What's more, I don't care. I'm bored. Can we go now?"

When writing my parents about the Tate Gallery, I omitted my Minnesota friend altogether. Since she appears in virtually every other letter I wrote from 1992 to 1994, I clearly intended the oversight. I didn't want to put into words how uneasy she had made me by putting her finger on a fundamental flaw in my undergraduate education: a blurring of the distinction between a given individual's thoughts, emotions, and experiences and the responses that anyone whatsoever would have when presented with the same situations, events, or texts.

To explain why this accusation was so upsetting, I need to backtrack. When I arrived at Harvard at age eighteen, I wanted to be a biochemist. I was soon converted to the study of literature by a series of unforgettable classes with Helen Vendler. In command of the whole English-language tradition from Geoffrey Chaucer to Seamus Heaney, she taught me that while verse might discuss or touch on the ineffable it is also eminently rational, composed with the rigor and forethought of a good crossword puzzle. Her lectures were dazzling but also logical and practical, accompanied by diagrams, mnemonics, and homey tips ("First, ask yourself . . ."). Poetry, as she presented it, was neither a hermetic nor an elitist art; any moderately literate person should be able to enjoy it. One came away from English 10 terrifically excited, indeed in a mood to proselytize. I remember bullying my roommates into attending John Keats day by saying, "He uses the word *adieu* in all his odes!"

Like many of Vendler's students, I could have followed in her footsteps and committed to the study of her favored writers, among them the Stevens-Ashbery-Graham lineage, the Bishop-Lowell-Plath cluster, and the Merrill pleiade. Many of my classmates went that route, and they have written first-rate criticism. My coursework in art history, however, deflected me, above all a class I took with Jean-Claude Lebensztejn, who was at the time a visiting professor from the Sorbonne. The topic—a general survey of twentieth-century avant-garde visual art—might not sound promising or compelling, but Lebensztejn excels at working with such a large canvas. He presented art history from Paul Cézanne to Brice Marden as a coherent aesthetic and philosophical endeavor. He assigned prodigious amounts of reading, much of it densely theoretical, in addition to what must have been thousands of slides. Tracing spatial, semiotic, and conceptual dilemmas across decades and national boundaries, he revealed unforeseen continuities and untangled knotty controversies. He was also able to begin with detailed commentary about an artwork—what it looks like from different points of view—and build toward giddy statements about the nature of being, the course of modernity, and the fate of humanism.

Lebensztejn introduced me to Continental philosophy, and he persuaded me that twentieth-century avant-garde artists engaged in a fascinating, intricate, erudite dialogue with thinkers in an array of fields, from anthropology to sociology to linguistics. I learned that one does not "apply" Jacques Lacan to Andy Warhol. One inquires into how arguments advanced by a particular Warhol might parallel, diverge from, or critique statements in Lacan's *Écrits* (1966). As the essays in this book demonstrate, my primary means of engaging theoretical texts has remained the visual arts. When asked, for instance, to explain Georges Bataille or Fredric Jameson, I am liable to do so via an example drawn from the history of painting or sculpture.

After such a transformative course of study I had a hard time returning to poets who appeared to lack intellectual ambition or who seemed disinclined to ask fundamental questions about the form and purpose of their writing. Three generations after Marcel Duchamp's readymades, how could anyone continue to write poetry as if the Victorian era had never ended? In the art world, few curators or critics would celebrate as a contemporary master an American or British painter who pretended that modernism had never happened or that the historical avant-gardes had not thrown into question the most basic assumptions about representation, artistic production, and aesthetic accomplishment. While, for instance, I might enjoy and respect a lyric such as Elizabeth Bishop's "In the Waiting Room" (1971)—and while I might perceive its value for discussions about gender, race, and citizenship ("black, naked women . . . Their breasts were horrifying" [159])—it simply could not hold my attention for long when presented with an alternative such as Gertrude Stein's "Susie Asado" (1913), which, while also exploring the relationship between language, exoticism, and desire, nonetheless exhibits a distinctly bolder, estranging sensibility. "Sweet sweet sweet sweet sweet tea" (*Geography* 13) goes Stein's refrain, echoing the fast-clicking footwork of the poem's inspiration, a flamenco dancer named Antonia Mercé y Luque ("La Argentina"). "Sweet SWEET sweet SWEET," coming to a stop, "sweet TEA," amid a shower of puns. The dancer is a "sweetie," a sweetheart, and she is a stimulating "drink." Not just any drink, moreover, but "sweet tea," a Southern delight that Stein likely knew from her years in Baltimore, an iced beverage made by first supersaturating boiling tea with sugar and conjures humid why-move-a-muscle summer days spent sprawling on the porch and sipping what seems the only cold thing in the world. Bishop's poetry might be psychologically acute and ethically insightful, but Stein was by turns thrilling, enigmatic, and forehead-slapping provocative.

My future was sealed one momentous day when I ran into Stephen Burt in the offices of the *Harvard Advocate*. He handed me a copy of the first edition of

Lyn Hejinian's *My Life* (1980). "Take a look at this," he said. "I came across it in the Widener stacks. Thirty seven sentences in each of the thirty seven chapters, all published when the author was thirty seven!" I opened it at random. "The red rose in its redness leaks no yellow" (64). "As for we 'who love to be astonished,' the ear is less active than the eye" (46). "I have been spoiled with privacy, permitted the luxury of solitude. A pause, a rose, something on paper" (29). Here at long last was contemporary writing that could plausibly be set alongside the art anatomized in journals such as *October* and *Artforum* without suffering in comparison. I put aside Rita Dove's *Thomas and Beulah* (1986) and Jorie Graham's *The End of Beauty* (1987)—until then my favorite poetry collections—and searched for more work by the mysterious notorious Language Poets.

As I began to read Hejinian and other post-World War II experimentalists, I again found myself falling back on Lebensztejn's teaching. During his classes he had shown me how to think and talk about strange, resistant, and mystifying works of art. In such instances, he maintained, simple description serves a crucial purpose. By pointing out what you see, sense, feel, or hear, and by ordering those impressions according to a certain scheme, you give your audience something to hang onto. Using this approach, initially enigmatic art quickly loses its perplexing otherness and becomes open to observation, notation, and speculation. Additional patient description can then uncover premises and possibilities that are integral to the artwork. As Louis Marin, a critic often in sympathy with Lebensztejn, once put it, one strives for "a description" of a given work "in its irreducible singularity," bringing to light any underlying "system," rudimentary, partial, or fully elaborated, that "make[s] it coherent" as well as "noncomparable" to any other similar work (293–94).

Here is a concrete example. Preparing to write an essay for Lebensztejn, I went to the Fogg Art Museum and stood for an hour in front of Kenneth Noland's *Hover* (1964), a painting made by "staining thinned pigment onto unsized canvas" (Fried 61). Such a technique leaves neither visible brushstrokes nor any other traces of the human hand. Instead of drawing attention to how it was executed, it places emphasis on the final results, in this case an extraordinary use of color: "the field is wine-red, the small central ellipse steely blue-gray and the elliptical band separating one from the other bright red" (62). I took notes furiously, trying to put into words how the colors pushed and pulled each other, and how they receded or advanced depending on where I stood. Michael Fried has a good account of what it is like to view the painting:

> *Hover* tends to appear dark, subdued and perhaps uninteresting at first glance. It is only after the beholder has looked at it hard for some time that the colors begin to become fully alive, and to involve him in their life. . . . The wine-red field appears to bring intense coloristic pressure to

bear on the central motif; and this pressure seems to account both for its ellipsoid shape as well as for the suspension at the heart of the field. At the same time, the bright red elliptical band seems both to menace the steely inner ellipse (which virtually disappears as we stare at the painting) and to be on the verge of expanding into the field. The result is perilous, constantly changing equilibrium that is at once coloristic and structural. (63)

One could consider such observations preliminary to the real work of a scholar, a trivial get-to-know-the-artwork exercise designed to ease a reader into a wider ranging, less subjective analysis. On the contrary, the optical experience offered by *Hover* has the force of an art-historical argument. It exemplifies and proposes a way of seeing and feeling that differs from other paintings. Unlike much geometric abstraction, *Hover* does not threaten to fade into the background or degrade into mere decoration. The unpleasantly clashing colors, the wine-dark background, and the cheesy bright red foreground are a brash request for attention that would interfere with any viewer's efforts at making a space feel integrated, intimate, or harmonious. It does not, to put it mildly, belong in a living room hung over a fireplace. Moreover, once a viewer does look closely at *Hover*, it blocks efforts to interpret it as a window looking out onto another, illusory reality. Unlike the Mark Rothkos, Jackson Pollocks, and other paintings that the Fogg's curators hung nearby, *Hover* resists being read as if it depicts a spiritual or mythic landscape. The weave of the canvas remains too visible, and the expanses of color are too unvaried, too flat, and too one-note. At the same time, despite the simplicity of its composition, it feels both dynamic and forceful. Noland, like the painters with which he is conventionally grouped (Helen Frankenthaler, Morris Louis, and Jules Olitski), might have a reputation for Apollonian restraint, but *Hover* suggests that an artist can stay true to the two-dimensionality of the picture plane without abandoning tension and edginess. Clement Greenberg famously characterized the 1960s "post-painterly" abstraction of Frankenthaler and company as exhibiting "clarity," "lucidity," and "openness" (195–96); if, however, one chooses *Hover* instead of works such as Frankenthaler's *Flood* (1967), Louis's *Claustral* (1961), and Olitski's *Tin Lizzie Green* (1964) to represent the genre, Greenberg's generalizations seem off-key, perhaps an attempt to sideline troublesome defiance in favor of luminous calm.

From observation to argument, in nice neat sweet neat sweet steps.

Road Block

When I visited the Tate Gallery in November 1992, my Minnesota friend's comments threw me for a loop partly because she challenged my default means of approaching, appreciating, and interpreting modern and contemporary art. As my letter shows, I was energized by Serra's *Weight and Measure*. It gave me license to walk around, to squint, to peer, to stand on my toes; in short it gave me a reason to inhabit the space in a self-aware and intensely embodied manner. My friend reminded me that such behavior is hardly universally practiced or esteemed, let alone automatic or innate. By that time I had read John Cage's *Silence* (1961), Rosalind Krauss's *Passages in Modern Sculpture* (1977), Michael Fried's "Art and Objecthood" (1967), and Maurice Merleau-Ponty's *Phénomènologie de la perception* (1945). Credentialed authorities told me that minimalist sculpture breaks with the traditional association between sculpture and the representation of the human form. Instead of depicting anything, it intervenes in a space. More specifically, it reconfigures the relationships within a space such that people experience that space newly, differently, and self-consciously. My letter home mischaracterizes a set of learned responses as a spontaneous, intuitive series of reactions. I had been led to expect and celebrate unmediated perception when in fact I was thick in the middle of an olio of discourses, institutions, and habits governing my experience of art.

While disturbing, this realization was only half the story. I could probably have handled matters if it had gone no further. I was already familiar with criticisms of the "transcendental subject" of phenomenology, that is, the assumption that people can make observations about the surrounding world as if from a disinterested Edenic point of view, unmarked and uninflected by their "prior . . . history" and "social conditions" (Eagleton, *Literary Theory* 50). I had even seen Lebensztejn challenged on precisely this point. Near the end of the semester, a group of students interrupted one of his lectures and demanded to know why he had included so few women artists on his syllabus. He awkwardly answered that, with a few exceptions, women had yet to create avant-garde art of sufficient quality or importance to feature in a survey course. It was the late 1980s. Every art student in the auditorium was familiar with such marquee names as Laurie Anderson, Jenny Holzer, Barbara Kruger, and Sherrie Levine. His argument was patently false. After that incident, it became impossible to believe that his aesthetic pronouncements rested solely on pure, unbiased, objective perception and judgment. I would not have reacted as viscerally to my friend's criticisms if she had simply exposed my unacknowledged prejudices and preconceptions.

What truly upset me: I had failed to persuade an intelligent, literate, articulate young woman to think and feel as I did. This lapse sent me tumbling back to square one of my humanities education, before I knew Picasso from Pollock or semiotics from structuralism. My friend had contradicted what I considered to be Vendler's unstated First Law: that any reasonable, educated person is likely to think and feel X or Y, much as you do, when presented with Z and appropriate accompanying explanations, illustrations, and evidence.

Of course, Vendler had never claimed, or even hinted, that such a precept should cover avant-garde experimentation as well as work within more conventional forms and genres, but as my definitions of *reason* and *education* had extended step by step since English 10 to include works such as *Weight and Measure*, I had unconsciously continued to believe that Vendler's Law, too, still applied. "[W]hat I assume you shall assume" (Whitman 24). Yes, my friend might have studied politics instead of art and literature but after I had told her how she was supposed to respond, why did she perversely refuse to do so? She could like or dislike Serra's installation. Ultimately, that didn't matter to me. But to refuse to engage his art, even provisionally, in the prescribed manner? That was preposterous. The problem was theoretical, yes. I had run up against the limits of old-school phenomenology. The problem, though, was pedagogical, too. My nascent sense of vocation was threatened.

How do you persuade adults to read (let alone keep reading and reread) texts sympathetically that at first might entirely fail to move them? Can you coax people into experiencing delight when their inclination is toward frustration, resentment, and boredom? Can you convince them to value feelings of exclusion or incomprehension as preludes to a breakthrough to new levels of appreciation and understanding? Are such goals creepily coercive? Do you risk confusing an insignificant difference in taste (*de gustibus non est disputandum*) with an opportunity for personal enrichment and/or political instruction? To avoid such quandaries, do you pull back and limit yourself to addressing only people who already think and feel as you do? Where would you find such a classroom? And in such a classroom would your lessons be redundant?

ABC 123

Terry Eagleton opens his book *How to Read a Poem* (2007) with a complaint fairly often overheard these days at conferences, in faculty meetings, and in other professional settings:

> I realised that hardly any of the students of literature I encountered . . . practised what I myself had been trained to regard as literary criticism. Like thatching or clog dancing, literary criticism seems to be something of a dying art. Since many of these students are bright and capable enough, the fault would seem to lie largely with their teachers. The truth is that quite a few teachers of literature nowadays do not practice literary criticism either, since they, in turn, were never taught to do so. (1)

Eagleton is combatively aware that expressing such sentiments are liable to make him sound old-fashioned and conservative, not only in terms of disciplinary trends but also in terms of his politics. For this reason, he takes pains to explain that he remains a convinced Marxist critic, and he rightly points out that there is no necessary conflict between an attentive, appreciative, and probing approach to literature and a radical political agenda. Cultural theorists from Bakhtin to Barthes and Jameson all "engage in scrupulously close reading" of literary texts and are "sensitive to questions of literary form." In contrast, though, he asserts, "most students today" have a drastically impoverished sense of the "material density" of language. They appear to think that "paying attention to form" amounts to no more than "saying whether the poem is written in iambic pentameters, or whether it rhymes" (2). "What gets left out" is any acknowledgment of "the *literariness* of the work" (3; his emphasis).

Eagleton's book is intended to help students cease trying to "disembody" poetic discourse in a rush to discover its concealed, buried meaning. He asserts that language is not "a kind of disposable cellophane in which the ideas come ready-wrapped. On the contrary, the language of a poem is *constitutive* of its ideas" (2; his emphasis). And contemplating a lyric's linguistic "thickness" leads one into, not away from, "social experience" and "history," since they provide the indispensable backdrop against which a poem's course and character stand out and acquire significance (164).

A recent special issue of the journal *Representations* (Fall 2009), edited by Stephen Best and Sharon Marcus, suggests that Eagleton's pedagogical argument reflects a broader shift within contemporary literary study. Teachers, of course, have been bemoaning their students' poor reading skills since well before St. Augustine's schoolmaster soundly thrashed him for his lack of progress in learning Greek. Eagleton's version of this age-old lament, however, targets what seems a relatively new problem, an overhasty desire to see through a text to a deeper stratum of significance. What for him spurs a polemic about the classroom has also prompted other professors to reassess what constitute valid research methods and meaningful scholarship. Speaking for their authors, all of whom received their Ph.D.s in English or Comparative Literature in the 1980s and '90s, Best and Marcus explain that:

> [W]e were trained to equate reading with interpretation: with assigning meaning to a set of texts. As scholars formed in the era of interdisciplinarity, we take for granted that the texts we read and interpret include canonical and noncanonical literary works. We also feel licensed to study objects other than literary ones, using paradigms drawn from anthropology, history, and political theory, which themselves borrowed from literary criticism an emphasis on close reading and interpretation after the linguistic turn of the 1970s. (1)

For everyone with this "shared training," the "idea of interpretation" was a "specific type that took meaning to be a hidden, repressed, deep, and in need of detection and disclosure by an interpreter." These academics, believing that they brought to light what had been "hidden, repressed, deep," implicitly cast themselves as diagnosticians, detectives, and truth-speakers, thereby lending their profession seriousness and social significance (1).

Best and Marcus claim that over the last decade, from *Bush v. Gore* onwards, this heroic self-presentation, and the interpretive practices on which it rests, have remained popular, but they have also become increasingly less tenable:

> The assumption that domination can only do its work when veiled, which may once have sounded almost paranoid, now has a nostalgic, even utopian ring to it. Those of us who cut our intellectual teeth on deconstruction, ideology critique, and the hermeneutics of suspicion have often found those demystifying protocols superfluous in an era when images of torture at Abu Ghraib and elsewhere were immediately circulated on the internet; the real-time coverage of Hurricane Katrina showed in ways that required little explication the state's abandonment of its African American citizens; and many people instantly realized as lies political statements such as "mission accomplished." . . . . Where it had become common for literary scholars to equate their work with political activism, the disasters and triumphs of the last decade have shown that literary criticism alone is not sufficient to effect change. (2)

The editors go on to announce a move in the humanities toward modes of analysis that circumvent or explode the old governing binaries of surface/depth, latent/manifest, and symptom/neurosis. Among these approaches, they mention the historical study of "books as things that link their producers, sellers, and users"; "studies of literature" that "attend to the material workings of the brain during the reading process"; "willed, sustained proximity to the text" that does "not seek hidden meaning but focus[es] on unraveling . . . the 'linguistic density' and 'verbal complexity' of literary texts"; "deferring" to texts and either charting one's "affective responses" or reaching through "receptiveness and fidelity" to their claims some ethical insight; and studies "breaking down texts or discourses into their components, or . . . arranging and categorizing texts into larger groups" (9–11).

Best and Marcus, one must admit, offer an overly simplified account of intellectual history. For instance, they badly underplay the influence of deconstruction. In the years that their cohort of professors were coming of age, high profile critics such as Barbara Johnson, Lee Edelman, and Eve Kosofsky Sedgwick were busily exposing, not falling prey to, the dangers of surface/depth binaries. In addition, the argument that one can no longer combine cultural critique and social activism would anger many of today's specialists in African American studies, Asian American studies, American studies, postcolonial theory, feminist theory, and queer studies. Nevertheless, the Fall 2009 special issue of *Representations* does provide an informative, albeit rough-and-ready, overview of the present moment. Its list of newly popular (or newly revived) literary-critical methods might not be complete, but it captures and codifies two undeniable tendencies within contemporary scholarship that eschew symptomatic reading.

First is what Franco Moretti in *Graphs, Maps, Trees* (2005) has called *distant reading*. In part, he has in mind histories of the book, both as a material artifact and as a focal point of social and economic networks. He also looks at the application of techniques more often associated with the social sciences, including statistical and quantitative analysis, to literature. According to Moretti, a critic subjects the "reality of the text," its phenomenal perceptible material and linguistic traits, to a "process of deliberate reduction and abstraction" (4). One could, for instance, restrict textual engagement to mapping place names mentioned in a group of novels, to graphing the total number of new novels released every year for a century, or to analyzing the titles of every novel published in a ten-year span. Such projects avoid the "synecdochic fallacy" common in the humanities, the assumption that a single text or artwork is representative of all cultural production in a period (Perloff, *Poetry* 19). As Moretti explains:

> [A] canon of two hundred novels . . . sounds very large for nineteenth-century Britain (and *is* much larger than the current one), but is still less than one percent of the novels that were actually published: twenty thousand, thirty, no one really knows—and close reading won't help here, a novel a day every day of the year would take a century or so. . . . And it's not even a matter of time, but of method: a field this large cannot be understood by stitching together separate bits of knowledge about individual cases because it *isn't* a sum of individual cases: it is a collective system, that should be grasped as such, as a whole. (Moretti 4; his emphasis)

For critics to grasp the "collective system," they must "distance" themselves from individual texts, concentrate on "fewer elements," and seek a "sharper sense" of those elements' "overall interconnectedness." "From texts to models," as Moretti summarizes the process (1).

Moretti is known as a fiction critic who has authored such influential monographs as *The Way of the World: The Bildungsroman in European Culture* (1987) and *The Modern Epic: The World-System from Goethe to García-Márquez* (1996).

Poetry, though, as Eagleton points out, depends for its effects on sound play, word play, and other localized features of language (*How* 21). Can one disregard these verbal traits and concentrate instead on systemic questions and still speak meaningfully about poetry? Studies as different as Eric Nebeker's work on Renaissance broadsides, Kelwyn Sole's exploration of contemporary South African verse, and Ana Parejo Vadillo's work on Victorian women poets demonstrate that one can do so and do it well. Indeed, Peter Middleton's *Distant Reading: Performance, Readership, and Consumption in Contemporary Poetry* (2005) attempts an intervention comparable to Moretti's in *Graphs, Maps, Trees*. He deemphasizes minute analytic scrutiny of individual works in favor of a combination of reception and performance history, a tracing of what he calls the "long biography" of particular poems (3).

More common within poetry criticism, however, remains the second kind of study that *Representations* surveys, namely, ones that involve "willed, sustained proximity to the text" (Best and Marcus 9). For instance, cognitive poetics has increased in popularity as scholars have sought to explanation the appeal of poetry's elaborate sound and word play using neurology and psychology. Likewise, in the years since Virginia Jackson and Yopi Prins published their manifesto "Lyrical Studies" (1999), debates over the history and nature of the lyric as a genre have provided a horizon for textual inquiry. Marjorie Levinson's "What Is New Formalism?" (2007) catalogues a variety of other relevant approaches, methodologically diverse but united around a "rededication" to the "problematic of form" (560).

Perhaps most typical are studies that argue that poetry cannot be properly understood when separated from the social, cultural, economic, and political milieu that helped shape it. To understand a poem, in other words, requires a reader to shuttle back and forth between a text and its contexts in a reciprocally illuminating process. For many critics, this mode of reading requires no justification; it represents business as usual in the wake of New Historicism. One can find samples of this positivist historicism in such journals as *Eighteenth Century Studies, English Literary History, European Romantic Review, Modern Language Quarterly, Modernism/modernity*, and *Victorian Poetry*. Other critics, such as Rachel Blau DuPlessis, Christopher Nealon, and Herbert Tucker, have proved much more self-aware, and, drawing on critical and cultural theory, they have spoken eloquently about why they pursue "reading strategies that . . . mediate between the historical terrain and the intimate poetic textures of a work" (DuPlessis, *Genders* 1). Essays such as DuPlessis's "Propounding Modernist Maleness" (2002), Nealon's "Camp Messianism" (2004), and Tucker's "Tactical Formalism" (2006), provide road maps for how one can look to historical circumstances to elucidate the ins and outs of a poem's rhetoric and vice versa.

As should be evident, scholarship on poetics in the new millennium has aggressively sought to identify and promote how best to read poetry. The essays in this book belong to this moment in the field's evolution. They draw on different thinkers and variously introduce historical fact in the service of clarifying how particular works of literature are put together and how they produce particular effects. They allow those works to set the bounds of inquiry; none of the pieces attempts to launch into a sustained, generalizable argument about nonliterary topics. Form is not a fetish, but it is a persistent puzzle. Why are these words in this order? What end does this arrangement serve? Why is it striking? Does it give pleasure? How so?

Hooked on a Feeling

The method pursued throughout is loosely phenomenological, that is, concerned with offering "a direct description of our experience as it is," "an account of space, time, and the world as we 'live' them" (Merleau-Ponty vii). Since the mid-1990s, phenomenology, as practiced by Edmund Husserl and later refined by other Continental philosophers, has undergone a widespread resurgence in the humanities. Moreover, whether one is talking about queer phenomenology (Sara Ahmed), phenomenology and new media (Mark B. N. Hansen), phenomenology and dance (Erin Manning), phenomenology and film (Malin Wahlberg), phenomenology and the visual arts (Caroline A. Jones), or phenomenology and literature (Rita Felski), this new scholarship presumes differential embodiment.[1] The perceiving subject has a history and an array of attributes and affiliations that uniquely inflect his or her experience of the world or, to put it more accurately, that prompt the world to disclose itself to him or her in a unique way.

One lesson of this return to phenomenology, particularly as practiced within disability studies, has been the value of narrative as a tool for conveying the intricacy, contingency, and richness of perceptual and affective experience.[2] Narrative can incorporate paradox, accident, and mistake in addition to laying bare causality, logical connection, and the mechanics of moral and ethical judgment. It registers intermittent doubts, changes in perspective, accumulations of knowledge, and alterations in mood. It records facts, counterfactuals, and impossibilities. Deciding what to include and exclude, what to highlight and what to downplay, narrators illustrate their interests, commitments, and zones of ignorance. For all these reasons, a narrative can both educate and persuade a reader. Here, it quietly asserts, is a possible plausible account of an event (or a life or a book) from a particular point of view. Authors can show audiences how they perceive and experience the world, that is, the manner in which, a Heideggerian might say, the world reveals itself to them as a world.

Narratives are also fictions in the etymological sense of the word: [Fr. *fic*-

tion (= Pr. *fiction, ficxio,* Sp. *ficcion*), ad. L. *fiction-em,* n. of action f. *fingēre* to fashion or form]. They are *made* by the teller. The essays in this book all take the form of stories. They present encounters with unusual texts in a tidied-up, more or less condensed fashion. The observations, speculations, and conclusions appear sequentially, as if an act of reading unfurls leisurely, easily, and straightforwardly in a no-space and no-time that also offers an uncanny quick access to illuminating data and pertinent block quotations. Middleton's *Distant Reading* pokes fun at this kind of literary-critical storytelling, which he contrasts with the messy unpredictable intermittent ways in which most people in fact engage poetry (1–2). As well-worn, readily recognized variants on the detective story, however, these essays seek to draw in readers, to entice them into by-ways and across barriers from which they might otherwise shy away. Here, here, and here, this book indicates, are places to which these writers can lead the curious and the open-minded. Explication and contextualization are not in themselves always sufficient to explain to skeptics how and why antirealist and antimimetic writing can be viscerally gripping, affectively powerful, and giddily illuminating in addition to distressing, disorienting, and infuriating. Sometimes skeptics benefit from a tour given by a believer. On such an occasion, they might come to sympathize, perhaps also imagine and conjecture, while also acquiring the background, tools, and resources needed to read with appreciation. Then they decide what next. They can rebut, recoil, or run in an unexpected direction. They can plunge.

Relying on narrative as a means of organizing literary-critical analysis does, however, leave one open to objections from a different quarter. Many of the poets discussed in this book are profoundly suspicious of narrative as a mode of cognition. From Stein to Caroline Bergvall, you can trace a poets' war against the lies that narrative encourages: its pressure to assert connection where there is only coincidence, its imposition of corseting coherence on libratory chaos, its tendency to favor a well-turned plot over the lyrical spots of time and fragments of eternity that cross-cut a linear life and open it outwards into new grand vistas.

In *Content's Dream* (1986) Charles Bernstein instructively addresses the problem of a dissonance between a commitment to radical poetics and the promotion of it via outwardly conventional literary-critical means:

> Different modes of writing, assuming as they do not only different readers but also modes of reading, kinds of information, and areas of investigation, have different domains of communicative and social power, and different limitations of these powers. The relation between the communicative and social power of a mode is always a complex one: the depth of communicative power of some recent verse is severely restricted in terms

of its social power by very limited dissemination, while it is the restriction of the full dimension of communicativeness, by a suppression of the acknowledgement of "modeness," that allows for the mass distribution of much writing whose social power is thereby secured. It seems important to me to break the closed circuit of a *forced* social insularity . . . not by writing a different kind of poetry but by taking a variety of other occasions to speak, to underscore this process of discrediting just what is most of credit, and to illuminate whatever discourse within which one finds oneself, to allow its forms and potential coercions to become apparent—to agitate, to question authority, not only in poetry magazines but in the workplace, the academy, the corridors of intellectual debate. (398–99; his emphasis)

Bernstein speaks here as a poet-critic, and he asserts his right to make tactical use of a variety of genres and discourses "to agitate" on behalf of an avant-garde poetics. Writing in multiple modes grants formally inventive writers a degree of authority that frequently eludes them as well as access to venues from which they are often barred. At the same time, they gain an opportunity to expose the political and aesthetic "limitations" of these more traditional genres, the very defects that often motivate them to pursue innovative form in the first place. They thus overcome the "forced isolation" imposed on artists who stray too far from mainstream expectations—while simultaneously encouraging the wider public that they reach to reevaluate how, when, why, and what they communicate.

I am not a poet-critic. I do not have Bernstein's gift for suturing unlike discourses, nor (to name just two revered examples) am I able to imitate Hejinian's nimble quick lateral thinking or Susan Howe's vertiginous intuitive leaps. The pieces in this book do not appreciably experiment with the format of the expository essay. They do, however, make use of a genre with a modicum of institutional clout, academic poetry criticism, to share projects, sensibilities, and poems that dissent from, express reservations concerning, and outright challenge language-as-usual in the American academia and the culture at large. If readers perceive that gap and would prefer to set these essays aside in favor of works that better exemplify in their warp and woof the values that they espouse, I would happily direct them to *Content's Dream,* Hejinian's *Language of Inquiry* (2000), Howe's *The Birth-mark* (1993), Christian Bök's '*Pataphysics* (2001), John Cage's *M* (1973), Guy Davenport's *Geography of the Imagination* (1981), Steve McCaffery's *North of Intention* (1986), Robert Smithson's *Collected Writings* (1979), and Rosmarie Waldrop's *Dissonance (if you are interested)* (2005). Sometimes readers outgrow familiar stories and are ready for more bracing fare.

Why do I persist in writing such essays when the poets whom I discuss might not highly esteem the results? In "Seja Marginal" (2008) Craig Dworkin amasses sobering data about the current state of poetry publication:

> The Poets House (New York), which aspires to acquire every book of poetry published in America, excluding vanity press publications, has shelved over 20,000 volumes from between the years 1990 and 2006. According to Bowker, the leading data provider to the publishing industry (the same company that assigns ISBN numbers), there were 37,450 poetry and drama titles between 1993 and 2006. Considering only books published during the last year: Poets House catalogued 1,971 titles with a 2006 copyright; Bowker registered 5,486 new titles under the category of poetry; and Amazon lists 9,444 poetry titles with that publication date for sale. (8)

Even excluding "reissues," "reprints," "nursery rhymes and children's books," "'inspirational' verse," "collections of song lyrics," and "thematic collections of light verse," the numbers remain truly daunting, if one aspires to comprehensive knowledge of contemporary poetry (8). A person would have to read several books a day, every day, in an effort to keep up. In addition, poetry today obeys "an economy of massive production without massive consumption." "[M]ore people submit their poetry for publication than purchase the publications of others"; a ratio of forty submitters per subscriber is typical for a "small magazine of modest reputation" (9). The overall impression is of a flood of new work out there, mostly unread, certainly charted in only the most rudimentary fashion.

After this set up, Dworkin considers Moretti's argument for "greater distance and further abstraction," and he acknowledges that such approaches have value, but he warns against any "dream" of an objective confident God's-eye-view "mastery" (14). The numbers suggesting a superabundance of poetry co-exist with statistics detailing its scarcity and the small size of its audience. "A National Endowment for the Arts survey in 2004 found that only 12% of adults had read any poetry in the previous year" (15), and, although there might be a large number of volumes published each year, they rarely have print runs above 1,000 and fewer still sell more than one hundred copies. "An exceptionally successful book of contemporary poetry might attain a readership equivalent to a mid-sized high school" (16). Under such circumstances, Moretti-style distant reading, while it undeniably adds to our knowledge of contemporary poetry's production and distribution, does not automatically help build an audience, academic or otherwise, for the phenomenon that it describes. Why read a systemic study of an activity so marginal that a single billboard on a state highway reaches more people than a "bestselling" volume? Dworkin concludes that "the conditions for poetry in the twenty-first century put increased pressure on its paratexts, those extra-poetic texts that can filter and link even part of the bewildering precession of published titles. That pressure comes to bear on criticism as well—a criticism, as we have seen, that needs to adjust its focus (whether closing in on the linguistic surface of a discrete text or pulling out to view the system of literary activity as a whole), to address the uninitiated, to educate as well as persuade its reader, and, more than ever, to stake its claim with scrupulously open clarity" (21–22). Dworkin advocates an above-board partisan criticism that informs would-be readers what they might want to read and why. When writing about poetry, especially neo-avant-garde poetry, scholars must be like investigative reporters, ferreting out what is of interest and significance, and they must be like sports commentators, explaining for the laity why a quad doesn't win you a gold medal and what the dividing line is in basketball between a charge and a block.

For some, this scenario might sound a little too much like Christina Rossetti's "Goblin Market" (1862). "Come buy our orchard fruits," the goblins cry, "Crab-apples, dewberries, / Pine-apples, blackberries, / Apricots, strawberries;—/ All ripe together / In summer weather" (1). I have no illusions, however, about the power of my writing to *compel* or *force* readers to do or feel anything. (I frequently circle those verbs in student papers and write "oh, if only!" in the margin. What if, for example, Shakespeare really did have the power to compel people to rethink patriarchal, racist, and heteronormative assumptions? I'd spam politicians around the world with extracts from *As You Like It*.) People who read this book can be Lizzies or Lauras. They can listen to the goblins or not. I've done my best to make the fruits tasty. I'll be glad if people are moved to read poetry by, or write about, these or other formally adventurous writers. I'll also be content if they, like my Minnesota friend back in 1992, do not. I've rethought Vendler's Law and rechristened it Vendler's Invitation. "Nobody should experience anything they don't need to, if they don't need [this] poetry bully for them" (O'Hara, *Collected* 498).

Contains Multitudes

The twelve essays in this collection are grouped according to the kinds of narratives that they pursue. First, in a section titled "Political Reading," come two essays—one on Carl Sandburg and 1930s modernism and a second on Tom Raworth and 1980s Thatcherism—that recount how the poets make use of formal devices to teach readers politically progressive ways of interacting with texts. In both cases, these efforts at reeducation become complexly entangled with aesthetics. Sandburg refuses to adhere to conventional notions of literary quality, but in the process he risks so repelling his audience that they turn against the revolution that he advocates. Raworth, too, pursues his poetic principles to extremes, but at times the pressures of the moment push him to qualify his radicalism, which in turn arguably (and paradoxically) results in verse both aesthetically superior and more politically efficacious.

The second section, "Sight and Sound," consists of four short pieces that treat the relationship between image, text, and technology. The topics covered include Ezra Pound's use of Chinese characters in the *Rock Drill* installment of the *Cantos;* Gertrude Stein's experiments with recorded and broadcast sound; Robert Grenier's graffiti-like ballpoint-pen-scribbled visual poems; and Caroline Bergvall's digitally recorded sound poem "Via" (2000).

The third part of the book, "Writers Reading," retells several episodes of intertextual encounter. Chapter 7, "Hart Crane and the Challenge of Akron," investigates how, in the years 1919–1920, the poet worked through and beyond nineteenth-century modes of composition in order to modernize himself. One inspiration, Sherwood Anderson, leads him in the direction of narrative and psychological realism, but then T. S. Eliot's early poetry shows him how to write poetry adequate to life in a Midwestern industrial boomtown. The next two chapters proceed to survey two other stories: Robert Duncan's decades-long immersion in Stein's writings and the end-of-the-century resistant reading of Crane undertaken by the African American poet Reginald Shepherd.

The fourth and final section of *Phenomenal Reading* is titled "Associative Reading," and it gathers three essays that perhaps best illustrate the method informing the whole of the book. They concentrate on particular authors, but each also veers into a discussion of another work from outside the realm of poetry in search of clarification. An analysis of Rosmarie Waldrop's use of collage, for example, leads to a discussion of Konrad Bayer's novel *Der Kopf des Vitus Berings* (1965). A discussion of John Ashbery's poem "Coma Berenices" (2005) proceeds by way of Mark Morris's ballet *The Hard Nut* (1991), and the book concludes with a meditation on Hollis Frampton's structuralist film *Zorns Lemma* (1970) that anchors a survey of twenty-first century efforts to displace free verse with predetermined forms.

These essays might appear under my name, but they are all collaborative works, to a greater or lesser degree. For their editorial acumen, I would like to thank Pam Brown, Andrew Feld, James Maynard, Michael Rozendal, and Demetres Tryphonopoulos. Individual pieces would never have existed without prompting from Albert Gelpi, Ping Guo, and Robert W. Sawyer. I am grateful to several of the poets who corresponded with me before and after the initial publication of these works: Caroline Bergvall, Tom Raworth, Reginald Shepherd, and Rosmarie Waldrop. Throughout these years I have pursued conversations with a number of friends, colleagues, and former students who deserve public thanks:

Robert Archambeau, Rachel Blau DuPlessis, Stephen Burt, Gabrielle Dean, Craig Dworkin, Stephen Fredman, Kornelia Freitag, Alan Golding, Amanda Golding, Michael Golston, Nicholas Halmi, Matthew Hofer, David Huntsperger, Meta DuEwa Jones, Lynn Keller, Angela Kim, Kimberly Lamm, Adalaide Morris, Susan Schultz, Lisa Simon, and Tim Yu. I have also benefited greatly from the support of people closer to home, in the English department at the University of Washington. I am especially thankful to Carolyn Allen, Linda Bierds, Herbert Blau, Jessica Burstein, Gillian Harkins, Jeanne Heuving, Monika Kaup, Heather McHugh, Joe Milutis, Pimone Triplett, and Kathleen Woodward.

Above all, I am indebted to three people. Two are Hank Lazer and Charles Bernstein, who have unfailingly stood behind my work and who both approached me about the possibility of assembling an essay collection. Third is Marjorie Perloff, whose name fittingly both begins and ends the story told in this preface. Her brilliance, generosity, and loyalty have amazed me again and again over the years. Without her, this book would not exist.

Phenomenal Reading

I
POLITICAL READING

1

Carl Sandburg and the Problem of Bad Political Poetry

In September 1936, Archibald MacLeish published a review of Carl Sandburg's book-length poem *The People, Yes* in the leftist journal *New Masses*. MacLeish praises Sandburg as a political visionary:

> *The People, Yes* ought to be required reading for every man in every American metropolis who thinks of himself as a radical. . . . It will teach him that the tradition of the people is not dead in this republic. It will teach him, further, that that tradition is the tradition upon which he must build if he wishes to build a social revolution which will succeed. (25)

The American masses, MacLeish explains, will not rise up until they are persuaded that revolutionary socialism has indigenous roots traceable back to 1776:

> We hold in our hands the growing thing, the true shelter for a great people, and yet it will neither grow nor shelter until it is grafted to the green wood of the people's lives. . . . What [Sandburg] says to those who have attempted to spell the name of their own cause out of the cracked letters of the Liberty Bell is this: Why turn back? Why say the people were right *then*? Why not say the people are right still? . . . He points out the one great tradition in American life strong enough and live enough to carry the revolution of the oppressed. That tradition is the belief in the people. (26; his emphasis)

MacLeish concludes his review with the ringing assertion that "the revolutionary party which can offer to restore the government to the people and which can convince the people of its sincerity in so offering . . . will inherit the history of this country and change it into truth" (27).

Not once does MacLeish comment on Sandburg's poetry *qua* poetry. He includes five long quotations from *The People, Yes,* but he neither praises nor analyzes them. They serve simply to illustrate or advance his argument. A case in point: while discussing the perennial fear of the masses that American politicians have exhibited, he turns to Sandburg for a civics lesson:

> Into the Constitution of the United States they wrote a fear
> In the form of "checks and balances," "proper restraints"
> On the people so whimsical and changeable,
> So variable in mood and weather (52; quoted in MacLeish 26)

Relying on Sandburg solely as an expert in politics, MacLeish evades the awkward duty of evaluating his technique. He does not have to draw attention, for instance, to the clumsy initial inversion ("Into the Constitution . . . they wrote a fear"), nor to the quick, clotted accumulation of four nonparallel prepositional phrases ("Into . . . In . . . On . . . in"). He overlooks both the verbiage (why use *both* "changeable" and "variable"?) and the stale metaphors (of course "weather" and "mood" are "variable"!). In short, MacLeish is guilty of a grievous sin judged by the standards of such contemporary poetry reviewers as Stephen Burt, Nicholas Jenkins, Marjorie Perloff, and Helen Vendler. He lauds Sandburg's content while disregarding its form.[1]

What Explains MacLeish's Crassness?

MacLeish and Sandburg were writing at a moment when, as Cary Nelson has illustrated, the nature and function of modern poetry, and by extension the role of the literary critic, were still greatly contested. When the famous Cleanth Brooks and Robert Penn Warren textbook *Understanding Poetry* first appeared in 1938, its disparagement of the "poetry of social protest" was far from an opinion universally shared among intellectuals (*Revolutionary* 64–65). Not until after World War II did it become accepted wisdom that technique, structure, diction, tone, and other formal aspects are crucial to judging the value of a poem, whereas its overt political and ethical commitments are of secondary importance. For those contemporary literary critics who wish to recover and celebrate the revolutionary leftist tradition in modern American poetry—scholars such as Nelson, Edward Brunner, Joseph Harrington, Walter Kalaidjian, and Michael Thurston—this 1940s and '50s academic consensus on what constitutes poetic merit represents the victory of an ostensibly apolitical formalism that in practice served to bolster a conservative, surveillance-mad Cold War regime. The diverse, vibrant radical poetries of the 1930s, which once flourished in such publications as *New Masses, Daily Worker, Contempo,* and *Anvil,* disappeared almost completely from view, unable to measure up to newly orthodox standards to which they never sought to adhere in the first place.

Nelson and his colleagues have devised a two-prong strategy to convince skeptical modern poetry specialists that the Old Left produced more than "formally conservative, thematically monochromatic, and theoretically wooden" verse rightfully consigned to oblivion (Nelson, *Repression* 102). On the one hand, this school holds that it is patently unjust for today's readers to judge 1930s politically radical art according to purportedly disinterested aesthetic criteria that were in fact originally and expressly instituted to devalue it. To "read noncanonical modern poetry fairly" means that one must "*relearn* how to read modern poetry" as well as rethink "the social meaning of a commitment to studying and disseminating literature" (Nelson, *Revolutionary* 64; his emphasis). On the other hand, these critics are unwilling to do away with the aesthetic as a category altogether. They wish to argue that poetry from the 1930s by the likes of Sol Funaroff, Tillie Olsen, Lola Ridge, Edwin Rolfe, and Genevieve Taggard deserves study because it offers different, differently grounded poetic virtues. As Nelson puts it, "understanding and evaluating noncanonical poems often requires a new and unfamiliar aesthetic vocabulary." One has to learn, for instance, to perceive value not in a poem's originality or autonomy but in its "contribution to a wider field of discourse," as when it "complicates or enhances a larger literary or historical dialogue" (164).

This two-front critical battle—disparaging one slate of evaluative criteria while advocating another—has been met with stiff resistance.[2] After all, there are numerous twentieth-century poems with overt political content—among them W. B. Yeats's "September 1913," W. H. Auden's "September 1, 1939," Robert Hayden's "Middle Passage," Adrienne Rich's "Diving into the Wreck," and Thom Gunn's "The Man with Night Sweats"—that have stood up reasonably well to present-day, post-New Critical demands for formal sophistication. Furthermore, when Nelson attentively, lovingly analyzes Langston Hughes's "Christ in America" or Michael Thurston Edwin Rolfe's "First Love," they demonstrate how steeped they are in the tradition of close reading that they wish to call into question.[3] Yes, elsewhere they discuss and defend a range of noncanonical and ephemeral verse, much of which would never reward *explication de texte,* but their residual faith in the usefulness of the aesthetic as a rubric—however qualified or rearticulated—and their periodic deployment of the very interpretive tools that they wish to historicize and problematize leaves them open to repeated, unwelcome objections that they perversely defend poetry that they couldn't *really* like all that much. Harvey Teres, for example, accuses Walter Kalaidjian of a "betrayal of his own skills as a reader honed over the course of many years" when he labels "inflated doggerel" such as Jack Haynes's "Scottsboro Boys Chant" "elegant and witty" (181).

When studying or discussing politicized poetry from the 1930s the problem of evaluation does almost inevitably arise, but it does not have to take the form of a struggle over its relative merits vis-à-vis canonical, mainline modernism. Such disputes have been productive, but they also tend to tilt over into sterile exchanges of the epithets "elitist" and "propagandist." This article proposes a different approach to the problem of evaluation: an inquiry into (overt, covert, or unintended) reasons why a 1930s poet might depart from standards for poetic accomplishment current then *and* now. The verse in Carl Sandburg's *The People, Yes* is, it must be confessed, rather egregious. Egregious, though, not only when held up to the standards of, say, Seamus Heaney or Jorie Graham, but also, crucially, when measured by a pre–World War II audience's sense of what lyric poetry should be. Yes, Sandburg's language is degraded, demotic, and clunky. So too, he would reply, is public language itself. Fighting for a subjective space apart from the pervasive, invasive discourses of the media and the market is a pyrrhic battle. Poetry, if it is to be modern, progressive, and redemptive, must first immerse itself in the tawdry discourse of industrial capitalism's cultural correlatives, Hollywood, the radio serial, and Madison Avenue.

Carl Sandburg's *The People, Yes* is a prime candidate for illustrating this dynamic, not least because it lacks the romantic allure of much 1930s political poetry. Sandburg was a national celebrity, a New Dealer, and a friend to presidents. Recovering his participation in the "rich cultural moment" of the 1930s may add to the "narrative depth and alternative meaning" that are lacking in treatments of the period in most "major surveys of modern poetry," but one does not come away with the thrill of championing a forgotten yet ideologically pure martyr to the cause of labor (Nelson, *Revolutionary* 61). Hence, there are fewer sentimental and political barriers to conceding the thoroughgoing *badness* of Sandburg's book. Poetry critics, whatever their party affiliations, can agree that *The People, Yes* is eerily mediocre—relentlessly so, over several hundred pages. This agreement permits one to see that the text solicits such an evaluation, only then to teach that such evaluative thinking is misguided. What matters is not taste *per se* but rather the structuration of thought that precedes and governs it, a patterning that in turn depends upon on an economic substrate. The "people" will only free themselves once they cease thinking of themselves as individuals, set aside their arbitrary personal preferences, and take reification to an extreme by uniting as a faceless mass. The people, empowered as a collective, will then "march." Sandburg reveals to us the hard—potentially repellent—truth that successful socialist revolution would require a paradoxical embrace of our alienated condition. Until we are just cogs in the machine, he ambivalently informs us, there can be no machine with the traction and power to overturn the present unjust order.

Who Was Carl Sandburg?

Carl Sandburg occupies a curious position in American literary history. He enjoys a celebrity status in American culture comparable to the likes of Robert Frost and Norman Rockwell. His prize-winning biographies of Abraham Lincoln, his earnest portrayals of Midwestern life, and his *Rootabaga* stories for children have combined in the popular imagination to grant him the image of a benign, plainspoken, apple-pie-wholesome sage. His picture appeared on the covers of *Life* (1938) and *Time* (1939); Bette Davis starred in a stage show celebrating his life and works; and he was a friend and correspondent of Franklin Roosevelt, Harry Truman, Adlai Stevenson, and John F. Kennedy.[4] Poems such as "Chicago" and "Fog" remain fixtures in high school English classes, and Connemara, his two hundred and sixty-four acre North Carolina ranch, is a National Historic Site that has become a national place of pilgrimage. According to the federal government, 34,617 people visited it in fiscal year 2001.[5]

Sandburg's popular appeal has not translated into enduring academic respect. The last twenty years have seen a surprising paucity of work on his writing. There has been one comprehensive biography—Penelope Niven's *Carl Sandburg* (1991)—one substantial book length study—Philip Yannella's *The Other Carl Sandburg* (1996)—a recent study of Sandburg's literary milieu—Lisa Woolley's *American Voices of the Chicago Renaissance* (2000)—and a handful of articles.[6] This meager showing cannot begin to compare to the literary-critical industries that have grown up around other American modernists such as Hart Crane, H.D., T. S. Eliot, Ezra Pound, and William Carlos Williams.

This list of secondary materials also displays a pronounced bias toward a single phase in Sandburg's long career, the years 1915–20. During that short span Sandburg published his best-known volumes of verse: *Chicago Poems* (1916), *Cornhuskers* (1918), and *Smoke and Steel* (1920). He was also more conspicuously involved in radical leftist politics than afterward. From 1915–18 he published forty-one pieces in the Chicago-based *International Socialist Review* that showed his ardent support for "the direct-action revolutionary tactics of the Industrials Workers of the World (IWW)" (Yannella xiv). Moreover, as a foreign correspondent based out of Sweden, he avidly supported the Bolshevik cause during and after the October Revolution of 1917 (123). With only one prominent exception—Sally Greene's "'Things money cannot buy': Carl Sandburg's

Tribute to Virginia Woolf"—critics have not inquired at length into Sandburg's post-1920 writings or politics. No one has wrestled with *The People, Yes* and its particular, Depression Era take on revolutionary politics. There appears to be an unspoken agreement among professors of modern literature that Sandburg peaked early as a poet and agitator.

Like most unspoken agreements, this one merits reconsideration. As Nelson never tires of reminding us, literary reputations of politically progressive writers rarely take shape neutrally or naturally. In those rare cases—like Sandburg's—in which they do manage to gain admittance to the American literary canon, their politics are almost always forgotten or misconstrued. And as Thurston's *Making Something Happen* and Nelson's *Revolutionary Memory* suggest, the present-day literary-critical unanimity on Sandburg's literary merit can be traced back to the immediate post–World War II era, when the equation "political poetry is bad poetry" was fast becoming orthodoxy.[7] Revisiting this moment of revisionism can help explain why subsequent literary critical attention typically focuses on only one, restricted moment in the poet's career.

How Did Sandburg's Academic Reputation Collapse?

The 1948 publication of Sandburg's autobiographical novel *Remembrance Rock* both confirmed his stature as one of America's most beloved authors and hinted that his reputation was about to decline precipitously among literary critics and East Coast tastemakers. Although the book was short listed for a Pulitzer Prize and occasioned a triumphant author tour of the Midwest, *The New Yorker* and other influential journals roundly panned it. Perry Miller, in a lead review in *The New York Times Book Review,* savaged Sandburg's "maudlin devices" and vulgarly "technicolor" imagination. His "blind assurance" in moral platitudes, Miller asserted, is no substitute for the fine craft necessary to "construct a novel" (qtd. in Niven 588–89).

This pattern—public acclamation on one hand and critical dismissiveness on the other—would repeat itself three years later in even more emphatic fashion. In May 1951 Sandburg's *Complete Poems* won a Pulitzer. In September, *Poetry,* the Chicago-based journal that had launched the poet's career in 1914, unexpectedly published a long, devastating review of the book by William Carlos Williams. Williams, an old friend of Sandburg's, followed Perry Miller's lead and blasted *Complete Poems* for its unforgivable technical failings. After this public dressing-down by a fellow modernist, the remainder of the 1950s saw a swift decline in Sandburg's representation in anthologies and textbooks. He virtually ceased to receive extended critical commentary (Niven 611). This fall from grace was so dramatic, so final, that its inaugural shove is worth examining in some detail.

"*Chicago,* his first brilliantly successful poem," Williams proclaims, "should have been his last" (346). Instead, he settled into a "sort of reporting" in a flat, formless delivery that is "just talk." Williams states:

> For twenty years he has kept this up with diminishing force, book after book. . . . It goes on and on from the Swede in the flat below, through railroad men, the farmer reaping his acres, the Texas ranger, slum dwellers, women, pimps playing the piano in whore houses, back to the sales girls in department stores in the big cities. In the end he sums it up, *The People, Yes,* and lets it go at that. (347)

Sandburg's career lacks development and direction, Williams argues, because he never sought to find or forge a new formal sensibility. Instead, he rested content with his initial innovations, heaving the pentameter and embracing the vernacular. Afterwards "technically the poems reveal no initiative whatever other than their formlessness" (345). His poetry over time "faded off . . . for lack of structural interest on his part, nothing to inform it, nothing to drive it forward" (346).

Importantly, the accusation that Sandburg's verse had "nothing to drive it forward" refers solely and narrowly to aesthetic motivations. Williams credits the "steady diminution of the poetic charge in his verses from about the period of *Cornhuskers* to *The People, Yes*" to a different kind of drive, his political commitments:

> Sandburg, convinced that the official democracy he was witnessing was rotten, abandoned his art to expose it. He suffered the inevitable results. . . . To have persisted as a pure poet would have maimed what to him was the outstanding thing: the report of the people, the basis of all art and of everything that is alive with regenerative power. (348)

Williams criticizes this position as fundamentally mistaken about an artist's proper role in society. He offers a stereotypically high modernist critique of Sandburg's populism:

> It is by his invention of new terms that the artist uniquely serves . . . . The poet in himself, tormented by the things which Sandburg evinces, dissatisfied with mere repeated statement, over and over and over reiterated

but undeveloped, digests that powerful incentive and puts it out as imaginative design, a new thing that embodies all their timeless agonies. It may
not seem as effective to the active tormented man as the direct outcry—
of an Okie in the desert, as Sandburg envisions him—but it has far more
carrying power. (348–49)

Williams rhetorically positions himself as doubly Sandburg's better. First, he
implies that his is a disinterested dedication to the pursuit of "pure" poetry,
whereas Sandburg falsely subordinates aesthetics to political expediency. The
result is degraded art, "just talk." Williams then turns around and condemns
Sandburg's "direct outcry" for its lack of "carrying power." Superior technique,
apparently, has the added, corollary benefit of producing a higher quality of
activist poetry, too. As Williams sees it, the quest for "a new thing" with an
"imaginative design" is the proper route to success, primarily literary but also
secondarily political.

Williams does concede that Sandburg's earliest, best work was "touched with
fire." That magic can, however, be attributed to the fact that he was writing "syn-
chronously" with the "upsurge of the modern impetus." This synchrony was
blind luck: he did not "know . . . what he was doing." Consequently, his subsequent decline does not license traditionalists to "snigger behind their hands"
and "rush back to their old respectable deadness." The "whole that [Sandburg's
early poetry] represents," that is, literary modernism, must be seen as a fundamentally distinct phenomenon from (and altogether superior to) the leftist politics that tragically misled this insufficiently self-aware poet (346).

Can We Blame the New Critics for Sandburg's Fall?

Acknowledging but belittling Sandburg, Williams engages in canonical policing
actions comparable to those that fill the pages of Nelson's *Repression and Recovery* and Thurston's *Making Something Happen*. Like Allen Tate, John Crowe
Ransom, and the other New Critics, Williams draws lines such that the aesthetic
falls within the purview of literary acceptability, whereas the overtly political
falls largely outside.[8] The particular contour that Williams ascribes to Sandburg's career—a plummeting descent from noble savagery to doctrinal medi-
ocrity—also reshapes it sufficiently to grant him, first, a place within the terrain
of the canonical while also, second, reinforcing the canon's distinction between
poetry that's bad because it's political (late Sandburg) and political poetry that's
good for reasons other than politics (early Sandburg). This nuanced reevalua-
tion concedes Sandburg's continuing popular appeal while also simultaneously
registering grave doubts about his value as a role model for aspiring writers.

Williams's argument was both straightforward and easily assimilated by those who wanted to depoliticize poetry in the 1950s. The powerful, formalist-leaning literary circles already inclined to challenge Sandburg's pre–World War II stature and authority—those circles that had savaged *Remembrance Rock*—seized upon Williams's thesis. After 1951, Sandburg's academic reputation was cemented as the author of a handful of sincere but clumsy 1910s lyrics best appreciated by readers uneducated in subtleties of form, technique, and tone. When his post-1920s work surfaces in criticism after mid-century, it almost always does so as a straw man or as a limit case, as in Burton Hatlen's "Regionalism and Internationalism in Basil Bunting's *Briggflatts*" (2000). Hatlen singles out *The People, Yes* as a work of "bad faith," proof positive that "rhetoric that affirmed the unity of the nation" had become "irretrievably corrupt" in the decades since Whitman (62). Hatlen then contrasts the "windy" vacuity of *The People, Yes* to the successful efforts of another American long poem—not coincidentally, Williams's *Paterson*—"to find the universal within the particular, to drive his foundation posts down as deeply as possible into the local ground, to build up from there with his bare hands" (63).

Nelson and Thurston might let the story rest here. "Sandburg: another politically-progressive victim of New Critical revisionism!" Williams himself, however, was neither a New Critic nor one of their literary protégés. His distaste for Sandburg's later poetry deserves more careful parsing. True, he may have been courting New Critical favor in 1951. He had suffered a severe stroke only months before his *Poetry* review, and he had yet to receive the plaudits that would later guarantee his renown as a first-tier modernist poet (Niven 608). Feeling vulnerable to shifts in the literary climate, he may have decided to distance himself from his old avant-garde comrade-in-arms as a means of repudiating his own, earlier 1930s sympathy for leftist activism evinced, for instance, by his 1937 essay "An American Poet," which lauds the communist poet H. H. Lewis (Nelson, *Repression* 49). Regardless, though, of any careerist efforts to portray himself as *au courant*, Williams's argument contains another important dimension. He makes it clear that he belongs to and speaks for a separate, older poetic constituency.

His betrayal of his former colleague blends a scorn for propaganda—an attitude typical of American literary pronouncements during the first decades of the Cold War—with a formal critique recognizably continuous with older Imagist demands for terse, clean, and original free verse.[9] Williams asserts a necessary (though unsubstantiated) connection between these two historically distinct sets of criteria. Radical political content not only renders Sandburg's 1930s verse *ipso facto* bad (a characteristically 1950s argument) but renders it bad in a very specific way, that is, by undermining the poet's ability to write the taut, effective *vers libre* that he, along with Williams and other modernists, had perfected in the 1910s. The forced correlation here between *two* periods' evaluative principles should alert us that the McCarthyite *Zeitgeist* cannot alone account for Williams's harshly critical review. Williams contends that a book such as *The People, Yes* could satisfy *neither* a Cold War audience *nor* a Progressive Era audience experiencing the first "upsurge of the modern impetus." The volume is *multiply* bad.

One has to keep this layering of histories in mind when considering Sandburg's reception in the second half of the twentieth century. When a critic such as Burton Hatlen—who had dedicated decades to the study of Williams, Pound, and other modernist and postmodernist American poets—dismisses Sandburg's *The People, Yes* as inferior to *Paterson,* he is not simply recycling literary historical clichés, nor is he restating ossified ideological positions.[10] Rather, he is espousing an ethics of writing whose high estimation of formal accomplishment derives, yes, partly from institutional memory of the New Critics but one whose values *also* descend genealogically from the Pound-Williams-Bunting insistence on precise versecraft. "[U]se absolutely no word that does not contribute to the presentation," as Pound enjoined in 1912.[11] Judged by such a rule, *The People, Yes* is indeed a horror, a muddle of words that fail to present any one "thing" clearly, concisely, or cogently. To read Sandburg's poetry from the 1930s with sympathy requires more than suspending post–World War II, post–New Critical academic demands for charged poetic language, as Nelson et al. would have us do. One must recognize, too, that *The People, Yes* bluntly, madly defies such demands, as well as earlier modernist injunctions regarding *le mot juste.* Only then can one begin to perceive the extent of its critique of public discourse. *All* language, including poetic language, has been "irretrievably corrupted," and the will to "drive foundation posts down as deeply as possible into the local ground" will ever be defeated, since no authentic "ground" remains, only detritus and slime (Hatlen 62-63).

Tell Us More about *The People, Yes*

Although Sandburg had already compiled a "portfolio" of poems for a prospective sixth volume of poetry by October 1932 (*Letters* 284), he did not begin working on *The People, Yes* in earnest until two years later, in October or November of 1934 (310). By mid-February 1935 the book had reached one hundred and twelve pages in typescript (312). He continued working on the poem through the summer and, after an extended fall lecture tour of the Midwest, South, and New York, sent a final draft to Alfred Harcourt in November (Niven 499).

In its final form, *The People, Yes* is a long poem of one hundred and seven parts, each of which ranges in length from one to nine pages. Each part is variably indented and heterogeneous in form, with three kinds of free verse predominating: end-stopped, sprawling lines; phrasally-lineated verse with occasional enjambment; and long line-paragraphs consisting of two or more sentences. There is little or no rhyme, meter, or other organized patterning of sound. The poetry depends instead on syntactical parallelism—especially in the form of lists, catalogs, and repeated phrases—to give his verse coherence and force. Sandburg betrays a particular fondness for asking one rhetorical question after another:

> Who can fight against the future?
> What is the decree of tomorrow?
> Haven't the people gone on and on always taking more of their own?
> How can the orders of the day be against the people in this time?
> What can stop them from taking more and more of their own? (187)

One can discern a rough plan to the book's contents. Its first third tends to look back to the mythic past, whether that be biblical or historical, especially the initial settling of North America by white colonists. The last third takes up the question of the future of "the people," with a repeated refrain of "Where to? What next?" The central third is a mishmash. Individual numbered sections are devoted to such ethnographic tasks as recording pieces of proverbial wisdom (42, 44); retelling tall tales (45, 47); providing samples of overhead conversation on a subway (61); and transcribing dialogue among newspapermen (69). Sandburg, when trying to explain this loose structure and miscellany of materials to his correspondents, resorted to outrageous portmanteau labels for the book: "a ballad pamphlet harangue sonata and fugue" (*Letters* 310); "an almanac, a scroll, a palimpsest, the last will and testament of Mr. John Public" (311); "a saga sonata fugue with deliberate haywire interludes and jigtime babblings" (312).

The most obvious precedent, however, is Walt Whitman's *Leaves of Grass*. Sandburg shares with Whitman not only anaphora-prone, prolonged free verse lines but also his ambition to present a synoptic vision of modern American life. Also Whitmanian are the catalogs, the abrupt transitions, and the "Song of Myself"-like structural tension between relatively self-contained, formally variable, individually numbered lyrical sections and the countervailing sense that one is reading a through-composed work with epic ambitions. Sandburg's authorial persona is quite different, though, much less Whitman's "Me myself" than a ventriloquist who serves as a conduit for a flood of anonymous prophecy, proverbial wisdom, statistics, and documentary observations on quotidian living. Accordingly, in 1935 he instructed Harcourt that it would be "not so apt" to advertise *The People, Yes* as "in the Whitmanian tradition." He wished to emphasize instead its debts to such near-anonymous, cobbled-together, poetic-historical surveys of national character as *Piers Ploughman*, the Norse sagas, and the Old Testament (*Letters* 330).

When correcting the page proofs of *The People, Yes* Sandburg expressed regret about its "curious craziness." He wished he could "go back and revise," especially the many sections where the "workmanship is slovenly," although it was much too late in the publication process to make such drastic changes (336). He later reconciled himself to its muddle and unevenness, claiming that he had put into it "the chaos and turmoil of our time and all time" (342). Whatever his own opinion of the work, *The People, Yes* had remarkable success for an American book of poetry that gloated over the Bolshevik execution of Tsar Nicholas II and celebrated the "hallelujah chorus" of "The people . . . Changing from hammer to bayonet and back to hammer" (*People* 222). A little over half a year after its release the book had already entered its third printing.[12] By the early 1940s it had been recorded as "a Decca album of six sides, twelve-inch" (*Letters* 411) and adapted as a one-act opera for broadcast on CBS radio (395). And surprisingly—unlike such famed 1930s volumes of leftist poetry as George Oppen's *Discrete Series*, Edwin Rolfe's *To My Contemporaries*, and Muriel Rukeyser's *U.S. 1*—it still remains available in bookstores today as a stand-alone volume.

But Is It Any Good?

Carl Sandburg's *The People, Yes* contains some extraordinarily bad poetry. Sandburg rarely introduces an idea without belaboring it. Combined with his earnestness, portentousness, and penchant for clichés, the results can be dreadful:

Money is power: so said one.
Money is a cushion: so said another.
Money is the root of evil: so said still another.
Money means freedom: so runs an old saying.

And money is all of these—and more.
Money pays for whatever you want—if you have the money.
Money buys food, clothes, houses, land, guns, jewels, men, women,
    time to be lazy and listen to music.
Money buys everything except love, personality, freedom, immortality,
    silence, peace. (166)

Fifteen mind-numbing lines later, Sandburg is still rumbling merrily along:

Money is welcome even when it stinks.
Money is the sinew of love and of war.
Money breaks men and ruins women.
    Money is a great comfort.
    Every man has his price. (167)

One could blame Whitman for this example of anaphora gone mad, but even at his worst Whitman never tries a reader's patience to this extent. Here the tap turns on, and the language bubbles merrily down the drain until, at some arbitrary point, Sandburg turns it off. The book as a whole feels much the same way. Why stop after one hundred and seven sections? Sandburg could have kept going, for many more pages, without either much adding to or detracting from the coherence or shapeliness of the whole. (The poet grew so tired of complaints on this count that he wrote George West that he was considering adding a pull-out-all-the-stops conclusion, "an appendix with the horns of municipal ownership contrapuntal to the woodwinds of collective bargaining, the entire orchestra in the finale giving three cheers for the C.I.O." [*Letters* 336].)

How does a critic respond when confronted with such amorphous, repetitious writing? One could read through *The People, Yes* in search of passages worth salvaging from the dross. Like such fellow Chicago Renaissance authors as Edgar Lee Masters and Vachel Lindsay, Sandburg debatably comes off best after an unforgiving editorial pen has vetted the verbiage. One could supplement the typical anthology pieces by Sandburg—such chestnuts as "Chicago," "Fog," and "Prairie"—with a few other neglected pieces—"Killers," "Billy Sunday," "Wilderness," "Four Preludes on Playthings of the Wind," and the scathing "Mr. Attila," perhaps—and plausibly claim to have assembled everything Sandburg wrote that is still worth reading. *The People, Yes* could yield a few passable passages to add to such a hypothetical list. Some recall the Midwestern laconic, stoic humor of *Chicago Poems* and *Smoke and Steel,* only now retooled to suit the thematics of an impending proletarian revolution:

We asked the cyclone
to go around our barn
but it didn't hear us. (260)

Other passages, such as the impressionistic closing lines of part 85, stand out because Sandburg attempts a more innovative style than customary:

tickets? where to?   round trip or one way?
room rent coffee and doughnuts   maybe a movie

suit-cases   packsacks   bandannas
names saved and kept careful
you mustn't lose the address
and what'll be your telephone number?
give me something to remember you by
be my easy rider
kiss me once before you go a long one
flash eyes   testaments in a rush
underhums of plain love with rye bread sandwiches (220)

The verse here features a range of devices otherwise rare in *The People, Yes*: a lack of punctuation and capitalization; irregular spacing internal to a line; pointillist compression ("flash eyes," "room rent coffee"); quick, unmarked movement between quotation and observation; neologism ("underhums"); and juxtaposition of the concrete and abstract ("plain love with rye bread"). One can also discern an unusual degree of soundplay for Sandburg, such as the assonance of long /i/ in the second half—"by," "rider," "eyes," "rye"—and the balanced rhythm audible in individual lines:

       /   /   ^   /   /   ^
    names saved and kept careful
     / ^ / ^ / ^
    be my easy rider.

Taken as a whole, this passage exhibits an improvisational feel that prefigures the 1950s poetry of Frank O'Hara, Philip Whalen, and Jack Kerouac. Like these later poets, Sandburg seeks a variable form adequate to the pace and crush of daily living in a busy, urban environment.

An editor, though, given the task of excerpting from *The People, Yes* would quickly conclude that, even at its best, the volume does not offer verse for the ages. The "be my easy rider" passage would never make it into an anthology of modern American poetry ahead of such tighter, more memorable examples of this lyric mode as O'Hara's "Personal Poem" and "A Step Away from Them." Sandburg's text simply does not display the polish, complexity, variable tone, and layered ironies that typify most anthologized verse from the twentieth century.

Wasn't Sandburg Himself an Anthologist?

A prospective anthologist who reads through *The People, Yes*, though, is likely to discover that the book is itself a curious kind of anthology, indeed, something of an anthology-of-anthologies. At times it sounds like a scrapbook, as in the section 57, in which Sandburg rather arbitrarily lineates prose quotations from Abraham Lincoln. Other times the book takes on a documentary feel, as in section 61, which collects representative statements by commuters, or section 69, which does the same thing for lawyers. This magpie method of composition could be construed as a natural, even logical, extension of Sandburg's inveterate habit of carrying with him travel notebooks in which to jot striking phrases, amusing anecdotes, or unfamiliar folk songs (Niven 444). He had already published one book using these found texts: *The American Songbag* (1928). Arguably, *The People, Yes* permits Sandburg to compile remaining materials within a flexible, capacious format that demands no consistency in rubric, subject, or style.

These borrowed, assembled fragments of language are frequently peculiar, perhaps innovative, and for that reason worthy of note—though one would be hard pressed to call them well written, let alone profound. This dilemma becomes acute during patches of the book that consist of nothing but reams of what Sandburg calls "proverbs."[13] These statements are authorless, ripped from any original context, and relatively self-contained. They include clichés, jokes, lyrical observations, and gnomic comments. Part 49 contains a fairly typical example:

Blue eyes say love me or I die.
Black eyes say love me or I kill you.
The sun rises and sets in her eyes.
    Wishes won't wash dishes.
May all your children be acrobats.
    Leave something to wish for.
    Lips however rosy must be fed.
    Some kill with a feather.
    By night all cats are gray.
Life goes before we know what it is.
    One fool is enough in a house.
Even God gets tired of too much hallelujah.
Take it easy and live long as brothers.
    The baby's smile pays the bill. (106)

Sandburg has arranged these fourteen sentences into an irregularly indented stanza with no set metrical or rhyme scheme. There is no readily apparent narrative, argument, event, dramatis personae, or setting that can help us understand the selection or ordering of the contents. A perplexed reader might conjecture, after the first three lines, that the passage describes a rocky love triangle, perhaps between the poem's speaker and two women, one blue-eyed and the other black-eyed. Abruptly, however, we are given a motherly admonition—"Wishes won't wash dishes"—followed by a bizarre curse or blessing. (Are acrobat children a good or bad thing?) Thereafter the connections between lines become increasingly fanciful and tenuous. The "wish" in "Leave something to wish for" harks back to the wishes to avoid housework, clearly, but in trying to parse a pairing such as "Some kill with a feather / By night all cats are gray," one has to resort to pure guesswork. Perhaps "kill" suggests the darkness of death, hence "night," and "kill" plus "feather" might lead to the idea of "cats"? The look of the page—that is, the arrangement of these lines into a discrete stanza separated by white space from the remainder of the text—provides us with a conventional visual cue indicating that we ought to be able to integrate its particulars into some kind of general statement. Instead, we are presented with stubbornly particulate statements related only partially or nonlinearly.

Unlike the "be my easy rider" passage, the stanza beginning "Blue eyes say love me or I die" is difficult to evaluate. What standards should one employ? Are there Arnoldian touchstones for such aberrant verse? By assembling statements whose authorship is credited to "the people," Sandburg prevents us from judging straightforwardly whether his contents are in themselves original or creative. They are offered up serially, without explicit comment, as things overheard or remembered. The procession of sentences is self-similar and repetitious. No matter which stanzas or runs of lines one chooses from the "proverb" sections of The People, Yes, they will sound remarkably similar in their pacing, delivery, and lack of logical connection and syllogistic progression. One could linger over or excerpt certain well-turned or pithy lines, in effect treating the text as a collection of quotable quotes and humorous one-liners. Such a selective reading, though, would violate the flow and integrity of the work, rendering Sandburg's contribution *as a poet* utterly peripheral. He would become a recorder and compiler, to be judged solely on the quality and aptness of his selected materials.

Sandburg would not necessarily consider such a job description a demotion. He regularly claimed that "poetry" was a misleading generic designation for *The People, Yes* (Niven 505). Indeed, one could argue that *The People, Yes* belongs less in the tradition of the American modernist long poem than in the company of such classic, multiauthored, mixed-genres collections as Alain Locke's *The New Negro: An Interpretation* (1925) and James Agee and Walker Evans's *Now Let Us Praise Famous Men* (1939). *The People, Yes*, like these other works, offers an unusual gathering of ethnography, sociological observation, original writing, and political commentary. In each case, the old notion of the solitary genius-artist is superseded by a notion of collective authorship (the edited collection, the collaboration, the scrapbook). The desire to represent a "people" in its entirety forces a recognition that no one individual can speak for the whole without doing violence to its superpersonal multiplicity. As Sandburg wrote Vachel Lindsay about his earlier compilation-text, *The American Songbag:* "It is not so much my book as that of a thousand other people who have made its 260 colonial, pioneer, railroad, work-gang, hobo, Irish, Negro, Mexican, gutter, Gossamer songs, chants and ditties" (*Letters* 246–47). *The People, Yes,* often restates this theme of collective authorship, most vividly in section 59. An "ancient clan" discovers that one of its "elders" had secretly begun "doing an eye-witness tale of their good and evil doings." He declares, "I will be the word of the people!" For his presumption, he is executed and his "bloody head" set "on a pike for public gaze" (142–43). The tale of the tribe can only be accurately told by a tribe, or, to put it differently, by a *plural* author, a choral voicing in which individual idiosyncrasies have been subsumed.

Although it is tempting—and partially correct—to read *The People, Yes* alongside the likes of Locke and Agee and Evans, any such attempt still must confront Sandburg's bizarre decision to present his populist *sententiae* in the form of long, undifferentiated, untitled, and unmarked lists. He does lineate the proverbs, and, as we have seen, he occasionally sculpts them into stanzas and verse paragraphs, but these formal traits relate little if at all, as we have also seen, to the contents, their ordering, or any underlying argument. *The People, Yes* is a modernist anthology of a kind, but also an anthology weirdly, cavalierly indifferent to the distinctiveness, representativeness, and comprehensiveness of its collection of found texts. It disregards their provenance, fails to note any previous publications, and lacks notation of any variants discovered during Sandburg's travels. Whether thought of as poet, editor, redactor, or student of oral literature, Sandburg in *The People, Yes* appears amateurish and inept. He churns out line after line, line after line, as if writing about "The People" required him to reduce his verse from an assemblage of lines to an assembly line that spits out interchangeable utterances at high speed.

Aren't You Being Overly Allegorical?

Sandburg wrote the bulk of *The People, Yes* in 1935, the same year that the Congress of Industrial Organizations (CIO) broke away from Samuel Gompers's American Federation of Labor (AFL) to pursue more aggressive policies toward owners and management. Sandburg was initially an avid supporter of John L. Lewis, the head of the CIO, and the spate of sit-down strikes that he orchestrated. Sandburg's wife reports that he saw in the CIO the rebirth of the working class movement that had fired his imagination in the 1910s, and he wept whenever he heard that another corporation, such as General Motors, had "yielded and began negotiating with Lewis' men" (Niven 516). She also reports that he began using his lecture tours as opportunities to tout union causes. On at least "eighty" occasions he brought up the subject of a garment workers strike in Chicago (516–17).

The People, Yes thus dates from a moment in Sandburg's career when he was acutely aware of class struggle. Moreover, after a decade and a half spent hymning the rural heartland of Abraham Lincoln, his attention was focused again squarely on factories, the proletariat, and ownership of the means of production. If in the 1910s, during his first radical phase, he had presented himself as a charismatic bard celebrating the anonymous and downtrodden, this time around he eschews such romantic posturing. The visionary, alienated "I" gives way to an "I" that is continuous with and indissociable from an anonymous, oceanic "we the people." This shift in authorial self-definition is matched by a shift in subject matter. *The People, Yes* is not a gallery of portraits and vignettes in the manner of an earlier volume such as *The Cornhuskers*. Instead, *The People, Yes* attempts something much more ambitious: to portray the divided, conflictual totality of American social relations.

This impulse is recognizably Marxist, whatever Sandburg's conscious political affiliations.[14] (In 1935 he wrote, "I belong to no political party and have not for 24 years. I belong to no organizations open or secret except the Veterans of Foreign Wars and the Authors League of America" [*Letters* 325].) Even more specifically, the desire to write a poetry in which "the people" are both speaking subject and object of depiction is consistent with the Popular Front aesthetic promulgated by the Seventh Congress of the Communist International in 1935. European communists, pressured by the rise of fascism, ruled that "solidarity" with "bourgeois democratic states" was "reasonable" under the circumstances.

> [This] policy shift resulted in rhetorical, organizational, and cultural changes in the American party. . . . [T]he party joined forces with many non-Communist progressive groups . . . in its efforts to make common cause with liberals and Socialists on such problems as race relations and threats posed by international and domestic fascism. Finally, the Popular Front loosened aesthetic prescriptions (and proscriptions) promulgated by party publications and critics so that nonproletarian writers who espoused even liberal reforms, writers often attacked in the past, were counted as allies in the education of the masses. (Thurston 177)

The People, Yes belongs to this moment of coalition building. "The people," for Sandburg, is a capacious, inclusive, elusive concept, transcending factional disputes, racial divisions, and ethnic boundaries. The book preaches unity and solidarity of *all* oppressed against their victimizers.[15]

To render its large-scale portrait of American society effective and affecting, Sandburg's book employs a variant of a strategy favored by many 1920s and 1930s communist poets, what Michael Thurston has called "serial interpellation." Works such as Hughes's "Advertisements for the Waldorf Astoria," Rolfe's "These Men Are Revolution," and Rukeyser's "The Book of the Dead," Thurston argues, "explored one way to capture collective consciousness and action": the "serial interpellation of worker-readers into provisional and tactical unity" (177). Lists of occupations, strings of monologues, and representative anecdotes "hail" readers who recognize themselves as addressed by and therefore included within a given poem's image of society. The poems move on to speak of multitudes, "the people," the masses, or other designations intended to reveal the solidarity of those oppressed by capitalism. Presumably, hailed readers would be carried along with this shift in rhetoric and, feeling united with hosts of other downtrodden men and women, experience a sense of empowerment (53).[16]

Thurston cautions that "serial interpellation" has obvious flaws. "As a strategy for building a counter-hegemonic coalition, this mechanical procedure alone is doomed to failure" (53). He takes pains to illustrate how Hughes, Rolfe, and Rukeyser all complicate, extend, and otherwise rise above the crudely "mechanical" aspects of the technique in their poetry. Sandburg, however, does no such thing. *The People, Yes* is uncannily machine-like in its production of list after list, lists within lists, intended, presumably, to "hail" its "worker-readers":

> The punch-clock, the changes from decent foremen to snarling straw-
>   bosses, the sweltering July sun, the endless pounding of a blizzard,
>   the sore muscles, the sudden backache and the holding on for all the
>   backache,
> The quick thinking in wrecks and breakdowns, the fingers and thumbs
>   clipped off by machines, the machines that behave no better no worse
>   no matter what you call them, the coaxing of a machine and fooling
>   with it till all of a sudden she starts and you're not sure why,
> A ladder rung breaking and a legbone or armbone with it, layoffs and no
>   paycheck coming, the red diphtheria card on the front door, the price
>   for a child's burial casket, hearse and cemetery lot (156–57)

The mention of death here is not, alas, the end of the catalog, which continues for another two pages, touching upon rush hour frustrations, the proper way to pour molten metal, and "the shine of spring sunlight on a new planted onion patch" (157). The authorial "machine" is like those in this passage that start and stop "and you're not sure why"; it interpellates anyone and everyone with no respect for such human failings as a limited attention span.

Mechanicity pervades the structure of the long poem. It deliberately "dumbs down" modernist techniques elsewhere employed to innovative ends. For example, like many twentieth-century long poems, *The People, Yes* depends heavily on parataxis as a compositional principle. That is, it links successive statements through the express or implied conjunction "and":

and the hangar night shift meets the air mail
and the steam shovels scoop gravel by the ton
and the interstate trucks parade on the hard roads
and the bread line silhouettes stand in a drizzle
and in Iowa the state fair prize hog crunches corn
and on the truck farms this year's scarecrows
lose the clothes they wore this summer. (275)

The parataxis here deserves comparison to the best-known modernist variant, the Poundian. Pound's *Cantos* assemble and juxtapose a tremendous diversity of historical and philological found texts. These texts jostle productively, inviting a reader to compare, to contrast, and to seek out illuminating connections, both linear and nonlinear. Sandburg's verse works quite differently. His "hangar night shift," "steam shovels," "interstate trucks," and "state fair prize hog" are images extracted in no particular order from an image bank labeled "rural Midwest." The rapid shifts in location, time of day, and season of year may be jolting but they are not especially epiphanic. Are the men waiting in the breadline presented as like or unlike the prize hog or the steam shovels? Are we supposed to be angry that the pig is eating corn while men starve? If so, the aestheticization of the breadline into "silhouettes" and the hint of childlike glee in "crunches corn" are both woefully out of place. One could reorder Sandburg's lines without appreciably changing their meaning. Alternatively, one could interject other clauses suiting the general topic without doing violence to the theme: "and the October cornhuskers toss ripe ears into bins," perhaps, or "and in Wisconsin the cows shift their feet at nightfall." Poetic language here loses its distinctiveness, aptness, and luster. Statements are ticked off, one by one, each serviceable but none unique. *The People, Yes* is a demonic undoing of Pound's ideogrammic method.

The People, Yes likewise echoes but flattens Gertrude Stein's principle of "beginning again and again." In a work such as "Sentences" Stein repeatedly reverts to a particular phrase, in this case the question "What is a sentence," in the midst of an idiosyncratic, inductive exploration of the limits of language: "What is a sentence. A sentence is an imagined master piece. . . . What is a sentence. A sentence furnishes while they will draw. . . . What is a sentence. A sentence is an anniversary of their begging them to be seen" (123). Part 72 of *The People, Yes* exhibits a similar organizational strategy:

> What is a judge? A judge is a seated torso and head sworn before God
>   never to sell justice nor play favorites while he umpires the disputes
>   brought before him . . . .
> What is a judge? The perfect judge is austere, impersonal, impartial, mark-
>   ing the line of right or wrong by a hairsbreadth . . . .
> What is a judge? A featherless human biped having bowels, glands, blad-
>   ders, and intricate blood vessels of the brain . . . . (188)

Unlike Stein, though, Sandburg does not use his repeated questions as oppor- tunities to strike out experimentally in ever-new directions. Instead, "What is a judge?" becomes the backbone of a droning welter of vague criticisms of the justice system in the United States:

> What is a judge? Another owns no more than the little finger of himself,
>   others owning him, others having placed him where he is, others tell-
>   ing him what they want and getting it, others referring to him as "our
>   judge" as though he is measured and weighed beforehand the same as
>   a stockyards hog, others holding him to decisions evasive of right or
>   wrong, others writing his decisions for him, the atmosphere hushed
>   and guarded, the atmosphere having a faint stockyards perfume.
> What is a judge? Sometimes a mind giving one side the decision and the
>   other side a lot of language and sympathy, sometimes washing his
>   hands and rolling a pair of bones and leaving equity to a pair of gal-
>   loping ivories. (189)

Curiously, Sandburg nests new Steinian "beginnings again" within these indi- vidual line-paragraphs. The first of the above two lines, for instance, is struc- tured by the repetition "Another . . . others . . . others . . . others . . . others." The second contains two such organizing structures, first the pair "sometimes . . . sometimes" and then, within the first "sometimes" phrase, "one side . . . other side." Sandburg could presumably extend *ad libitum* the writing at any of these levels, adding further "others," other "sometimes," more "sides," or further itera- tions of "What is a judge?" The form is rigid and repetitious but also modular and expandable, accordion-style, to fill whatever space desired. Steinian writing- to-the-moment, dependent for its success on her ingenuity and wit, gives way to a writerly format amenable to quick, predictable, measurable production of verse. As Sandburg puts it later in *The People, Yes*, in this book the "efficiency expert" and the "poet" at last meet (212).

As this assertion suggests, Sandburg's mechanization of modernist technique is self-consciously related to his chosen content. He draws attention to the intimate connection between his modular, paratactic mode of writing; the economic system whose unjust division of labor has led to class conflict; and the proletariat who are both the object and subject of the book:

> The people? Harness bulls and narcotic dicks, multigraph girls and soda-jerkers, hat girls, bat boys, sports writers, ghost writers, popcorn and peanut squads, flatfeet, scavengers, mugs saying "Aw go button your nose," squirts hollering heads, hops, cappers, come-ons, tin horns, small timers, the night club outfits helping the soup-and-fish who have to do something between midnight and bedtime.
> The people? A puddler in the flaring splinters of newmade steel, a milk-wagon-driver getting the once-over from a milk inspector, a sand-hog with "the bends," a pack-rat, a snow-queen, janitors, jockeys, white collar lads, pearl divers, peddlers, bundlestiffs, pants pressers, cleaners and dyers, lice and rat exterminators. (252–53)

Occupations, licit and illicit, exotic and prosaic, pile up paratactically. The likes of pearl divers jostle with accountants, pants pressers, and rat exterminators. Authorial alter egos—"sports writers, ghost writers"—are plunged in among the rest. The selection and ordering of list items comes across as almost willfully arbitrary, despite the local instances of sound play ("hat girls, bat boys"; "janitors, jockeys") and a consistent preference for trochaic job titles ("soda-jerkers," "cappers, come-ons, tin horns," "pack-rat," "snow-queen," "cleaners," "dyers"). The sound-linkages accentuate the heterogeneity of "the people" insofar as they underline the absence of any rational, narrative, or other, extra-linguistic motivation for such occupational groupings. Consonance, assonance, and meter cannot substitute satisfactorily for the lack of coherence in the list-responses to the *faux*-Steinian reiterated question "The people?" Sandburg eventually breaks out of this catalog to address the obvious, deferred question: if the people are an assemblage of men and women with different job descriptions, what is a job anyway?

> In uniform, in white collars, in overalls, in denim and gingham, a number on an assembly line, a name on a polling list, a postoffice address,

a crime and sports page reader, a movie goer and radio listener, a
stock-market sucker, a sure thing for slick gamblers, a union man or
non-union, a job holder or a job hunter,
Always either employed, disemployed, unemployed and employable or
unemployable (253)

"The people" consists of human beings robbed of individuality. They are interchangeable bodies dressed up to fulfill specific tasks ("In uniform, in white col-
lars, in overalls"); they are bundles of quantifiable needs targeted by advertisers
("a movie goer and a radio listener"); they are points in space locatable by name
and number ("a name on a polling list, a postoffice address"). Above all, they
are reducible to their labor and labor-status, "employed, disemployed, unemployed." Sandburg's randomized catalog of occupations reflects the underlying
reality that, at the present stage of capitalist development, the division of labor
rather arbitrarily forces humans into pre-defined job categories. Distinctions
between individuals matter only for purposes of optimally matching laborers to
specific kinds of labor; we are all just "number[s] on an assembly line," workers
in the mill that is Depression-era America.

The People, Yes thus employs serial interpellation, but it does not work in the
manner of Rolfe's "These Men Are Revolution" or Rukeyser's "The Book of the
Dead." Instead, serial interpellation functions within the service of a more general formal strategy elucidated by Barrett Watten: poetry can model "productivity" in its construction. How a poem is put together instantiates a particular
relationship between producer and thing produced; this relationship can in turn
serve as a synecdoche for the (possible) totality in which it (imaginatively) participates (618). *The People, Yes* hails its readers into a wordscape that, in its very
warp and woof, conveys the alienation wreaked on the proletariat. Recognizing
yourself in its catalogs is as likely to result in a shudder of horror as a sense of
comradeship. You are interpellated into an undifferentiated, indifferent mass.
That mass has power, that mass can take action, but whatever action it takes will
have no necessary relation to your own, specific, individual wants and needs.

The bleakness of this dynamic may seem foreign both to the volume's cele-
bratory, affirmative tone and to Sandburg's reputation for genial, naïve humanism. But *The People, Yes* repeatedly registers its scorn of the individual *qua* individual. It portrays the self as inescapably enmeshed in a brutal system of
quantification, commodification, and exchange:

Weighing 150 pounds you hold 3,500 cubic feet of gas—oxygen, hydro-
gen, nitrogen.

> From the 22 pounds and 10 ounces of carbon in you is the filling for
> 9,000 lead pencils.
> In your blood are 50 grains of iron and in the rest of your frame enough
> iron to make a spike that would hold your weight.
> From your 50 ounces of phosphorus could be made 800,000 matches
> and elsewhere in your physical premises are hidden 60 lumps of
> sugar, 20 teaspoons of salt, 38 quarts of water, two ounces of lime,
> and scatterings of starch, chloride of potash, magnesium, sulphur,
> hydrochloric acid.
> You are a walking drug store (162)

Capitalist logic has so radically penetrated and contaminated the self that no one is safe from its alienating effects, even in his or her very blood and marrow. In the United States the individual, like it or not, is *already* lost in the "Niagara" of "the bargain sale crush, the subway jam, / The office building emptying its rush hour stream" (238).

Is Lyric Poetry Possible under Such Circumstances?

Most leftist poets of the 1930s, Cary Nelson writes, continue to presume that the lyric is "a special site for expressive subjectivity." Not only do they use their verse as a platform for agitation, they also feel free to register their personal thoughts about the revolutionary struggle, including their doubts, despair, and dissent (*Repression* 151). For such writers, poetry as a genre possesses an authenticating stamp: these emotions, it guarantees, are valid and profound. *The People, Yes* implicitly rejects this idea as obsolete romanticism. Poets, like everyone else under industrial capitalism, have lost ownership of themselves. Their thoughts, feelings, and words are every bit as contaminated by reification as their bodies.

The People, Yes emphasizes the agency of the mass media in this degradation of contemporary interiority. The "people" today consist of "millions at radio sets for an earful" and "millions turning newspaper pages for an eyeful" (238). Publishers (and the economy as a whole) work hard to insure that this vast, carefully cultivated market remains pliable, gullible, and uncritical, mere "boobs" (171). Through decades of refinement, the media have perfected Orwellian techniques of thought control. They manipulate reality through agenda-setting and the seductive appeal of the spotlight: "All I know is what I read in the papers" (234). We see (and imitate) whatever receives hype, until (in order to keep sales up) a new fad takes center stage: "Yo yo charmed till yo yo checked out. / The tree sitters climbed up, came down" (215). The rhetoric of advertising, stardom, and newspeak has become reflexive at all levels of society:

> One movie star arches her eyebrows
> and refers to "my public."
> One soda-jerker arches his eyebrows,
> curves malt-milk from shaker to glass
> and speaks of "my public." (214)

Section 68 of *The People, Yes* is the most acute passage of media-critique in the volume. It is given over entirely to an imagined conversation between newspaper "rewriters" who speak in nothing but nails-on-the-blackboard clichés and bad jokes: "I love a few individuals . . . but I've got a grudge against the human race"; "it takes a smart man to be a crook"; "The way to be a big shot is don't know too much"; "Lord give me this day my daily opinion and forgive me the one I had yesterday" (176–79). The news media here is portrayed as thoroughly inauthentic, derivative, and cynical—and cheerfully so. Any verse to see print in such a milieu would be empty and formulaic, mere retreads of "The Ole Swimmin'-Hole" and "Little Boy Blue."

Sandburg's attack on mass media can sound prophetic insofar as it anticipates in important respects the writings of Guy Debord and Jean Baudrillard. The 1930s, in fact, saw a proliferation of modernist texts—among them Edward Dahlberg's *From Flushing to Calvary* (1932), John Dos Passos's *Big Money* (1936), Nathanael West's *Day of the Locust* (1939), and Richard Wright's *Lawd Today!* (1937)—that reacted with prescient horror to the trivialization, homogenization, and standardization of language and subjectivity stemming from ever-greater, media-abetted penetration of commodification into every sphere of life.[17] Lyric poetry, too, contributed to this critique. Rita Barnard has detailed Kenneth Fearing's proto-Situationist techniques for subverting a "mass culture" that he saw as "an all-pervasive grid of alienation, manipulation, and censorship" (73). In "1933," "Twentieth-Century Blues," and other poems, he challenged the commodification of "emotions, and culture itself" through pastiche, collage, code switching, and a variety of other disorienting devices (89).

Sandburg, though, does not share Fearing's confidence in the creative imagination. Fearing's puckish gaming depends on surprise, vertigo, and other virtuoso effects. In contrast, Sandburg's modular verse excludes the possibility of pyrotechnic craft. In Sandburg's view, a poet's claim to profound originality is as misguided as his or her claim to communicate "unique," authentic, and affective experience. Nothing prevents their interior lives from being debased by the same economic forces at work on everyone else in society. In line with this position, section 93 of *The People, Yes* offers a deflationary myth of poetic origins. It extols the "name givers," the anonymous somebodies who invented the words that we now use to refer to things. The section then proceeds to illustrate the delights of Adamic creativity by listing flower species:

> The toadflax, the ox-eye daisy, the pussy willow, rabbit bells, buffalo clover,
> swamp candles and wafer ash,
> These with the windrose and the rockrose, lady slippers, loose-strife, thorn-
> apples, dragon's blood, old man's flannel,
> And the horse gentian, dog laurel, cat tails, snakeroot, spiderwort, pig
> weed, sow thistle, goose grass, moonseed, poison hemlock,
> These with the names on names between horse radish and the autumn-
> flowering orchid of a lavish harvest moon—
> These are a few of the names clocked and pronounced by the people mov-
> ing of the earth from season to season. (244–45)

As throughout *The People, Yes,* the verse here is strangely mechanical. First, it literalizes the etymological meaning of "anthology"—a gathering (*legein*) of flowers (*anthos*). Sandburg reduces a favorite Classical and Renaissance metaphor for a volume of verse into an artless, two-page paratactic avalanche of vegetation. Second, when not choosing flower species wholly at random, he relies upon arbitrary rules to generate them. In this passage, he gives us two runs of flowers that include animals in their names: toadflax, ox-eye daisy, pussy willow, rabbit bells, buffalo clover; horse gentian, dog laurel, cat tails, snakeroot, spiderwort, pig weed, sow thistle, and goose grass. Both of these lines—the first and third in the above passage—also end by naming two further species that do not refer to fauna: "swamp candles and wafter ash" and "moonseed, poison hemlock." Sandburg praises the creativity of "the people," but their creativity turns out to parallel the mechanical generation of verse that the text as a whole exhibits. Significantly, the names that the people generate are "clocked," that is, measured and quantified in the manner of workers' labor as they clock in and out of a factory. When "the people" speaks, it does so thoroughly informed and compromised by the economic forces that determine the rhythms and structures of their daily lives. Imagination, myth, and verse provide only pseudoescapes. They, too, remain constrained and structured by the social realities that they purport to negate.

The strings of authorless, decontextualized "proverbs" that keep recurring in *The People, Yes* are further instances of this dynamic. They are like blats of lyricism packaged and delivered serially, indifferently, *ad nauseam.* A reader consumes them, one after the other, with no time or space to reflect, sort, weigh, or judge. Instead of the genius prophet-poets who tower over the nineteenth century—Shelley, Byron, Whitman, Dickinson—we now have near-faceless, interchangeable author-functions whose poetic ejaculations are routinized and commodified.

The thoroughgoing mechanization of Sandburg's style represents a conscious capitulation to what he presumes to be history's iron law. The inhumanity of the volume's interminable lists, tinny cheeriness, and indifference to quality are indices of what he considers a sobering truth. Poets must realize that, at the present time, regardless of their efforts to craft a uniquely personal, expressive oeuvre, they are *already* and *inevitably* sitting at the assembly line of the culture industry. If they are to participate in the impending revolution that will someday enable *truly* authentic self-expression, they must, like all workers, cease to lie to themselves about their distinctiveness as individuals and lose themselves in "the people." This final sloughing-off of any residual (now merely ideological) trappings of individuality is the necessary precondition for the proletariat's coming fully to consciousness of itself as a collective agent, that is, *as a class*. This group awakening will at long last empower the working masses to transform society in its totality. "The people . . . are in tune and step / with constellations of universal law," as Sandburg intones (285). "The steel mill sky is alive. / The fire breaks white and zigzag . . . . Man is a long time coming. / Man will yet win" (286).

Williams believed that when Sandburg chose politics over art his art suffered. Sandburg limns the options differently. As he presents it, 1930s poets must decide between two hellish alternatives: (1) a hypocritical, inauthentic artistry that obfuscates its complicity in injustice and (2) a degraded, inauthentic artistry that serves the cause of eventual justice.

Why Are Those the Only Options?

Sandburg's diagnosis of the situation may seem extreme, even if one agrees with certain of his premises, such as the corrosive effects of media conglomerates on public discourse in the period of industrial capitalism. A Marxist thinker such as Georg Lukács, for example, would take Sandburg to task for overstating the depersonalization demanded by revolutionary politics. As he puts it in *History and Class Consciousness* (1922), "the category of totality does not reduce its various elements to an undifferentiated uniformity" (12). The specific and the concrete do not lose their "apparent independence and autonomy" once they are understood as participating in larger categories and processes. Rather, they are reinterpreted as "involved in a dynamic dialectical relationship with each other" as well as redefined as "dynamic dialectical aspects of an equally dynamic and dialectical whole" (12–13). In short, poets can believe in and actively participate in the proletariat revolution without having to become anonymous automata.

Sandburg's overly mechanistic understanding of social dynamics reflects the time and place of the composition of *The People, Yes*. Walter Kalaidjian has recounted how, eager to transform the U.S.S.R. into a modern industrialized state, the Communist Party of the 1920s and 1930s "embraced Fordism's accelerated pace of production" and imitated the "dehumanizing regimen of the American factory." As usual, Comintern and American communist rhetoric followed Moscow's example, and they, too, made the "production line" serve "as a symbol for cultural output as such" (126). Sandburg's mid-1930s assembly-line poetics belong to this era of Soviet dominance over American leftist thinking.[18] He had no recourse to the many persuasive Western Marxist critiques of Stalinism's fetishization of "technical rationality" that date from the 1920s and '30s. *The People, Yes* sacrifices quality and makes itself over as a mass-produced, inauthentic work—a perverse decision in hindsight, perhaps, but also an intelligible one, given its immediate literary context, the dawn of the Popular Front era in the United States.

The willed, willful badness of *The People, Yes* might also represent a potent if unintended means of protesting this intellectual climate. The book is so unvarying in its flatness, repetition, and predictability that an experienced reader of poetry cannot help but eventually turn away from the spectacle in boredom, disorientation, disgust, or anger. *The People, Yes* first interpellates its audience, only then to alienate it. When one turns away, one also rejects the image of society that it proposes. It offers us, on the one hand, an unacceptable status quo of oppression and victimization and, on the other hand, a revolution by and in the name of a nameless, boundless, philistine multitude. Closing the cover on *The People, Yes*, one disavows its pessimism, vulgar materialism, and dualist cosmology.

This strategic use of "badness" could represent a period- and nation-specific literary phenomenon. Fredric Jameson, following Jean-Paul Sartre, has argued that another 1930s American modernist work—John Dos Passos's *USA* trilogy—likewise owes its importance to its profoundly distasteful style. Dos Passos adopts a newspaper-like tone, exhibiting the "breathless enthusiasm" and "vacuity and distraction" of a "social column." The narrative begins to sound as if it were the "very embodiment of the 'objective spirit' of our society, of inauthenticity become public opinion." The implied, cynical narrator proves unable to convey "lived experience" in its subjective richness; instead, he provides us with "impersonal accounts of anonymous destinies" played out against the background of a "stylization of events" (99). This eerily objectifying writerly style provokes "horror" in Dos Passos's readers because it meretriciously violates their intuitive belief in an individual's autonomy and uniqueness: "In the movement of the narrative sentences we are able to watch our subjective experiences transformed into . . . inauthentic collective representation; we watch our own private feelings turn into those of anybody at all" (101). Dos Passos's readers eventually turn away in revulsion, refusing further involvement in the inhuman, inhumane process by which media outlets (of all political affiliations) mechanically produce sham histories out of individual human lives.

Jameson concludes that this "reaction is evidently not a political one; yet it touches that vision of ourselves and the world which is the very source of political action" (101). If during the 1920 and 1930s Europeans such as Theodor Adorno, Walter Benjamin, and Antonio Gramsci strove to free themselves conceptually and philosophically from the face-off between two dehumanizing ideologies—American industrial capitalism and Soviet communism—American writers such as Sandburg and Dos Passos wrote themselves into a kind of *affective* rebellion. Denotatively, they defend existing brands of utopian leftism. Stylistically, they dissent, pleading for better, more just visions of the present and future.

The People, Yes is verifiably bad poetry. But its badness should not be transvalued, rearticulated, mitigated, or ignored. Nor should it serve as a pretext for consigning the volume to history's dustbin. *The People, Yes* records a vexed, ambiguous moment in modernism's unfolding. A modernist text, driven into an ideological cul-de-sac, brazenly betrays the spirit and aesthetics of modernism in hopes that its readers will be horrified enough to act recklessly, even anarchically, to prevent themselves from succumbing to the same fixed killing patterns of thought. I can't go on, it says. You find another way.

2

Tom Raworth and Poetic Intuition

While studying at Essex University, Tom Raworth published several volumes of experimental verse, among them *The Big Green Day* (1968), *Lion Lion* (1970), and *Moving* (1971). His poetry of these years, Peter Middleton asserts, represents "the purest product of sixties culture that appeared in Britain" ("Silent Critique" 14). It features a "good-natured and inarticulate incomprehensibility" redolent of the era's counterculture, which sincerely (if naively) tended to presume that "a revolution capable of overthrowing the capitalist state was imminent" (14–15).[1]

Times change, as do authors. After completing his M.A., Raworth lived abroad until 1977. He returned to England to take the position of visiting poet-in-residence at King's College, Cambridge. In his absence, UK politics had taken a turn toward the dire. James Callaghan's Labour government was engaged in a slow, painful process of self-destruction. A bitter series of strikes and disputes in late 1978—the infamous "Winter of Discontent"—was followed by a vote of no confidence in March 1979. In May, in the largest reversal of power since 1945, the Conservatives under Margaret Thatcher won a forty-five-seat majority in Parliament. The new government set about privatizing state-owned industries; reducing public expenditure on education, health care, and housing; and implementing legal restrictions on unions.

Initially, Thatcher's policies were quite unpopular. Unemployment doubled. Inflation reached twenty percent. She would likely have lost the general election in 1983 if not for the Falkland Islands War. The fervent British nationalism provoked by Argentina's 1982 invasion of the South Atlantic colonial outpost guaranteed Thatcher an electoral landslide.[2] She increased her majority to one hundred forty-four seats. With renewed vigor, she pursued a "state-directed withering away of the state" of a sort never envisioned by Marx (Sheppard, "Whose" 193).

During 1982–1983 Raworth wrote the long poem "West Wind," which speaks out vigorously against the *Zeitgeist*:

> we are pieces
> of percentages . . .
> for credit
> is as far
> as machines
> can trust
> what you own
> and what you'll earn (*CP* 360–61)

Raworth's depiction of the prime minister is particularly harsh. Perhaps recollecting Neville Chamberlain's umbrella, he unflatteringly refers to her by the name of another accessory, her "handbag" ("a handbag / strutting between uniforms / such slow false tears" [360]; "the poor / said handbag / are lucky to be alive / breathing my air / contributing nothing / to profit" [372]). He denounces as deluded the widespread support for her efforts to "restore our former glory"; her economic policies, after all, will necessarily reduce the majority of her now-enthusiastic followers to "a global servant class / too poor / to see the crown jewels" (374).

Raworth's political commentary made "West Wind" "a kind of anthem of resistance" in the mid-1980s and won him many admirers among younger poets (Sheppard, "Whose" 199). "West Wind," though, does not resemble the better known, more aggressively vernacular protest poetry found in Linton Kwesi Johnson's *Inglan Is a Bitch* (1980) and Tony Harrison's *v.* (1985). Its grammar is often unparsable. Punctuation, other than a few question and quotation marks, is spotty to nonexistent. The verses are interrupted by curious doodle-drawings. There is no clear sequence of events, no consistent speaking voice, and no sustained cumulative argument. One could say that Raworth persists in the "articulate incomprehensibility" characteristic of his 1960s verse, albeit shorn of its prepossessing, genial whimsy (Middleton, "Silent Critique" 15).

So much has happened since Margaret Thatcher's 1983 reelection—the Poll Tax, the Treaty on European Union, the fall of John Major, the rise of New Labour, the death of Lady Diana, two wars in Iraq—that Raworth's outrage can seem quaintly dated. There are, however, important disciplinary reasons for this glance backwards. Until recently, a handful of renowned figures—among them

Philip Larkin, Ted Hughes, Geoffrey Hill, Craig Raine, and Seamus Heaney—
has almost entirely dominated academic discussions of post–World War II British verse. As Keith Tuma's preface to the Oxford University Press *Anthology of
Twentieth-Century British and Irish Poetry* (2001) explains, this curious reduction of fifty years of writing to a list of "tokens" was largely the consequence of
an unreflective understanding of "tradition as unconflicted and uncontested"
common among experts in the field. For such critics, "tradition" also narrowly
signified a national tradition, either the "continuous tradition of 'Englishness'
in English poetry" descending from Thomas Hardy or the corresponding Irish
genealogy issuing from W. B. Yeats (xxiv–xxv).[3]

What twenty-first century scholar could defend such assumptions? Cultural
studies, postcolonial studies, African diaspora studies, and other interdisciplinary areas of inquiry have repeatedly demonstrated that culture is a zone of perpetual "contradiction" in which variably sanctioned, differently originating narratives about history and identity emerge, circulate, merge, and collide (Lowe
96). In the wake of such classics as Dick Hebdige's *Subculture* (1979) and Paul
Gilroy's *There Ain't No Black in the Union Jack* (1987), it is nigh impossible
to speak of a single, uncontested British culture. There are simply too many
national, regional, racial, ethnic, religious, gender, class, and other differences
among British subjects for such a normatively unitary culture to exist, except
as a fiction promulgated by conservatives dreaming of a rural, Anglo-Saxons-only
past. For similar reasons, it is impossible to assemble a shortlist of the premier
British poets of the last half-century without inviting controversy. A diverse,
larger sampling of poetries is required before a critic can even hope to gesture
toward the art form's heterogeneity. Tuma's anthology, for instance, although
including generous selections by the old guard, devotes the bulk of its space to
introducing a prodigious range of sub- and noncanonical authors: dub poets,
eccentrics, experimentalists, feminists, performance poets, punk rockers, Scottish nationalists, South Asian immigrants, working-class bards, and many others that elude easy categorization.

For a poetry critic, this drastically expanded purview of what qualifies as
contemporary British poetry is both exhilarating and daunting. Aside from such
suspect distinctions as prizes, laureateships, and newspaper puff pieces, there
are few available means to help make sense of this unsorted avalanche of writing.[4] This chapter responds to this literary-historical dilemma in two comple-
mentary ways. First, it focuses on a prominent but little-studied author and
a challenging, ambitious long poem in relation to an undeniably central feature of recent British history, "the postwar establishment of a welfare state and
the subsequent erosion of this ideal" (Perril 108).[5] Raworth, born in 1938, belongs to the first generation to benefit from the remarkable, immediate post-

Blitz consensus that privileges once limited to the wealthy—such benefits as a postsecondary education, reliable health care, convenient transportation, and a comfortable retirement—should be the right of every British subject. He has also lived long enough to witness the *coup de grâce* to that consensus, the pit closures of 1983 and the ensuing strife between the National Coal Board and the National Union of Mineworkers. Reading a poem such as "West Wind," a critic necessarily grapples with questions of revolutionary longing, dystopian fear, communal solidarity, egotistical greed, and other states of mind and shades of affect that are grounded in and responsive to the particulars of British history. As scholars attempt to remap the contours of British verse, little could be more rewarding than attention to the interplay between literary production and the perduring social forces that occasion and shape it.[6]

Such interplay, though, as any literary critic knows, is inherently, even inordinately, complex. Literature never simply reflects society. A poem can be imagined as a space traversed by many forces, each of them vectoral, that is, pushing in a particular direction with a certain degree of insistence. And a poem, like any medium, variably refracts or obstructs these vectors. The results are unpredictable and hybrid. "West Wind," for example, does more than react to agonizing structural shifts in the British political economy. It also participates in the uneven, contested British reception and transformation of Euro-American avant-garde traditions. Moreover, it belongs to a particular stage of that process, namely Raworth's inquiry into a peculiar form, a "long, skinny poem" that combines short line length—often no more than a word or two—with a substantial page count—often filling an entire book (Wilkinson 146). This essay's second strategy for moving beyond the present impasse in the study of contemporary British poetry is to examine a poem that stands at the intersection of multiple compelling historical trajectories, each with their distinct, knotty problems of interpretation.

A Closer Look at "West Wind"

The lyric's allusive title is a tempting place to begin reading Raworth's poem. It immediately establishes an intertextual tie to Percy Bysshe Shelley's "Ode to the West Wind" (1819). On the surface, though, connections are not obvious. Shelley's poem is a five-part romantic ode written in terza rima. Raworth's poem consists of eleven, mostly unrhymed verse paragraphs of varying length, accompanied by four interpolated drawings. There are few verbal echoes of or traceable allusions to Shelley's ode beyond stray references to "dry leaves" (*CP* 357), "the breeze / this winter" (359), and "screaming blossoms / in a coy spring" (368). The title "West Wind," Simon Perril has argued, chiefly serves to announce a correspondence between the time of its writing and the historical "background to second-generation Romanticism." In both cases, a period of "revolutionary zeal" (the 1790s/1960s) is succeeded by an age of "a new conservative orthodoxy" founded on "a fiercely combative national identity" and "cultural insularity" (the 1810s/1980s). Moreover, Raworth's title makes clear his opinion about the "changes in political climate" since the 1960s. He implicitly assumes a Shelley-like, apocalyptic stance toward the decadence of the present moment (118).

These moorings in the British canon, as well as the neatness of the historical parallel, can make "West Wind" sound like ideal anthology-fodder, a comfortable participant in the "continuous tradition of 'Englishness' in English poetry" (Tuma xxv). Its opening lines quickly dispel that impression:

> the moon
> is blacker than the sky
> memories move
> in abandoned armor
> corridors of such interest
> of mirrors and cut glass
> night
> a few lights
> outlining motion
> a city's blue glow spikes
> from shadows fanned
> by airbrushed fingers
> restarting ink
> with a thumb (*CP* 355)

The form is easily described. These uncapitalized, punctuation-free lines vary between one and four stresses and follow no set meter. The subject matter, however, is more difficult to pin down. The first two lines propose a paradox (a moon that is black instead of white) that hints at something horribly awry in the cosmos. The following assertion, "memories move / in abandoned armor," although a bit of a non sequitur, nonetheless fairly straightforwardly suggests a further turn from the external (the night sky) to the internal and subjective, and there is a striking, ghost-of-Hamlet's-father tinge to the image that evokes the uncanny return of things long forgotten. Thereafter, matters become murkier. How does one interpret the next line, "corridors of such interest"? Whose "interest" are we talking about? What kind of interest anyway—monetary? aesthetic? parti-

san? Is the phrase a sentence fragment describing where the armored memories wander? Or does this line point ahead to the next bit, "of mirrors and cut
glass / night"? The poem possibly (but not necessarily) compares a starry night
to a darkened hallway spot-illuminated by flashes from mirrors and the fiery
edge-glimmer of "cut glass." Then, for a brief few breaths, the setting and action become relatively accessible and stable: "a few lights / outlining motion / a
city's blue glow spikes / from shadows." One can envision a speaker on the out-
skirts of a large city, perhaps in a car traveling down a road with widely spaced
streetlights. The "shadows" here, though, turn out to be "fanned / by airbrushed
fingers / restarting ink / from a thumb." The nighttime scene we have just been
contemplating turns out to be somebody's drawing ("fingers," "ink," "thumb").
The frame break is jolting. Why remind us so early in the poem that we are reading a work of pure imaginative artifice? Why not let us first settle into a coherent story, setting, or point of view?

　　Little here is reminiscent of Shelley, let alone Hughes or Heaney. No conventionally first-tier British poet resorts to such a hasty agglutination of unfinished
thoughts. True, formal analogues to "West Wind" do exist within the wider
canon of twentieth-century British verse. The lineation recalls Basil Bunting's
First Book of Odes (1966) and parts of Roy Fisher's *City* (1961). The unpunctuated piling-up of clauses and phrases resembles stretches in David Jones's *In
Parentheses* (1937), and some of David Gascoyne's 1930s verse exhibits a similar aversion to capitalization. Such precursors, though, are notably eccentric
to the lineages of Hardy and Yeats. They depend on foreign models, whether
French surrealist (Gascoyne) or American modernist (the others). Moreover,
these writers tend to favor regional over abstractly British allegiances, Bunting
to Northern England, Jones to Wales, and Fisher to the industrial Midlands. In
other words, if the verse in "West Wind" is detectably British, it belongs to an
outsider tradition that places a premium on modes other than a stoic, quietly
virtuosic inhabitation of inherited forms.

　　It must be pointed out, though, that even when classed among the writings
of outliers and experimentalists, the poem's speedy shuffling-through of topics,
settings, and frames of reference remains unique to Raworth. There seems to
be a roving, spotlight-like center of attention with drastically curtailed knowledge of what has come before and what is to follow. The poem's form sub-
tly reinforces this impression. The sound play tends to be inventive but also
highly local in application. The first few lines, for example, interlace voiced na-
sals (MooN, MeMories, abaNdoNed, iNterest, Move, arMor, Mirrors) and velar
plosives (blaCKer, sKy, Corridors, Cut, Glass). Next, long *i*'s predominate: night,
lights, outlining. After a line whose chief sound-effect is a thud-parade of mono-

syllables ("blue glow spikes"), two new consonants move to the fore: *f*'s (From, Fanned, Fingers) and *r*'s (fRom, aiRbRushed, fingeRs, RestaRting). The poem's sound patterning operates throughout in this tag-team fashion, particular configurations emerging and vanishing with alacrity.

One might expect this forward-propulsive mode of writing to yield a chaotic mess. It does not. "West Wind" remains intently engaged with the time of its writing. Fleeting leftist political commentary enters the poem's flow again and again. There are generic digs against the Thatcher era: "corruption / divides dis / from uninterest" (359); "colourless nation / sucking on grief" (360); "the homeless state . . . the nation with no pain" (361); "dangerous age . . . future / an unreliable tense" (372). There are jokes about the short-sightedness of the British electorate ("if I can't / take the dog in / i won't vote"—372), the swaggering stupidity of the nationalists ("proud to be / neanderthal / it's my bomb / i'm taking it home"—356), the vacuity of the press ("puffs of unrelated news"—374), the duplicity of spin doctors ("'it wasn't a mistake / it was an oversight'"—365), and the presumption of the Tories ("'are you / the other side?' / asks / our conservative canvasser"—369). Raworth laments Western Europe's intimacy with the United States ("two burger kings / on the champs élysées"—361) as well as the unreasoning paranoia that motivates that alliance ("lucky / no russians called / while we / were in the south atlantic"—374–75). Above all, he resents the Thatcherite rhetoric of cost-benefit analysis, which mechanically strives to maximize gain ("computer city / edged upward / twenty points"—365), ignores human wants and needs ("the computer acts / on limited knowledge / anaesthetised / by not knowing more"—356), and grants the power to make life-altering decisions to the "dry thin-lipped zombies / waffling in ice-shadows" that "money . . . attracts" (362).

Raworth's opposition to Thatcher provides "West Wind" with other kinds of coherence. He employs repeated, related images that lend the poem, if not a plot, then an overall, satisfying arc. As we have seen, Raworth begins with the image of a moon "blacker than the sky" (355). Midway through, between verse paragraphs five and six, after "handbag" (Margaret Thatcher) has dramatically entered the poem "strutting between uniforms," another moon appears, in this case a large, black, inked-in rectangle labeled "new moon" (360–61). We knew from the start that all was not right with the world; now we know who is to blame. Near the poem's end the speaker recalls a different celestial prodigy: "a ring / around the evening sun . . . brown to purple / edged by a rainbow / lacking red and orange / clouds almost clear / streamed from the horizon." This glorious melancholy instant, the beauty of a day in its vanishing, is opposed to the menacing gloom of what now impends: "we don't know night / to fear it" (374). The final two lines of "West Wind"—"fragments / of black spider motion"—end the poem on a horror movie note, with monsters stirring as Thatcher's dark night falls.

"West Wind"'s association between Thatcher and wicked-witch imagery (blackness, moons, arachnids) can come across as misogynist.[7] One could blame it on the rhetorical position in which Raworth finds himself. How does a male poet criticize a female prime minister without sounding unchivalrous? The fairy tale symbolism has a more important root cause. It originates in a binary fundamental to the poem that brings personal and public into painfully close conjunction. Verse paragraphs eight and nine concentrate on a second, contrasting female authority figure: the poet's mother, Mary Raworth née Moore. He recounts the hospitalization that preceded her death in 1983. He begins the story at the point when she is no longer able to recognize her son, or his gender:

thirties white concrete
glass shattered
in rusty frames
my mother sits
inside the door
first bed
next to the lavatory
under a fan
her flowers wilt
her fruit crinkles
'are you audrey's sister?' (367)

Distraught over his mother's squalid surroundings and forced to confront the fact of her bodily and mental decay, Raworth feels primally bereft:

sweet smell of death
forget-me-not
'is this the hospital
Hello   is this the hospital'
'we like to tilt them back
so we can see their eyes'
gangrene
shuddering
flecked with yellow
red-rimmed eyes
no patience

with death
no breast-feeding (368)

There is simply no consolation, not even theological, for his looming loss: "who made you? / god made me / no / my parents made me" (368). And his sense of powerlessness is exacerbated by the fecklessness of the National Health Service (NHS), which has been so gutted by Tory cost cutting that it can no longer provide the minima of medical care: "no chart / at the foot of her bed / the doctor / is at the other hospital" (369).

Grappling with an atavistic, child-like fear of abandonment, Raworth personifies and vilifies the forces that would deny him happiness. He assigns Thatcher, the miser in charge of the NHS, the attributes of a nursery-rhyme villain. Her handbag, like the witch's oven in the Hansel and Gretel story, takes on a horrible fascination as a demonic inversion of a mother's fruitful womb. As Robert Sheppard reminds us, Thatcher famously kept "the nuclear 'button'" inside her purse ("Whose" 195). The poem makes the possibility of a "war three" to follow "world war one / war two" immediate and tangible by documenting Thatcher's inhumane assault on the very people—like Mary Raworth—that a British prime minister ought, logically, to protect and nurture (CP 359). Thatcher, having shown herself "educated in empire" and a master of "internal colonialism," appears capable of any outrage (373). The answer to the rhetorical question twice-repeated in verse paragraph eleven—"whose lives does the government affect?" (372, 373)—is implicit in a message "nailed to a fence" that the speaker encounters in the poem's closing lines: "beware of the bomb" (375). Thatcher might preach less government, but she also holds—quite literally at hand—the power to change the future of the planet irrevocably.

Raworth's feelings of private and political powerlessness account for the final respect in which his anti-Thatcherism unifies "West Wind." At constant work in the poem is a tension between an impulse toward immersion in history and a desire to flee its horrors altogether. The instances of political commentary, which exemplify immersion, are played off against other moments, in which Raworth longs to escape the agony and mire of contemporary life. Frequently— and here the title's romanticism again becomes pertinent—this escape involves flight into the countryside:

baa
gibbets ahead
sweet rocket
rue
rubbed lemon balm

a snake
thoughtless as a bird
thud rolled hibiscus bloom
onto a plastic cover
water violets duck (372)

* * *

rose red
set yellow
what distance
between the double orange lines
of a roman wall?
ground ivy
smothers bluebells
golden moon (369)

Intimations of mortality and violence persist in these pastoral interludes—
"gibbets," "snake," "smothers"—but they appear not as specific evils wreaked by
culpable individuals but as timeless facts. Et in Arcadia ego: Death is inevitable
even in a latter-day Eden. Such truisms have their own consolations. Life proceeds predictably, and even its bumps and interruptions are if not foreseeable
then readily intelligible. Unlike the unnatural "new moon" regnant in Thatcher's London, the "golden moon" that shines in such places obeys natural laws.

Raworth associates these rural interludes with a second, devoutly wished
form of escape, into the contemplative life, where the only "noise" is the buzz
of "thinking":

simple things
warm sunlight
a cloud
thinking
the noise
of mind
leaves wrestle
stalks green
matchsticks
descriptive words
verbs
directions
spherical geometry
the comfort of nouns (362–63)

Raworth aches to lose himself in free exploration of what, to him, are truly the "simple things": "descriptive words," "verbs," and "nouns." If only he could slough off the world and write without worry or consequences, give himself up entirely to the delights of sound and word play . . . but his mother lies dying, and the Iron Lady rules. "West Wind" cannot in good conscience remain fixed on "warm sunlight / a cloud." Contemporary history exerts a centripetal force on "West Wind" that consistently tugs its peculiar, antinarrative waywardness back into the ambit of protest, documentation, and lament.

To date secondary literature on Raworth has placed little emphasis on the kinds and causes of coherence in his poetry.[8] In fact, critics have typically dwelled on the opposite, its resolute resistance to sense-making. They have described its refusal to differentiate lesser from more important passages; its lack of temporal and causal signposting; its multiplication of points of view; its accumulation of specifics in the absence of organizational rubrics; its tumbling collocation of words, phrases, and lines that rarely group themselves into complete sentences; its lack of opportunities for a reader to pause and reflect; and the difficulty of remembering what one has just read and anticipating what will come next.[9] Secondary criticism has not, admittedly, had much to say about "West Wind." Other long poems have drawn the bulk of the attention, especially *Ace* (1974), *Writing* (1982), and *Eternal Sections* (1993). "West Wind"'s unifying anti-Thatcherism could represent a departure from Raworth's more characteristic writing style, in which "the poetry remains stubbornly open" (Davidson 219).

This idea has merit. Indeed, we will be revisiting it near the end of this essay. For the moment, however, one should note that the coherence of "West Wind" can easily be overplayed. There are many parts of the poem that diverge from, interrupt, or undermine its structural binaries, symbolic armature, and thematic uniformity. The two page-sized drawings are the most obvious example. The first, which intrudes immediately after the passage about "simple things / warm sunlight," depicts an amorphous, protean shape subdivided into irregular regions. It looks somewhat like a tissue sample viewed under a microscope, or better yet a free-hand rendering of a map of administrative divisions (e.g., the counties of Ireland or the departments of France). A reader might expect this visual graphic to illustrate the text in some manner. It does so only partly and parodically. The speaker has just expressed his wish to escape to a pastoral neverland. The drawing immediately thereafter provides us with a bizarre maybe-map marked with a wild assortment of possible place names: nouns ("malnutrition," "consequence," "height"); proper nouns ("Argus," "Jane," "Scobie"); verbs ("am," "ate," "compare"); adjectives ("aloft," "half-hearted," "slip-shod"); an adverb ("devoutly"); words not easily identified as a certain part of speech ("bugle," "darn," "Druze," "hike," "string"); and a French loan word ("on-

cle") (365). This curious diagram could be intended to extend the preceding verse paragraph's association between pastoral spaces and poetic composition, but the word selection here is so aleatory that it conveys less reverie than vertigo. Moreover, the lines that separate the words, as well as the words' clashing spatial orientations, suggest a poetics of hermetic isolation in which ideas relate only contingently and provisionally. In short, this page evokes not Raworth the incisive political commentator but the nonmimetic, anarchic writer familiar from secondary criticism.

If the first page-sized drawing is an anti-map of an impossible zone, the second is an aggressive anachronism. It consists of a large rectangle that contains roaming spirochete-like squiggles. The word "MENSHEVIKS!" appears along the rectangle's bottom edge. This drawing tropes the Bolshevik, and latterly Soviet, tradition of the propaganda poster as practiced by Nikolai Dolgorukov, Gustav Klutsis, and other graphic artists. Superficially, it might not bear

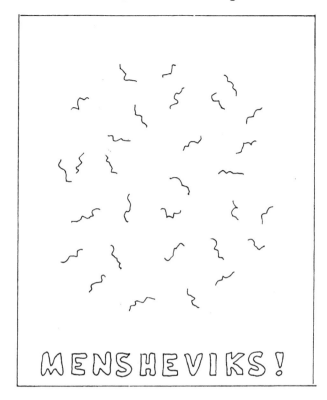

much resemblance to such posters—there is no photomontage, no futuristic sans serif font, no bold primary colors—but it employs recognizably similar semiotic strategies. Seen on a factory wall in Tomsk circa 1950, its message would have been transparent. It denounces an enemy using common CPSU shorthand for counterrevolutionary activity. ("Menshevik" originally referred to a wing of the Russian Social-Democratic Workers' Party, led by L. Martov [Julij Tsederbaum], that opposed the Bolsheviks in the years 1903–22.) It also bluntly compares this enemy to subhuman vermin, worms, or bacilli. Viewers of such a poster are exhorted to be vigilant and to help authorities exterminate a pernicious threat.

Thatcher's Britain, however, is not Stalin's Russia. Importing Bolshevik-Soviet visual rhetoric into a poem written by a British subject is profoundly disorienting. Who is the intended audience? Who is its implied author? Raworth does not appear to be attacking Thatcher herself. He uses *Menshevik* in the plural; besides, the word implies outward or erstwhile espousal of (flawed, insufficiently developed) socialist beliefs—hardly a charge one could level against the prime minister. More apt but still problematic scenarios exist. One could imagine, for instance, a hard-core socialist supporter of Labour accusing centrist-leaning colleagues of being Mensheviks, but even in its pre-Blair days party members rarely flung Soviet slang at each other so cavalierly. Alternatively, Raworth could be portraying himself as a hard-liner denouncing former advocates of the welfare state who now vote Tory. Such posturing, though, would hardly change the minds of Thatcherite converts. Or—yet another alternative—the poster-doodle could be a way for Raworth to poke fun at his poem's stridency by associating his anticapitalist rhetoric with communist propaganda at its most egregious. Why invoke the Bolshevik-Menshevik split, though, as opposed to, say, the battles between Reds and Whites during the Russian Civil War? Posters such as El Lissitzky's *Klinom krasnym bej belykh* (Beat the whites with a red wedge, 1920) dramatize a conflict between socialists and capitalists that would appear much more germane to the situation in 1982–1983.

To put it simply: whether one chooses to read it as a serious or parodic statement, the "Mensheviks!" drawing does not align well with political realities in the months when Raworth was writing "West Wind." The interplay of us/them upon which the coherence of the poem depends thereby loses crispness and effectiveness. Raworth, at such moments, seems intent on undoing what he elsewhere achieves. He permits "*nacheinander,*" the principle of "setting down" one thing "after another," to proceed without check despite results that refuse integration into consistent messages (Skinner 175). This lack of consistency has led one critic, John Barrell, to conclude that the "voices which express the fragments of an anger against . . . the organised injustices of international capitalism" are a red herring. "[I]f there is a politics in Raworth's poetry, it is as much deferred and contradictory as everything else in his writing" (409).

One does not have to agree with Barrell to recognize that he has pinpointed a problem in Raworth's poetics. Why undertake an anti-Thatcher polemic only to muddle the message? What does Raworth gain by refusing to make a straight-ahead, easy-to-follow argument? To answer such questions, one must situate "West Wind" within a different trajectory than British political history. The poem must be read in relation to postwar literary history, more specifically the British reception of American postmodern verse.

Before "West Wind"

Tom Raworth belongs to a cohort of British poets who "first appeared in the sixties and seventies" that includes Andrew Crozier, Lee Harwood, Christopher Middleton, Wendy Mulford, Douglas Oliver, and Denise Riley. This group of writers rebelled against the conservative "good old solid English tradition" that they associated with Larkin and the Movement more generally. To free themselves from parochialism, they paid close attention to the most provocative overseas literature to which they had ready access: "what was going on in the States" (Hollo 80–81). More specifically, they read, discussed, and imitated the writings produced by the loosely affiliated, mid-twentieth-century avant-garde poetry circles retrospectively called the New American Poetry (a label lifted from the title of an influential 1960 anthology edited by Donald Allen).[10] The British poets found much to admire in the writings of each of the various subsections of the New American Poetry (hereafter NAP): the Beats, the Black Mountain School, the San Francisco Renaissance, and the New York School.[11] They particularly esteemed the NAP's antiestablishment ethos, disregard for decorum, delight in popular culture, vernacular diction, ludic youthfulness, and rigorous practice of a mode of free verse in which form is everywhere finely calibrated to subject matter.

Raworth's involvement with the American avant-garde dates back to 1961–64, when he edited a journal named *Outburst* that published Gregory Corso and Robert Creeley. A close friendship followed with the Pond-hopping Black Mountaineer Ed Dorn, and, while at Goliard Press (1965–67), Raworth accepted books by several NAP authors: Creeley, Paul Blackburn, Charles Olson, Ron Padgett, and John Wieners. Given such contacts, it is hardly surprising that Raworth's early poetry is unapologetically indebted to NAP precedent.[12] He characteristically employs an irregular, mostly left-justified lineation derived from William Carlos Williams via such Black Mountain intermediaries as Creeley and Dorn. Likewise Black Mountain-esque are his departures from standard punctuation, spelling, and capitalization; his interest in notating the rhythm and intonation of speech; and his rapid pacing, which exemplifies Charles Olson's "much-quoted dictum . . . that one perception must directly lead to another" (Ward 22). Moreover, he renders overt his literary affiliations by regularly referring or alluding to such premier NAP writers as Creeley, Padgett, Ted Berrigan, Kenneth Koch, and Frank O'Hara.[13]

Raworth's indebtedness to NAP models in no way implies slavish imitation. An illustrative example: *Penguin Modern Poets 19* (1971) published selections by Raworth alongside verse by the New York School poet John Ashbery. Certain early Raworth lyrics, such as "Inner Space," do indeed recall Ashbery's elusive not-quite-allegorical dreamscapes:

in an octagonal tower, five miles from the sea
he lives quietly with his books and doves

all walls are white, some days he wears
green spectacles, not reading

riffling the pages - low sounds of birds and their flying

holding to the use of familiar objects
in the light that is not quite (*CP* 34)

Raworth gives specifics (*octagonal* tower, *five* miles, *white* walls, *green* spectacles that vividly sketch an imagined scene. The actions that take place, though, are muddled. Two blandly inexpressive verbs ("lives," "wears") give way to a trailing, ambiguous syntax: three dangling participles ("reading," "riffling," "holding") and a floating noun phrase ("low sounds of birds and their flying"). This vague reportage leaves readers unsure what moral to draw about "inner space." Should we imagine the mind as a tower in which the intellect flips through books without reading them? Or rather flips through them every once in a while, on "some days"? What does it do on other days? If "books" stand for knowledge or memory, as appears likely, what then are the "doves"? Emotions? Flights of fancy? The white walls could refer to the bones of the skull, but why green eyeglasses? Are they related somehow to rose-colored ones? Like Ashbery in "They Dream Only of America" and "Houseboat Days," Raworth's narrative brings readers to the verge of quick paraphrase only to strand them amidst quandaries. Depending on one's inclinations, the result is either frustration or a detour into mystery and fantasy.

Unlike a typical Ashbery poem, however, "Inner Space" investigates the varied poetic effects made possible by manipulating a page's white space. After the words "not reading," a blank space interrupts the poem. We are, appropriately, deprived of anything to read for a bit. Later, another stanza break occurs after the mention of the "low sounds of birds." We are given a respite in which to imagine cooing and fluttering before the poem resumes. Finally, Raworth ends the lyric in the middle of a phrase, just after an adverb: "in the light that is not quite." Not quite *what*? We could supply the missing conclusion. The word "right" is particularly tempting, since it would echo "light" and "quite." Alternatively, we could construe "is not quite" as a skewed way of saying "does not quite exist," willing a finality, of sorts, on the poem by arresting it and its message (its "light") in the flickering nowhere between presence and absence. There are analogues to Raworth's experimentation with layout in NAP writings—Frank O'Hara's "The Day Lady Died," for instance, ends abruptly *sans* period after the declaration "and we all stopped breathing" (325)—but Raworth's three, differently valenced interruptions of "Inner Space" break with the NAP's predominantly speech-imitative versification by displaying a recurrent, pronounced interest in a poem as a visual construct of words arranged on a page.

Robert Sheppard has argued that Raworth's early poems "valorise intuition over intelligence" ("Poetics" 83). Understood properly, this assertion accounts both for Raworth's initial attraction to the New American Poetry and for his (over time increasingly evident) departures from its precedent. The 24 January 1971 entry in Raworth's fragmentary prose-and-verse piece "Notebook" declares that "Intelligence become reflex equals intuition" (93). The remainder of "Notebook" can help clarify this crucial gnomic statement. Intelligence, we learn, is a quality prized by "critics" and "explainers." Such people overvalue "meaning," which they confuse with "mathematical" regularities. Meaning, though, is, strictly speaking, ubiquitous: "*any* piece of language / contains *meaning.*" No larger pattern, structure, or context has to exist before readers can attribute *some* degree meaning to a word. Moreover, "any piece of language / will fuse with any other." Words can be strung together without an overall plan or intent. Such haphazard combinations might lack a "centre," and therefore vex "explainers," but an artist, "scan[ning] for the new," will delight in the consequent, unforeseen interplay of meanings. He or she has no worries that the words' ordering might violate logic or common sense. They know that while composing, "you / can't / contra / dict / your / self" (99–101; his emphasis). Furthermore, artists feel no need to arrive at an integral understanding of a given word-string: "Intuition skips language it doesn't 'know' and reappears where the words fit again" (95).

The explainer/artist binary is, thankfully, neither absolute nor static. "Art can always attract attention from intelligence" (91). And with persistence, explainers can begin to appreciate that artists are striving "to get something that isn't a thought around something that isn't an idea" (89). They see that "meaning," as they have traditionally understood it, is precisely what artists are "fighting against" (101). They are then free to redirect their will-to-analyze. Instead of aiming at a global account of a given work, they discover that they can analyze without preconception or goal its "constant flowage from meaning to meaning, and . . . slideslippage between meanings" (95). Once old-style critical intelligence becomes transformed to "reflex," that is, a constant, instinctual response to this rapid unceasing flow, intuition at last takes over (93).[14] "We are free now to delight in the surface of language" (95).[15]

Raworth's celebration of intuition resonates with the Black Mountain emphasis on keeping things moving. In a poetics of intuition, one perception immediately leads to another without fear that such speed entails overlooking important pieces of "the whole picture" ("Notebook" 99). His delight in "slideslippage" also accounts for his fascination with the quick, improvisatory shifts in tone, setting, diction, and persona associated with the New York School. Poets such as Ashbery, Koch, and O'Hara regularly make use of unexpected transitions, unbelievable coincidences, brute juxtaposition, surreal happenings, comic asides, and mismatches between rhetoric and subject matter. Little in British verse since W. H. Auden's *The Orators* (1932) could offer Raworth such an archive of applied intuition, a "flowage" of language fully alive to its course, obstacles, rapids, and eddies.

Significantly, however, neither the Black Mountain nor the New York School habitually takes the war against "meaning" (as understood by "explainers") far enough for Raworth. He envisions a poetics of surplus that enforces "skip[ping]" around and investigating a poem piecemeal ("Notebook" 95). Most NAP writings are too invested in conventional meaning-production to satisfy this demand. They usually reward being read from beginning to end without omissions. Similarly, Raworth's distrust of elevating the poetic self to centrality put him on a collision course with the NAP. He believed the self to be not a master of its environment but a crossing point for multiple, external, unknowable forces: "we *are* / the switching of relays" ("Notebook" 95; his emphasis). "Maybe there are four forces using our 'self's. All that information" (100). While many New American Poets—among them Creeley, O'Hara, and Olson—undoubtedly questioned the epistemological grounds of selfhood, the biggest names also succeeded, via their writing, in reinventing themselves as larger-than-life figures whose personae frequently overshadow their verse. Creeley's anguished assault on the pronoun "I" in lyrics such as "The Language" (1967), for example, might point toward a postmodern conception of the self as a relay-switcher, but it is difficult not to imagine *Creeley himself*, self-doubting bard and tormenting-tormented lover, suffering through the agonizing dissolution of identity that his lyrics recount. Raworth sought a truly impersonal poetry that would bar "explainers" from offering autobiographical interpretations that might smooth over his works' disjunctions, incongruities, and other challenges to the intellect.

From *The Relation Ship* (1966) to *Ace* (1974), he sought to craft a form long enough to permit selective reading; a form impersonal enough to forestall looking to the author as guarantor of meaning; and a form flexible enough to provide maximal opportunities for unlike things, words, and images to abut. He experimented with a diaristic mode ("Six Days," "Stag Skull Mounted," "Logbook"); an epistolary format ("Love Poem," "Letters from Yadoo"); and modular sequences ("My Son the Haiku Writer," "Formal" 1–7). Although fascinating, rewarding, and innovative, none of these works fully satisfied his underlying program. They remained either too identified with the poet as implied author (diary, letter) or too amenable to classification, comparison, and other modes of "explaining" (haiku, quatrain).[16]

In a clutch of lyrics written just before *Ace* and later collected in *The Mask*

(1976), Raworth made one last raid on the New American Poetry in quest of a solution. He borrowed the serial form of Creeley's *Pieces* (1968), perhaps the most radical NAP experiment with language.[17] Its short, abstract, discrete segments offer little in the way of narrative, character, moral, or passion. They more closely resemble puzzles or riddles than compressed poems. If there is a rule that guides the ordering of segments, it is a perversely negative one: sections must possess few or no obvious causal, logical, temporal, or dramatic connections. In the following extract from "Perpetual Motion," one finds Raworth gleefully adopting this mode of writing:

reception

*

je ne veux pas
les biscuits de chocolat

*

warp
lines

*

a cat's concept of mind
that could make it dance
and sing by editing film

*

mary
was assumed
into heaven (*CP* 180)

Read straight through, the writing is nonsensical. What does the Assumption have to do with chocolate biscuits or dancing cats? Matters improve slightly when sections are read individually. The doggerel French couplet suggests an English speaker amused at discovering an internal rhyme ("pas" / "chocolat") while talking with a waiter on the Continent. The freestanding word "reception" is phatic, that is, a means of making a reader contemplate the relation between author, text, and audience (are we "receiving" the message?). The monosyllables "warp / lines" could also be knottily self-reflexive. The "lines" of the poem could be said to constitute its "warp"—a comparison between poem and cloth licensed by the etymological link between the words *text* and *textile*. Similar speculations could be made concerning the import of the singing felines and the avowal of Catholic dogma. Intuition, in other words, has opportunities to run riot. In contrast, intelligence is paralyzed. It simply cannot unify such heterogeneous nuggets of verse.

Indeed, for Raworth's purposes, intelligence proves to be overly paralyzed. Nothing in "Perpetual Motion" tempts readers to seek larger patterns of meaning. Its sequence of mini-poems is too aleatory, too disjunctive, to entice a reader's intelligence into the repeated process of trial-and-error that precedes its elevation into intuitive "reflex." Raworth's *Ace* (1974) solves this problem. Like *Pieces,* it presumes that anything can follow anything. Unlike *Pieces,* it limits the number of articulated segments. The book-length poem has four parts. Each part consists of a lengthy, narrow, uninterrupted column of verse:

> puts wind
> to back
> as light
> ups
> sail
> for life
> laughs
> to sky
> original
> out
> standing
> art in
> junction
> expounds
> only
> one
> love
> is well
> we are here
> before the standard
> planes (*CP* 206)

The first eight lines of this excerpt seem to depict an excitable person on a sailboat. That vignette blurs into what might be an "in / junction" about "love" that "out / standing / art" "expounds." The words, though, can be fit together in any number of ways. It could be that person on the sailboat who is "out / standing" while "laugh[ing] / to sky." The word "love" potentially functions both as the direct object of "expounds" and the subject of "is well." And "we are here" could either be a dependent or independent clause, depending on whether a "that" has been omitted after "is well." The word "standard" is either a noun (as in "battle standard") or an adjective describing "planes." *Ace* teases readers with multiple, possible, non-exclusive ways of configuring its short lines into plots, descriptions, soliloquies, and other conventional elements of literary expression. If the asterisks in "Perpetual Motion" signal ruptures—moments when Raworth announces that an intelligence cannot bridge this gap—in *Ace* every line break becomes an invitation for intelligence to strive after explicable meaning. And, as readers soon discover, it is impossible to make use of every such invitation. To keep from going mad, they have to pick and choose when to ask questions and be content with less-than-complete answers. As Raworth would put it, the poem's incessant "flowage" stops readers from thinking like critics and encourages them to think like artists.

"West Wind" in Theory

Since *Ace,* the "long skinny poem" has remained the favored format for many of Raworth's most ambitious works, among them *Bolivia: Another End of Ace* (1975), *Writing* (1982), *Catacoustics* (1991), *The Vein* (1991), *Blue Screen* (1992), and "Meadow" (1999) (Wilkinson 146). In fact, the form has become Raworth's trademark, his distinctive contribution to the Anglo-American poetic avant-garde. He strikes a balance between sense and nonsense such that readers are inescapably (albeit sometimes begrudgingly) made aware of their active role in determining the boundary between the two. He thus ensures that the focus falls less on him as an author than on the phenomenology of reading, that is, how people interact with the words on the page in front of them. Numerous poets, including Charles Bernstein, Miles Champion, Adrian Clarke, Allen Fisher, Lyn Hejinian, Drew Milne, and Maggie O'Sullivan, have looked to Raworth's disjunctive techniques to help further their own efforts to disrupt "vocal consistency" (Ward 19).

"West Wind" occupies a singular place within Raworth's series of long-skinnies. It reprises, as we have seen, the form's discontinuities and other disorienting devices. Yet it differs fundamentally from the rest. *Ace,* like "West Wind," contains an array of politicized utterance, but, unlike "West Wind," the movement between frames, narratives, voices, and thoughts is too rapid for a coherent, stable political statement to emerge. There is no recurrent villain, no extended lament for a dying relative, and no straightforward governing binaries. It might be possible, though, following Robert Sheppard, to argue that *Ace* offers a covert ethical message. Its disconcerting, proliferating ambiguities encourage new patterns of thinking ("intuition") that could carry over into other interpretive contexts (when viewing a television show, when perusing the Sunday paper, and so forth). With luck, the result would be a heightened tolerance for the unknown and the unknowable in the world. When confronted by irresolvable difference, the reflexive response would become not a will-to-master but an impulse to let-be.[18]

"West Wind" portrays such problem-free letting-be as desirable but ineffectual. Such an ontological stance, it implies, belongs not to the world of engaged action but to the escapism of the pastoral. In 1982–1983, Thatcher is prime minister, and no matter how much Raworth might compassionately, nonjudgmentally stand alongside his ailing mother, that alone cannot give her ease. In his extremity, he resorts to autobiography and polemic, two modes of writing that he had avoided since *Ace*. Moreover, this seeming violation of his aesthetic principles occurs in the United Kingdom as a consequence of British events in a poem written in a "foreign" style, that is, one that emerged in dialogue with American poetic models and that was perfected during 1972–1977, the years in which he lived as an expatriate in the United States. In "West Wind," he butts up against the ugly possibility that his career to date had been founded on flight from home and from the difficult work of making that home livable and just. Thatcher has begun dismantling the British welfare state—but didn't he, too, abandon it long before? An American detour in the giddy age of Haight-Ashbury, Andy Warhol, and Neil Armstrong might have held promise, but in the era of Reagan-Thatcher it can appear an irresponsible act. In 1982–1983 he reexamines the course his career has taken. He chooses to place "West Wind" at the end of *Tottering State: New and Selected Poems 1963–1983* (1984). After "West Wind," Raworth wrote little verse for three years. When he began again, he struck out in a new direction. From 1986–1990 he wrote reams of fourteen-line "sonnets" (Sheppard, "Whose" 202). Looking across Raworth's *oeuvre*, "West Wind" is more than an anomaly. It is a rupture.

He recovered from the stumble, though. Long-skinnies feature prominently in his major late 1990s publications, *Clean and Well Lit* (1996) and *Meadow* (1999). To understand both the interruption and the resumption of this form in Raworth's writings, we have to address a question skirted in the last section. Why was Raworth so partial to intuition in the 1960s and '70s? Raworth's writings on poetics from the period are scanty and evasive (Middleton, "Silent Critique" 8–9). Not even the otherwise invaluable "Notebook" has much to say on this key point, beyond linking intuition, greater creativity, and improved artistry. In search of an explanation, one could turn to a triumvirate of critics—Peter Bürger, Andreas Huyssen, and Fredric Jameson—whose updates of Frankfurt School sociology have dominated recent discussions of postmodern art and literature. All three men charge that capitalism's development has reached a point that disruptive formal strategies formerly identified with modernism and the avant-garde have lost their ability to shock or otherwise express opposition to the status quo. Such provocations have now become commodified, freely available in the marketplace like any other prepackaged experience. From this point of view, Raworth's poetics can appear regressive. His praise of irrationality, one might contend, usefully diverts attention from the awkward fact that fractured grammar, plural voicing, and abrupt changes in subject matter no longer advance leftist politics in any meaningful sense.

This line of argument, however, places a strangely high valuation on novelty. It faults postmodernists and neo-avant-gardists for hollowly, uncritically recapitulating the formal strategies of their precursors. As we have seen, though, Raworth is not driven by the imperative to "make it new." His primary end is didactic, to alter how readers think about and read poetry. Such retraining requires a hyperbolic practice of one's analytic intellect to the point that it becomes reflexive, an automatic process pursued *ad libitum* regardless of conscious, rational, or purposive intent. If a given form abets this end, its degree of novelty is irrelevant.

There is a second school of thought concerning the postwar avant-garde that is better suited to evaluate Raworth's project. Critics such as Yve-Alain Bois, Craig Dworkin, Rosalind Krauss, and Steve McCaffery, instead of dwelling on breakthrough, senescence, and repetition, have concentrated on elucidating the economics of signification at play in particular artworks. They have taken as their starting point the French thinker Georges Bataille.[19] McCaffery's argument is most pertinent for our purposes. Foundational to his thinking is Bataille's distinction between a "restricted economy," one whose "operation is based upon valorized notions of restraint, conservation, investment, profit, accumulation and cautious proceduralities in risk taking," and a "general economy," which includes "all non-utilitarian activities of excess, unavoidable waste and non-productive consumption" such as "orgasm, sacrifice, meditation, The Last Supper, and dreams" (*North* 201–3). According to McCaffery, "the single operation of writing" is "a complex interaction" of these "two contrastive, but not exclusive economies" (203). Most writing, admittedly, is intended to participate in a restricted economy—people, after all, generally tailor what they write to attain particular ends—but that does not preclude seemingly utilitarian texts from also inadvertently conveying "wasted" meaning through accidents such as rhyme, punning, typos, and so forth.

McCaffery argues that lyric poetry's innate emphasis on the materiality of language makes it a genre in which the interplay between general and restricted economies can assume greater urgency than usual. A poet, unlike a philoso-

pher or a memo writer, cannot rely upon the "language of instrumental reference" to "repress" the fact that language is forever producing "wasteful" meanings inadvertently (204–5). Since poets attend to such features of language as
the sound, rhythm, and spelling of words, they are forever confronting (if not
necessarily recognizing) the fact that language communicates in an array of
nonsemantic ways, many of which may appeal to the senses but fail to convey
utilitarian, paraphrasable meaning. Nothing, of course, prevents poets from
downplaying this aspect of their art, or citing aesthetic, intellectual, political,
and/or theological commitments to justify why they write as they do. Certain
exceptional poets, though, delight in their art's wastefulness. They take a stand
on behalf of verse that exhibits "deployment without use, without aim and without a will to referential or propositional lordship" (214). They strive to offer "a
linguistic space in which meanings splinter moving fields of plurality, establishing differentials able to resist a totalization into recoverable integrations that
would lead to a summatable 'Meaning'" (220–21).

McCaffery here could be describing *Ace* or any of Raworth's other long
poems, including "West Wind." To McCaffery, works such as Raworth's are important because they bring to light the contested coincidence of writing's general and restricted economies. Such standout texts do not, it is crucial to note,
eliminate that binary opposition, nor do they achieve an anarchic, entropic victory of a general economy over the constraints of a restricted one. As Craig
Dworkin explains, "General and restricted economies are not . . . easily separable alternatives which one might simply choose between; they ceaselessly ir-
rupt within one another" in every act of writing. Cross-grain, eccentric, aleatory,
and other nonstandard reading practices can reveal that "every text threatens to
sacrifice itself in an ecstatic loss of meaning," even as the "meaninglessness" of
eccentric, aleatory, and other nonstandard texts "can always be accounted for
(even if only as the meaning of 'meaninglessness')" (*Reading the Illegible* 81).
True, Raworth might typically dwell only on the libratory potential of the inter-
implication of general and restricted economies. But he has practical reasons for
this one-sided approach. He hopes to show that every statement nominally in
line with instrumental reason, capitalist efficiency, and political expediency can
in fact, with ingenuity, be read otherwise, as participating in a utopian, pyrotechnic surplus of possibility. One simply has to read selectively, speculatively,
perversely, or in any other manner that refuses "summatable 'Meaning.'" To
put it differently: he preaches the indispensability of "intuition" in navigating a
world with a monstrously unbalanced, ideological preference for the categoriz-
able, disciplined, and profitable over the hybrid, wayward, and improvident.

Raworth wrote "West Wind" in a time of personal and political crisis. Intended to redress concrete, particular wrongs, the poem ends up possessing an

unusual degree of thematic, symbolic, and polemical coherence. Having just spent nearly a decade, though, seeking a form that forestalls "recoverable integrations," how could Raworth find this outcome anything but suspicious? The sudden return of "logic" after its deposition years prior ("logic is not thin king for your self") had to feel like a retreat ("Notebook" 94). Yet "West Wind," as we have seen, is far from a seamless or unified text. The "Mensheviks!" doodle-poster and the labeled maybe-map derail line-by-line explanations of the poem. Other aspects of the poem comparably defeat integration: the periodic interjection of phrases in French, German, Spanish, and Italian; the abrupt jumps between viewpoints, locations, and discursive registers; and the unpredictable shuttling between memory, present-tense observation, and counterfactual speculation. Yes, "West Wind" tilts further in the direction of establishing restricted economies than *Ace*. For that reason, it probably rewards a reader's "intelligence" more than the earlier work. But "West Wind" also contains more than enough jolts, surprises, and perplexities to provoke intelligence toward reinvention as "intuition." Both long poems make overt the opposition between restricted and general economies; they differ solely in the relative degree of emphasis that they place on those two economies. After ceasing to write long-skinnies for several years, Raworth was able to return to the form and discover that its virtues remained unimpaired. "West Wind," soberly judged retrospectively, was seen to reveal no fatal flaws in the long-skinny format.

True, aficionados of avant-garde verse are likely to rate "West Wind" a lesser achievement than *Writing*, *Ace*, or *Eternal Sections*. Those poems capture Raworth at his most formally and syntactically daring. They are radical experiments that rigorously unsettle conventional reading practices. In the last half-century, only a few works—perhaps Clark Coolidge's *The Maintains* (1974), Karen Mac Cormack's *Quirks and Quillets* (1991), and Steve McCaffery's *The Black Debt* (1989)—can rival their acetic aversion to purely instrumental uses of language.

One can acknowledge the merits of such a ranking without accepting it. In "El Lissitzky in Vitebsk" (2003), Raworth's old Essex University tutor, the art historian T. J. Clark, illustrates that one can fairly evaluate formally innovative art without presuming that its quality depends solely on the extremity of its novelty. His argument is worth repeating here in brief: Clark posits that El Lissitzky's paintings, although undoubtedly pushing much further the non-Euclidean spatial experiments of his mentor Kazimir Malevich, typically display "deeply limiting . . . good manners" (199). In comparison to Malevich's work, they are too "rarefied," exhibiting "too much mere difference and advantage" (203). One major exception is a propaganda board that Lissitzky painted in spring or summer 1920. It combines geometric shapes—rectangles, triangles, and an enormous dark circle—with a text that orders workers to return to factories and to "move production forward" (199). The "three-dimensional plotting" suggested by the superimposed shapes is "at loggerheads" with the two-dimensionality of the Russian script. The flatness of the words, it turns out, exerts a "palpable gravity" that resists, and therefore accentuates and energizes, the shapes' spatial gaming (203). For this reason, the overall tone is heroic striving, not the effortless aimless play conveyed by other Lissitzky paintings. Clark stresses that the aesthetic success of this work stems directly from the exigencies of War Communism. "Doing propaganda in extremis pushed the artist's modernism to its most intense and most effective state" (206). Lissitzky's then-ardent Bolshevism translated pictorially into a saving "pull of everything back onto the flat." Clark concludes, "If there simply are no strong vectors or figures of totalization . . . then the viewer will not see the centripetal activity *as* centripetal" (209; his emphasis).

"West Wind" is Raworth's equivalent of Lissitzky's propaganda board. The personal and public pressures on the poet spurred him to write in a more sustained, focused manner than usual. His recurrent themes, symbols, and polemical targets provide a stable backdrop against which affects such as humor, pain, and rage achieve deeper, more memorable expression than elsewhere. In contrast, the comparatively context-free lines of *Ace*, *Writing*, and *Eternal Sections* have a tendency to glide frictionless past the eyes. "West Wind"'s overall push to cohere similarly renders dispersive, anti-lyrical moments such as the maybe-map and the poster-doodle much more viscerally effective than similar visual interruptions in long-skinnies such as *Catacoustics*, where non sequitur is closer to the norm. The "strong vectors" in "West Wind," to adapt Clark, make more dramatic its "centripetal activity *as* centripetal" (209).

Posterity will answer whether "West Wind" is for the ages. It stands, though, at the intersection of two histories—the story of the British welfare state and the story of Britain's transatlantic involvement with American avant-garde verse—whose crossing produces a richly complex blend of motives, motifs, and melodrama. Any academic treatment of 1980s British culture will benefit from wrestling with the poem's particular demands, oversights, and accomplishments, and all future overviews of postwar British verse will have to account for works like "West Wind" that, however little regarded at Faber and Faber, succeed in being by turns haunting, moving, bewildering, hortative, hermetic, discerning, and pleasurable.

II
SIGHT AND SOUND

3

Ezra Pound's Utopia of the Eye

"Verse now, 1950, if it is to go ahead, if it is to be of *essential* use, must, I take it, catch up and put into itself certain laws and possibilities of breath." So begins Charles Olson's influential manifesto "Projective Verse." For Olson and for many avant-garde writers of the 1950s the breath was indeed considered fundamental to rethinking contemporary poetry. Consider Ginsberg's experiments with the long line, Williams's struggle to find a typography expressive of the variable foot, or Olson's use of spacing on the page to register intervals of silence.

But, as many scholars have noted, one major avant-garde figure seems to have dissented from this trend. As Table 1 illustrates, Ezra Pound, whom Olson repeatedly praises in "Projective Verse" for his good ear, more and more frequently uses Chinese characters in the sections of the *Cantos* published during the decade.[1]

Flipping through *Section: Rock-Drill* or *Thrones,* confronted by columns of Chinese, one is understandably tempted to say that Pound's typographical innovations concern the look of his poetry more than its sound. Closer analysis tends to confirm this impression. The Chinese characters often function in the *Cantos* in complex ways that can only be seen, not heard. One exemplary instance occurs on the first page of *Section: Rock-Drill*:

chih[3]

a gnomon,
Our science is from the watching of shadows (563)

Table 1. Frequency of Chinese Characters in Ezra Pound's *Cantos*

Section of *The Cantos*	Year Published	Number of Characters	Average # per Canto
I-XXX	1930	0	0
XXXI-XLI	1934	1	0.09
XLII-LI	1937	2	0.2
LII-LXXI	1940	50	2.5
LXXIV-LXXXIV	1948	39	3.6
LXXXV-XCV	1955	217	19.7
XCVI-CIX	1959	116	8.3
CX-CXVII	1969	8	1.0

The character here, $chih^3$, has two vertical strokes, one taller than the other, which to Pound suggest a pole and its shadow, hence the next word, "gnomon," referring to the pointer of a sundial.[2] Such a visual link between two words has no place in a poetry founded solely on the physicality of the voice.

This essay proposes, however, that the distinction between the speech-based poetics characteristic of the 1950s avant-garde and Pound's contemporary yet highly visual experimentation is not as straightforward as it might at first appear. Contrary to what some critics have argued, Pound does not simply invert prevailing assumptions by championing writing over speech. This chapter will argue that Pound, like other 1950s poets, is in fact interested in the spoken word, but that in his case the question of breath and page, ear and eye, becomes a productive ambiguity, not the set of value-laden binary oppositions that Olson's "Projective Verse" seems to suggest. In the *Cantos* Pound multiplies the means of communication in his poetry in order to demonstrate their variable potential for conveying information. Different languages, different discourses, and different alphabets come together, producing a disorienting welter that forces his audience constantly to wonder what kind of reading the text demands. Oral performance, like every other conventional sort of reading, is put into question.

The Chinese characters are only one participant in this larger, deafening congress of sign-systems. Concentrating on *Section: Rock-Drill*, the portion of the *Cantos* in which Pound's use of Chinese is at its height, this chapter investigates why many discussions of the ideograms have been inadequate and will examine the particular role that the Chinese writing serves in the poem, which is to break down syntax and interrupt the linearity of traditional reading.[3] These devices enable Pound, ever forward-looking, to move beyond the limitations of a poetics of the breath and, through what one might call his "art of noise," to inaugurate a new era in American experimental art.

Translatio Studii

In order to understand Pound's breakthrough in *Rock-Drill*, the necessary first step is a new approach to Pound's treatment of his source material. For decades critics have emphasized Pound's willful misreading of his Confucian source texts. The technique of "etymosinology" that Pound learned from Fenollosa's "The Chinese Written Character as a Medium for Poetry" has remained a favorite target.[4] True, Fenollosa was wrong about how to read Chinese. His explanation is an Orientalist fantasy with a long genealogy, extending back through Emerson to Leibniz and Francis Bacon (Kenner 223–24; Jung 212). But is it helpful to compare Pound, even implicitly, to more conscientious readers or translators of Eastern tongues?

A good yardstick against which to measure the *Cantos'* success as a translation is Kenneth Rexroth's *One Hundred Poems from the Japanese*, published by New Directions in 1955, the same year as *Section: Rock-Drill. One Hundred Poems* aspires to be correct, consistent, and informative. On a given page of Rexroth's work appear an English version of a Japanese poem, an italicized transliteration of the original, then a romanization of the poet's name, and finally his or her name in *kanji*. The book's back matter includes scholarly notes and a bibliography. A long introduction puts forward a developed theory of translation as well as a succinct literary history of Japanese poetry.

Pound's *Cantos* is an entirely different animal. It, too, may give readers citations, annotations, dictionary definitions, and so forth, but all these elements occur in exploded, scattered, unsystematic ways. Moreover, Pound's dynamited Rexroth appears jumbled among any number of other recycled reading materials: history, economic treatises, political propaganda, and autobiography, even the lyric. Confronted with this confusing mixture of literary forms, a critic of almost any disciplinary background can find parts of the *Cantos* that look familiar, but every such genre is invoked (or *provoked*) in such a way that it strikes a specialist as annoyingly amateurish. *Annoying*, that is, because Pound does not fulfill all the necessary generic demands, and *amateurish* because he seems not to know or care what such rules might be. Hence, Chinese comparatists feel drawn to critique Pound's use of Chinese, just as medievalists, too, consider him an interloper into Provencal.

If one considers Pound no more than a bad translator, there is no way to avoid reiterating empty value judgments about the intentionally inconsiderate game that the *Cantos* plays with genre and the academy. The rudeness of the *Cantos* ultimately stems from its reliance on the logic of collage, in which, as Marjorie Perloff explains, "objects, object fragments, and materials drawn from disparate contexts" are juxtaposed in such a way that the "process inevitably alters their individual appearance and signification" (*Dance* 35). Rather than as a translator, as a failed Rexroth, one should conceive of Pound in *Rock-Drill* as someone closer to a Dadaist like Kurt Schwitters or Marcel Duchamp, picking up whatever he finds that might suit his aesthetic purposes and incorporating it into his artwork.[5]

Videre et Audire

Pound undoubtedly employs visual criteria when plundering Confucius for his "found objects." If Pound was interested solely in the denotative meaning of the two hundred fifty or so different characters that occur in the *Cantos*, he could, presumably, have used transliterations, just as Eliot did with the Sanskrit in "The Waste Land" (1922). Indeed, as Hugh Kenner notes, "the Chinese in *Rock-Drill* . . . and *Thrones* . . . is as likely to appear in phonetics as in ideographs" (226). Thus, when a Chinese word appears in the *Cantos* as an ideograph rather than in romanization, one can safely say that Pound is consciously choosing to emphasize its look. But how should one interpret this turn toward the visual?

Generally, critics explain Pound's motivation for including written Chinese in the *Cantos* by reference to Fenollosa's theory that ideograms can be broken down into concise, concrete metaphors or mini-narratives that depict an action. Scholars have assumed that characters thus optically convey something visceral and immediate that a commonplace word could not. It is certainly true that individual characters often figure visually into the metonymic play of Pound's poetry according to Fenollosa's precepts. Carroll Terrell's *Companion to the Cantos* fairly exhaustively details how Chinese characters in the poem behave according to Fenollosa's (or Matthews's) pseudo-etymologies, so there is no need here to itemize anew the extent of Pound's ingenuity.[6]

But the problem with this level of analysis—treating every character as an application of Pound's so-called "ideogrammic method"—is that one forgets that Chinese characters are only a single element in Pound's larger collage-text. This oversight can lead to overstatement. That is, some critics have argued that Pound, by inserting ideograms in his verse, subverts an age-old Western prejudice by giving writing priority over speech.[7] Derrida's *Of Grammatology*, for instance, contends that Pound's "fascination" with the ideogram indicates an "irreducibly graphic poetics" that signals a "breach" in speech's dominance in Western culture (92).

Nevertheless, *pace* Derrida, Pound considers the Chinese in the *Cantos* to be neither purely visual nor silent. In the introduction to his 1954 translation of the *Shih-ching*, he writes, "there can be [no] real understanding of a good Chinese poem without knowledge both of the ideogram reaching the eye, and the metrical and melodic form reaching the ear or aural imagination" (xii). Indeed, in the *Cantos* Pound usually pairs an ideogram with a transliteration. Ever the pedagogue, he sets about teaching his readers how to pronounce his Chinese characters.

Derrida is correct to state that through visual play Pound calls into question traditional hierarchies involved in reading and writing, but he oversimplifies matters because, as part of his critique of phonocentrism, he wants to make a sharp distinction between Western phonetic alphabets and Eastern ideographic writing. As Pound fully recognizes by 1955, however, the association between a Chinese character and its spoken equivalent may be arbitrary, but one could say the same about Arabic numerals or everyday symbols like the dollar sign or ampersand. Accordingly, beyond merely experimenting with ideographic scripts, Pound's later writings also repeatedly emphasize the disjunction between spoken and written *English*. In his letters and in the *Cantos* abbreviations such as "sd/," "vb/," and "EP" proliferate. Any oral rendering of the *Cantos* must navigate these sorts of typographical transgressions. A person reading aloud must also decide whether to voice or suppress the ever-multiplying, unpredictably placed dates, annotations, and marginal notes.[8]

Critics often fail to perceive the subtlety of the *Cantos'* broader inquiry into the relation between speech and writing because they forget that the ideograms are only one aspect of the epic's visual play. The Chinese and English scripts simply are not straightforward binary opposites in the *Cantos* but instead coexist and clash with many other systems of writing. In *Rock-Drill,* there also appear the Greek alphabet, emphatically oversized Roman letters (585, 588), playing card glyphs (609), medieval musical notation (630), pictographs (Ra-Set's boat, 632), and hieroglyphs (643, 646–47, 651, 655).

What is significant about this array of means of communication is that each performs certain functions better than the others. The musical notation in C91 lends an added dimension of sound to Pound's Provencal, thereby restoring song to poetry. The Greek alphabet and Egyptian hieroglyphs reinforce the sense that the text presents us with actual, unmediated extracts from historical documents. Pictographs like the boat in C91 or the card glyphs in C88 are what Charles Pierce would call icons; that is, unlike phonetic or ideographic writing, they refer directly to that which they depict by reproducing its appearance in a stylized image.[9] The assorted ways of writing in the *Cantos* variously supplement the capabilities of the standard Roman alphabet to convey Pound's message, whether phonetically, visually, or otherwise. What the *Cantos* highlight is the contingent and partial quality of any and all means of communication.

Scripsi

The dramatic increase in Pound's use of Chinese characters in *Rock-Drill* must be seen as only one feature of this larger linguistic endeavor. In particular, they should be understood in relation to Eva Hesse's observation that the later parts of the *Cantos* encourage a novel approach to the written page, which in Cantos 85 and 87 Pound calls *contemplatio* (566, 596). Pound borrows this concept from the medieval mystic Richard of St. Victor, who held that while engaged in contemplatio, which is the ideal mode of reading, the mind acts by *liber volutas* (free flight) and pursues the *mira agilitate circumferri* (the wondering encirclement) of the contemplated object (Hesse 48). Richard licenses Pound to imagine escape from the rapid, unimpeded sequentiality of contemporary reading practice, which Pound distrusts, because he believes it encourages the unreflective acceptance of suspect ideas (Yee 248–50). In rebellion against centuries of tradition, Pound proposes an alternative, freer mode of engagement with a text: a wandering, wondering perusal of a poem, in which the eye moves as readily backward, upward, or diagonally as well as down or to the right.

The Chinese characters are crucial in realizing this project. From his earliest encounter with Fenollosa's notebooks, Pound appreciated the way in which uninflected ideograms allow for a breakdown of the linearity of syntax. In *Rock-Drill*, with its emphasis on contemplatio, Pound applies the asyntactical potential of Chinese writing as never before. Pages 660–61 provide an elementary demonstration of the principles at work throughout *Rock-Drill*. Pound illustrates how the simple repetition of the same character (here

wang wang, or "king king") can express any number of syntactical relationships in English. The text pairs *wang wang* with a variety of English constructions: an order ("the king . . . shd/ be king," 661), a list of emperors ("ANTONINUS" and "SEVERUS," 660), and, elsewhere in *Rock-Drill*, an exchange ("Name for name, king for king," 611). In other words, two free-standing characters can potentially be placed in relation through hypotaxis ("for"), through parataxis (the list), or through an expression of identity (inserting a copula such as "shd/ be").

As syntax becomes distorted, so too does the page layout that conventionally mirrors it. Specifically, the columns of Chinese create lines of force that challenge the horizontal impetus of the English. Consider the layout of an example cited in the last paragraph:

that the king 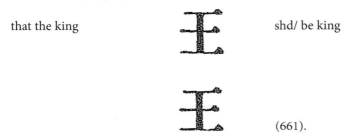 shd/ be king

(661).

Here the characters *wang wang* split apart, like an ax or a rush of water, the two halves of the clause "that the king . . . shd/ be king." In the extreme case of Canto 85, the conflict between Chinese, Roman and Greek scripts, and marginal annotations becomes so dramatic that, bewildered, one has to wonder in what order to read them. The literal meaning of this canto—an edifying mix of quotes by prominent ministers and descriptions of battles virtuously won, mostly drawn from Couvreur's *Chou King*—at times seems secondary to the startlingly unusual page design. Pound teaches us that one way to MAKE IT NEW is to make it look new.

Through its ideograms *Rock-Drill* thus calls into question every unit of contemporary poetic practice. The word itself can be broken down into an interplay of graphical elements via Fenollosa's etymosinology. The horizontal line shatters in collision with verticals. The page loses its defining hierarchy of elements. With the intensification of such definitional chaos, the eye is free to roam where it so desires—as the *Cantos* puts it, "UBI AMOR IBI OCULUS EST," where love is there flies the eye (609).

Pound seeks to reshape American poetry by asserting the plane, not the line, as its geometrical imperative. It should be no surprise that at one time he considered having the *Cantos* end with a square of sixteen ideograms (Kenner 535). Presented with such an array, the eye could start and end where it chose, traveling in any direction. The ideal type toward which the later *Cantos* tend would thus be a realization of Pound's desire, expressed early in his career in "Gathering the Limbs of Osiris," to make a poem a "switchboard" of words to direct variously the flow of the "latent energy of Nature" (23–25).

Radix

At the beginning of the century in *Un Coup de Dés* Mallarmé proposed that the poem was a constellation of words, winking at each other across the white emptiness of the page. Pound's mid-century utopia for the eye is more energetic, more machine than celestial chapel, an arena for a clash of sign-systems. By lifting the boundaries between tongues and scripts, by defying disciplinary boundaries, Pound raises to a deafening level the "interference" that convention strives to suppress. Lost in a sea of noise, with one's moorings undone, one drifts at will across the page in any direction. One could argue that Pound presents us with a surprisingly forward-looking poetry, perhaps an instance of what Michel Serres would call *cacography* (*Hermes* 66). Pound offers us a mode of art opposed to the lingering romanticism in much modern literature, which manifests as the stubborn refusal to abandon the dream of the mystified, individual speaking subject, standing lone and separate from the linguistic and communicative chaos of late twentieth-century life. Starting with *Rock-Drill* Pound pushes beyond Fenollosa and the speech-based poetics of contemporaries like Olson. He prepares poetry for the age of information overload.

4
Gertrude Stein Speaks

Much to Gertrude Stein's surprise, the publication of *The Autobiography of Alice B. Toklas* (1933) made her a celebrity. And fame—if she could properly harness it—promised access to the mass audience that she had long coveted. How, though, would people encounter her writing? What control would she have over that process? On the advice of her literary agent William Aspinwall Bradley, she quickly installed telephones at 27 rue de Fleurus in Paris and at her summer home in Bilignin. She wanted to make it easier for presses and journals to contact her (Goble 129). Few if any representatives of the publishing world sought her out, however. In the winter of 1934–1935, tired of waiting, she went on the offensive. She traveled to the United States for an extended author's tour. She visited nearly thirty college campuses from Massachusetts to South Carolina to California, and she gave a series of talks rushed into print under the titles *Lectures in America* (1935) and *Narration* (1935). She was also interviewed repeatedly by print and radio journalists. She found the latter experience especially revelatory: she was "smitten" by the "distinct form of communication" that radio creates, that is, a "feeling of everybody" everywhere listening to her speak (Wilson 263). Obeying Wordsworth's dictum that great poets create their own audiences, Stein learned to use celebrity as a vehicle for disseminating the skills and information necessary to appreciate her experimental writings.

The best-known record of this phase in Stein's career is *Everybody's Autobiography* (1937), a memoir in which she meditates on how writing a bestseller changed her life. There is a more useful document, however, if one wishes to learn about her immediate response to American celebrity culture and its promotional apparatus. In 1956, the record label Caedmon released the LP *Gertrude*

Stein Reads from Her Work, which includes a handful of recordings all made in "New York, winter, 1934–35": "Matisse," "If I Told Him: A Completed Portrait of Picasso," "A Valentine to Sherwood Anderson," and extracts from both the novel *Making of the Americans* and the libretto *Madame Recamier*. These recordings capture Stein in the process of retooling for mass-reproduced oral performance her earlier, limited-circulation page-based work.[1] Conveniently, too, they remain readily available down to the present day, easily downloaded from websites such as PennSound, Ubu.com, and Salon.com.[2] Accordingly, they offer a high-profile, readily accessible means of investigating the innovative soundscape of Stein's verse, as adapted to a new medium.

How should a literary critic approach these recordings, though, let alone interpret them as windows on 1934–1935? They are not original compositions. They are oral renditions of texts that, in many cases, were written a decade-or-more previous. Granted, in the course of reading these works aloud, Stein could selectively reveal aspects of her 1910s and 1920s artistry that might otherwise prove elusive. In other words, one could credit the recordings with the ability to clarify what had been present all along. (Martina Pfeiler repeats a scholarly commonplace when she asserts that the "meaning of [Stein's] poems unfolds itself much better when heard" [59].)[3] Could one, though, proceed differently? Could one permit a one-off dramatic reading of a piece to displace or replace its prior textual incarnation(s) as an object of literary analysis? If so, in what sense and to what degree?

In *Everybody's Autobiography* Stein herself downplays the value of oral performance. Back in Europe and writing just before the outbreak of the Spanish Civil War, she is acutely aware of the propaganda skirmishes underway between fascists and communists. In response, she draws a distinction between her work—which she characterizes as page-based and self-consciously writerly—and the belligerent, populist, speech-oriented media culture that surrounds her. She assures her audience that she has "never owned" a radio, indeed has never wanted one (253–54), and she predicts that cinema, too, is well on its way to becoming "just a daily habit and not at all exciting or interesting" (292-93). She maintains that "really being alone with reading is more intense than hearing anything" (263). Even the sounds of a text, she counterintuitively asserts, are best perceived via the page, that is, by "hear[ing] with the eyes" and not "with the ears" (90). ¡Arriba la literatura, abajo la voz!

Two years earlier, however, an ocean away from Franco, Mussolini, and Stalin, Stein seems to have been working from another set of starting principles altogether. Asked on the radio to explicate "Van or Twenty Years After: A Second Portrait of Carl Van Vechten" (1923), she reads (or recites) several lines:

Tied and untied and that is all there is about it. And as tied and as beside, and as tied and as beside. Tied and untied and beside and as beside and as untied and as tied and as untied and as beside. As beside as by and as beside.[4]

She then upbraids the interviewer for trying to "understand" this portrait:

Look here. Being intelligible is not what it seems. You mean by understanding that you can talk about it in the way that you have a habit of talking, putting it in other words. But I mean by understanding enjoyment. If you enjoy it you understand it. And lots of people have enjoyed it so lots of people have understood it. . . . But after all you must enjoy my writing and if you enjoy it you understand it. If you do not enjoy it why do you make a fuss about it. There is the real answer.[5]

Stein here makes the familiar modernist argument that the aesthetic value of an artwork becomes apparent as one attends to the specific qualities of its constituent materials as well as the unique manner in which they have been altered, arranged, or reconstituted. The interviewer errs when expressing a desire for an "intelligible" interpretation of "Van or Twenty Years After," which would be no more than a mundane everyday utterance, something said "in the way that you have a habit of talking." She suggests that, instead of explaining away or smoothing over the bizarre idiosyncrasies in her writing, one should observe them closely, study the ins and outs of their construction and function, and "enjoy" the spectacle of their alterity. In short, she discourages hermeneutic engagement with art in favor of a richly phenomenological experience of its sensuous particulars.

What does this have to do with the 1934–1935 recordings? When "enjoyment" is a writer's (and an audience's) chief goal, any differences that might exist between an original and a copy, or between a written score and an oral performance, cease to be grounds for asserting a hierarchical distinction. Both options can be "enjoyed" fully on their own terms. Reading "Van or Twenty Years After" as it appeared in *The Reviewer* in 1924 offers one kind of experience. Listening to a portion of it on the radio in 1934 provides a different one. While there will likely be overlap between these experiences, they will nonetheless remain "singular," as Derek Attridge would describe it. He would go on to label these two moments of reception as separate but related "events," which count as "literary" insofar as their audiences become aware of "new possibilities of meaning and feeling (understood as verbs)" (59).

Thought of as "events," the Stein recordings can be construed as documents of the winter of 1934–1935. True, they are also in some manner connected to the moments when Stein composed the print-based works that inspire them, as well as to any and all subsequent listenings (for instance the present moment, when the author of this essay has them playing on his I-Pod). A "literary work" is "never entirely separable from the act-event (or act-events) that brought it into being," nor is it "entirely insulated from the contingencies of the history within which it is projected" (Attridge 59). As a series of performances datable to one stretch of time, however, they do make available a historically specific bundle of decisions that Stein made (or chose to adhere to) while she was being recorded.

A comparison between the print and oral versions of one of Stein's most famous works, "If I Told Him: A Completed Portrait of Picasso" (1924), can illustrate this point. On the page, one is immediately struck by its anomalous layout. Some parts are emphatically prose: they are horizontal, reaching toward or wrapping around at the right hand margin: "Exact resemblance. To exact resemblance the exact resemblance as exact as a resemblance, exactly as resembling, exactly resembling, exactly in resemblance exactly a resemblance, exactly and resemblance" (*A Stein Reader* 464). These sections alternate with others that are strikingly vertical, suggesting line breaks:

As trains.
Has trains.
Has trains.
As trains.
As trains.
Presently.
Proportions.
Presently. (465)

The "conspicuous tension" between these two vectors of movement makes one unusually aware of the two-dimensionality of writing (Haselstein 738). Words unfurl in orderly fashion on a plane—much like pigment applied to a canvas. Stein invites readers to think about her poem as an analogue to a Picasso painting. Does she advance a critique of "resemblance" on par with his? What kinds of "proportionality" exist in writing that parallel or depart from those available to a visual artist? When one places the word "trains" repeatedly down a left hand margin, does that constitute a drawing of train tracks or of a train in movement? Why or why not?

One could imagine Stein striving to preserve the horizontal/vertical binary in oral performance, perhaps by employing two distinct pitches, volumes, accents, or other methods of vocally marking difference. She does not. Instead, as recorded, "If I Told Him" comes across as a much more heterogeneous composition, consisting of sequential sections that obey distinct formal logics and proceed according to disparate rhythms. The first "module," for instance, has a questioning intonation, and it relies heavily on chiasmus (ABBA), as the following annotated transcription illustrates:

if I told him [A] would he like it [B] / would he like it [B] if I told him [A] / would he like it [A] / would Napoleon [B] / would Napoleon [B] / would / would he like it [A] / if Napoleon [A] / if I told him [B] / if I told him [B] / if Napoleon [A][6]

The delivery seems stuck on idle, as if the repetitions and mirrorings could continue *ad infinitum*. Stein then, without transition, launches into a second segment: "now / not now / and now / now." The tone is emphatic, as if she were issuing orders. "Now" take action! But this "now" appears in isolation, decontextualized, so it is not exactly clear how it is to function as a command—unless, perhaps, Stein is directing listeners to attend to "now" itself, that is, the moment of utterance. Of course, strictly speaking, once such a present tense "now" is pointed out, it ceases to be "now." That is, once singled-out for attention, it inevitably becomes a "then," a moment receding ever further into the past. Thus, paradoxically, every "now" is, at one and the same time, "not now." One cannot hold onto the present moment. The most one can do is register the series of nows as they tick by ("and now / now"). Just as an audience begins to absorb this complex temporal lesson, this procession of nows abruptly give way to another type of now altogether, a third segment of the portrait: "exactly as as kings / feeling full for it / exactitude as kings / so to beseech you as full as for it / exactly or as kings." This time, the sentences end with falling intonation, and the mood is declarative, not imperative. As performed orally, "If I Told Him" provides a listener with discrete, well-demarcated slices of time that resist being integrated into a larger governing scheme such as the prose versus verse binary suggested by the print version. Instead of evoking Pablo Picasso's *Ma Jolie* (1911) or Georges Braque's *The Portuguese* (1911)—works whose parts are meant to be perceived in subordinate relation to a whole that can be visually taken in all at once—Stein's recording more closely resembles cell-based musical compositions such as Steve Reich's *Music for Eighteen Musicians* (1974–1976) and John Adams's *Phrygian Gates* (1977)—works in which each interval of time is characterized by a repetitive pattern sustained long enough for a listener to perceive and appreciate in isolation its distinctive rhythm, melody, and mix of timbres.

These cross-media comparisons can be taken one step further. On the page, the repetitions in "If I Told Him" have a tendency to disrupt linear progression through the text by creating rectangular "blocks" of words that one's eyes take in all at once. For example:

> He he he he and he and he and and he and he and he and and as and as he and as he and he. He is and as he is, and as he is and he is, he is and as he and he and as he is and he and he and and he and he (*A Stein Reader* 465).

Here, one sees a field that consists of a small number of words: "he," "and," "is," and "as." At a glance, one can distinguish such a segment from another: "Shutters shut and shutters and so shutters shut and shutters and so and so shutters and so shutters shut and so shutters shut and shutters and so. And so shutters shut and so" (464). The words "shutters" and "shut" here appear so often that they leap out at a reader; it's as if an artist has applied a broad horizontal swipe of a single color. The verticals behave the same way:

> The first exactly.
> At first exactly.
> First as exactly.
> At first as exactly. (465)

The recurrences of "exactly" line up, much like the trace of a brush's sweeping downstroke. The overall effect of Stein's juxtaposed "blocks" of text can be compared to Picasso's employment of different jostling fragmentary "planes" in his canvases during the analytic phase of cubism. One encounters a surface of busy push-and-pulls between elements that refuse to cohere into the familiar illusionistic space to be found in most post-Renaissance portraiture.

The recording of "If I Told Him" operates differently. Its constituent parts necessarily unfold over time. Listeners are barred from skipping around or pondering the whole of its design simultaneously. *Faute de mieux*, they are likely to end up concentrating on the moment-to-moment specifics of the composition. And, when approached in this manner, one discovers something peculiar. She speaks in short rapid bursts, consisting of one to six words, separated by very brief pauses (occasionally by quick breaths). Each burst employs one of only a small number of intonational arcs. Here, for example, is how Stein reads the passage quoted above beginning "He he he he and he." At first each word receives individual identical emphasis, like dollops of sausage meat on an assembly line: "he / he / he / he." Then, interspersed with a few more one-word bursts, comes a string of two-word phrases, in which the voice rises or falls on the second word:

and ^{he} / and ^{he} / and / and ^{he} / and ^{he} / and ^{he} / and / and $_{\text{as}}$

Matters quickly become more complex. Three- and four-word units begin to proliferate:

and $_{\text{as}}$ he / and $_{\text{as}}$ he / and $_{\text{he}}$ / he ^{is} / and $_{\text{as he}}$ is / and $_{\text{as he}}$ is / and $_{\text{he}}$ is / he ^{is} / and $_{\text{as}}$ he / and ^{he} / and $_{\text{as he}}$ is

Stein rounds the section off by returning to one- and two-word phrases and then signals closure with falling intonation:

and ^{he} / and ^{he} / and / and ^{he} / and $_{\text{he}}$

If one were to assign a letter to each of these intonation-curves, the passage could be rendered schematically like so:

A A A A B B A B B B A C D D C B E E D B D B E B B A B C

The underlying rhythmic logic is made clear. As give way to Bs, then a C signals a shift to Ds and Es before Bs and at last A return. A musician might say that Stein states a theme, varies it, then returns to the opening theme. Granted, her use of pitch and rhythm can appear simple and straightforward when judged by the standards of Beethoven, Brahms, and Schönberg. Then again, so too is Steve Reich's in a masterpiece of *musique répétitive* such as *Drumming* (1970–1971), which experiments throughout with the variation and permutation of short rhythmic phrases. Like Reich (albeit less systematically), the Stein recordings of 1934–1935 make it possible for "structural process" to "be clearly perceived by the listener" (Schwartz 376).

To sum up: visually, the text of "If I Told Him" encourages a reader to think about levels of organization and meaning that fall above the lexical level. Horizontals, verticals, and repetition create "blocks" of words that relate dynamically to one another within an overall composition. Arguably, one is thereby nudged to think about the meaning of the piece *in toto*. How does this layout of text compare to a Picasso portrait of the same period? Does the frequent mention of Napoleon serve to praise or mock the famous artist? What might "exact re-semblance" mean when so many traditional mimetic devices have been casually discarded? In contrast, when listening to the recording, it is relatively easy to forget that "Picasso" is the declared referent. A listener attends more closely to the idiosyncratic selection of words and their peculiar sequential arrangement. Local effects consequently predominate over the gestalt. Orally, the following passage is rather humorous: "one I land / two I land / three the land / three the land / three the land / two I land / two I land / one I land / two I land." Stein stumbles around Longfellow's "one if by land, two if by sea," never quite nailing it. "I land" keeps replacing "by land," and "three" supplanting "sea." "Paul Revere's Ride" (1861) would seem to have little or nothing to do with Picasso; why interject such a strange trivial aside into the portrait of an influential avant-garde artist? But who cares? Once one places "enjoyment" ahead of "intelligibility," as Stein does in her 1934 interview, the goal is to delight in the here and now ("now / not now / and now / now"). Chiasmus, off-rhyme, near-repetition, almost-allusion, and other rhetorical devices are to be savored as they parade by.

Some of the divergence between the written and performed version of "If I Told Him" is ascribable simply to the change in medium. There is more to it than that, though. In 1934–1935 Stein chose a manner and pacing of delivery that slanted her own compositions in particular ways. She catches her listeners up in a series of time-intervals that they are encouraged to experience in a heightened state of attention. Each of these intervals offers a richness of sound and word-play, and the audience moves from one to another at unpredictable junctures. The totality of the work never comes into view. As Krzysztof Ziarek puts it in another context, Stein thereby demonstrates "the temporal non-coincidence of the present with itself." An audience experiences the flow of time as consisting of a series of discrete non-identical nows. Because the composition places so much emphasis on its processual unfolding—and places so little stress on any kind of end goal or final form—its listeners are positioned within a "freeing horizon." They begin to sense that "futurity," the incipience of an unforeseeably new present within the existing present, is a "transformative vector." A person leaves herself open to whatever comes, an orientation toward time that necessarily "alters the dynamic matrix of power relations constitutive of the present" because those power relations are shown to be not eternal and static but (*in potentia* at least) wholly mutable (98).

"If I Told Him" ends by saying, "Let me recite what history teaches. History teaches" (*A Stein Reader* 466). In print, this statement can come across as a final ironic touch. Stein assumes briefly the persona of a history teacher, a profession antithetical to the radical novelty that she and Picasso espouse. Orality ("Let me recite") is associated with empty didacticism and rote repetition ("history teaches history teaches"). Implicitly and by contrast, visuality—as explored either on the page or on the canvas—is connected with modernity. Aroynt thee, History, and leave the new dawn to us visionaries! Curiously, in the recording, this same final line, coming after a pageant of nows-that-are-not-nows, leaves a different impression. Stein hints that the moral of history, its punch line, cannot ever be pinned down. Instead, one discovers a process of repetition and variation, a succession of resounding and re-sounding restatements ("And now. Now") that will extend indefinitely into the future. As a performative event instead of a textual artifact, "If I Told Him" affirms not "Make It New" but "It Will Be Otherwise." In other words, instead of advocating an impossible redemptive-utopian future, it invites listeners to rejoice in whatever will be. As Ziarek explains, the goal here is not empowerment. One seeks to become "power-free," no longer bound by the conceptions of governance and order prevalent in the (perishable) present (91).

Stein herself, as we have already seen, could not maintain pure openness to whatever comes when she returned to Europe after her American tour. She ceased her optimistic embrace of the "enjoyment" of mass-reproduced oral performance after becoming cruelly reacquainted with the ways that mass media can manipulate an audience's pleasure toward ideological and teleological ends. The 1934–1935 recordings, however, continue to testify to a special moment when, after receiving a crash course in the modern "technological organization of power," Stein created an "outside within," that is, a way of using mass media that superficially resembles but in fact runs counter to their function of educating and informing (a.k.a. disciplining) a public (Ziarek 99). Hers was an anarchic anti-pedagogy, instructions on how to embrace the vulnerability of not-knowing and the freedom that arises from a lack of control. One is left to wonder: did the politics of the later 1930s invalidate Stein's momentary optimism—or did they quash an important new development in the international avant-garde? Do Stein's recordings anticipate the current academic romance with performance as a mode of critique—or should they serve as a caution against such fascination? Let me recite what Stein asks. Stein asks.

5

The Baseness of Robert Grenier's Visual Poetics

I begin with something grossly unfair, because it made me think. In his common-place book of the postmodern, *The Tapeworm Foundry* (2000), Darren Wershler-Henry records the following flippant, anonymous recommendation for how to write a poem: "stick a magic marker up your asshole and then scuttle around like a crab in order to write texts resembling the later visual poems of robert grenier" (n.p.). As someone who has twice had the pleasure of witnessing Robert Grenier present his 1990s poetry in the context of cheery, meandering slide-lectures—complete with sunny snapshots of Northern Californian meadows—this line from *The Tapeworm Foundry* initially struck me as an adolescent remark made in ignorance of the poetry's value and spirit.

On further reflection, though, I realized that in its very vulgarity this squib might have hit upon something significant. Yes, *autoerotic, scatological*, and *bestial* are hardly adjectives that one associates with Grenier. In fact, as presented in his slide-lectures, such works as *rhymms* and *POND I* can seem, well, wholesome, caught up in an optimistic Emersonian affirmation of the essential goodness of nature, art, and humanity. But in these lectures Grenier also tends to treat the poetry as if its odd look were somewhat incidental to its intended meaning. That is, although he regularly emphasizes the ambiguities produced by the palimpsesting and stylizing of his handwritten words, he also sequentially and narratively reveals that each page, however chaotic in appearance, nonetheless proffers a message that can be deciphered. With Grenier as a guide, the poetry's unruly appearance thus becomes a puzzle capable of solution, an analogue, perhaps, of how we, in nature, are to study the enigmas around us so that, with delight, we can discover the Word concealed behind or within them.

The situation is very different when one confronts such works as *for Larry Eigner* [sic] and *GREETING* in the hard-to-find color-xeroxed editions, available online at Karl Young's *Light and Dust Mobile Anthology of Poetry*, or, best of all, in manuscript. In such circumstances, the latent content of the writing is frustratingly difficult to access. One asks: Is that an *N* or a *R*? Has he omitted "is" in this sentence? Why underline that word? Moreover, once one tentatively resolves these paleographic problems, their original purpose can still remain mysterious. What, for example, could Grenier possibly gain in *for Larry Eigner* by interfering with a reader's ability to appreciate Eigner's gently ironic pun "[the] typewriter [is] quiet an instrument" (20)?

One might argue that aesthetics motivate Grenier to write in such an unusual manner. By making us attend to the physical reality of his writing, Grenier could be reminding us of writing's comeliness, rich tactility, or sensuousness. The poetry, though, resists recuperation in these terms. There is nothing painterly or calligraphic about Grenier's penmanship. He uses ballpoint, which produces a wavering, scrawny, hard-to-follow line. After a Grenier talk at New College in San Francisco, I overhead one poet whisper to another, "We really ought to get Bob some colored markers for Christmas." The poetry, it seems to me, deliberately solicits this kind of reaction. Opting for an amateurishness of execution by settling for at-hand materials (he reputedly lifts the pens from the law office where he works), Grenier produces a poetry noticeably less visually appealing than he might otherwise. Why do so? And why then insist upon holographic reproduction—which in practice entails limiting the distribution of these books to non-traditional media (the slide lecture, World Wide Web)—if the net result is to promulgate "ugly" verse?

The perversity of this project presumably motivated Grenier's anonymous detractor in *The Tapeworm Foundry* to accuse him of scatology. Yet, as any aficionado of the avant-garde recognizes, there is nothing new about art taking a turn toward the lower digestive tract (think of the Calypso episode in Joyce's *Ulysses*). Nor is there anything novel about an equation between a handwritten scrawl and base matter. Rosalind Krauss's fascinating 1995 article "Le cours de latin" investigates the purpose and function of this equation in the works of the painter Cy Twombly. She analyzes the way in which Twombly employs graffiti as a reference point in his "excremental" assault on the pieties of high art. She particularly concerns herself with the sketchy, uneven, random inscription of proper names such as "Virgil" and "Dionysius" across his canvases. Krauss argues that such graffiti-like writing concentrates a viewer's attention not on the intrinsic beauty or appeal of language's materiality but rather on its stubborn, disruptive role as a trace of the writer's presence. We perceive that the mark which is writing does violence to a surface, irrevocably separating the "before" in which this surface was an unmeaning part of the timeless order of things-as-they-are and an "after" in which it belongs to the order of human temporality. In short, the act of writing induces a (violent) fall into history. Krauss credits such Twombly works as *Olympia* (1957) with "desublimating" the nasty reality behind the glorification-of-the-artist's-hand that played such a foundational role in the 1940s myth of the action painter. In other words, after Twombly, Jackson Pollock is just another tagger. For Krauss, Twombly thus exemplifies the logic of what she, following Bataille, labels the *informe:* the strategic manipulation of the inferior, "marked" term of a binary opposition (here, drawing versus graffiti) to counter their joint sublation into a more general, elevated third term (Art). By foregrounding lowness and violation as inescapable features of writing's materiality, Twombly blocks his audience from subordinating that materiality to, or erasing it within, higher, transcendental orders of experience (aesthetic or spiritual).

Does this model apply also to Grenier? He has long emphasized that poetry is an embodied art. More than twenty years ago, in "A Packet for Robert Creeley," he posited:

> Language, a thought "in action," as it popularly goes, it senses, one to another, one step at a time, an epistemology of language as organ of body process, talking, the linear structure of words occurring as *as* literal a condition of experience as the structure of the eye, producing & defining a common "human" continuum of particulars continuously present, "here," continuously presencing world, "one." (424; his emphasis)

"Language as organ of body process"—in 1978 Grenier conceived of language as an extension of the human *soma,* as concrete, physical, and immediate as "the structure of the eye." In recent years he has acknowledged the potentially embarrassing grossness that is the corollary of this position. In the 1998 poem-manifesto "ON THE EMPTY / SUBLIME" he wrote,

> FUCK, SHIT, THINK, PISS ETC.
> EMPTINESS, more empty than all of the measles of dead things, totals
>   TODAY.
> EMPTINESS is 'bigger' than all blight. BY FAR ! !
> Therefore REJOICE - in weird ability to LOOK AROUND BRIEFLY —
>   & LIFT UP THINE EYES (above your 'threshold limit') to SPACE,
>   wherein ('below') you still have 'time' to love the local individuals
>   ('SKULLS') (n.p.)

If language is an "organ of body process," it is part of an excretory system, no different, really, from other corporeal means of eliminating waste (perspiration, micturition, defecation). Poetry, then, belongs to the mortal, corruptible realm, to the land of "SHIT" and "SKULLS." Poetry may point to a "SPACE" above or external to this realm, but that space is, in the final analysis, pure "EMPTI-NESS," an absence that cannot be confused with the fullness of God's presence. The only available choices are the degradation that is Samsara and the hollow nothing that is Nirvana. Not much of a choice when, as a poet, one feels a voca-tion for "thought in 'action'"! Grenier here opts for the path of the Bodhisattva: to "love" and "REJOICE" amid the "SKULLS" in full awareness that this deci-sion means embracing what is worthless, that is, "SHIT."

This paradoxical stance plays itself out in Grenier's 1990s work, most no-tably in the long poem *for Larry Eigner*. It grapples with his friend's difficult life and death, confronting the reality of the "chaos / noise" of the world's ac-tuality (42). The poem ultimately ends, though, by celebrating the fortitude of the "Heart / in / dark," in other words, by affirming the human(e) fight against entropy. As such, *for Larry Eigner* traces the conventional course of an elegiac poem. Like, say, Milton's "Lycidas" (1638), Grenier's poem first faces the hor-ror of the body's dissolution but then moves on to stake a claim on behalf of the power of heart (and by implication art) to redeem fallen existence. But, as we have seen, this kind of recuperative move is, according to Rosalind Krauss, precisely what art that follows the logic of the *informe* cannot permit. Accord-ingly, the appearance of the graffiti-like final page of *for Larry Eigner* belies the ostensible optimism of its message. The *a* in "heart" does not resemble the *a* in "dark." On the contrary, the first *a* more closely resembles the *n* in the second word, "in," stricken through as it is by the line meant to underscore "heart." The *a* in "dark" in turn replicates the odd, reverse-Z-shaped *a* of three pages prior, where it occurs in the word "chaos." And, a final touch of *bizarrie,* the word "dark" looks like nothing so much as "Oz[a]rk," introducing an utterly irrele-vant frame of reference. By distracting readers, by making them ponder irra-tional connections, Grenier's peculiar handwriting thus defeats the text's move toward a unitary moral. The wobbly irregularity of the letters causes them to deviate from the "proper" meaning that they "ought" to express in a satisfying, stable manner. The page "Heart / in / dark" may instruct a reader to "LIFT UP THINE EYES" but at the same time it also tugs that reader's eyes toward a dis-persive immersion in the vagaries of a wayward pen. Not coincidentally, the only color ink used to write "Heart / in / dark" is red. Grenier reminds us that ink can be heart's blood, not only in the conventional sense of representing an author's intimate thoughts, but also in the sense that poetry is the waste product of "an organ of body process," a defilement of the abstract purity of "SPACE."

It might be the height of perversity to suggest that *for Larry Eigner*, let alone a quietist work such as *POND I*, belongs in the same class as such celebrated showcases for the excremental grotesque as Matt Collishaw's *Bullet Hole* (1988), Tracey Emin's *Everyone I Have Ever Slept With 1963–1995* (1995), and Damien Hirst's *The Physical Impossibility of Death in the Mind of Somebody Living* (1991), a fourteen foot tiger shark in formaldehyde. The affect is all wrong. Grenier never adopts the sneering, angry pose of the *enfant terrible* bent on bringing low the high. Rosalind Krauss, though, cautions that one must not confuse *informe* with "abjection," the Kristevan rubric that has served as an intellectual imprimatur for the contemporary tide of offal-as-art. The fact that Grenier's handwritten verse does not convey the same feelings of defacement and criminality as a Cy Twombly canvas in no way disqualifies it from operating according to a comparable semiotic strategy. Insofar as his ballpoint scribble-scrawl obstructs or counters the transcendentalist urges present in his verse, Grenier has found his own way to stage a radical, insuperable split between spirit and matter. He might not deny transcendence with the rigor, verve, or thoroughness of the artists anatomized in Krauss's (and Yve-Alain Bois's) *Formless: A User's Guide* (1997), but the *bassesse* of his handwritten poetry should be understood along similar lines: as a demonstration of the deconstructive potential of an improper (or perverse, untimely, inexplicable, inconvenient, deviant, etc.) emphasis on writing's materiality.

6
Caroline Bergvall Begins Again

In summer 2000, the British poet and performance artist Caroline Bergvall, working together with the Irish composer Ciarán Maher, recorded a piece titled "Via." Patiently and equably, she reads forty-seven English translations of the famous opening tercet of Dante Alighieri's *Inferno* (1321): "Nel mezzo del cammin di nostra vita / mi ritrovai per una selva oscura / ché la diritta via era smarrita," or, as her first source renders it, "Along the journey of our life half-way / I found myself again in a dark wood / wherein the straight road no longer lay."[1] These passages appear alphabetically, from "Along" to "When," and each is followed by a terse but sufficient indication of its source, the last name of the translator and the year of publication. The above translation, for instance, is credited to "Dale 1996." A quick library database search will turn up Peter Dale's *Divine Comedy: A Terza Rima Version*, published by London's Anvil Press.

Over the course of ten minutes, a listener is treated to a remarkable, sustained exercise in repetition and variation. Certain words and phrases recur insistently—"midway," "I found myself," "dark wood"—creating a stable backdrop against which variations from the norm stand out with unusual vividness. One notices immediately when "dark" is replaced by alternatives such as "darkling," "darksome," "in darkness," "drear," "gloomy," "gray," or "obscure." Alphabetization creates a reassuring predictable pattern that is counterbalanced by the thoroughly randomized series of dates: 1998, 1893, 1995, 1854, 1915, 1884, and so forth.

Proper names appear and disappear with alacrity. Literary celebrities such as Seamus Heaney, Henry Wadsworth Longfellow, and Dorothy Sayers receive no more emphasis than forgotten Victorians and Edwardians. This uninter-rupted, undifferentiated flow makes it difficult to weigh the merits of the indi-vidual translators. For example, by the time a listener fully appreciates that she has heard the opening lines from one of today's standard classroom editions of the *Inferno*—John Ciardi's, Allen Mandelbaum's, or Robert Pinsky's—Bergvall is typically already one or more items further along in her list. Under such circum-stances, textual specifics quickly begin to blur into one another, making any at-tempt at compare/contrast a futile exercise. In fact, over time, the bibliographic data tend to become altogether dissociated from the poetry. What sticks in the mind, for instance, is less Ciardi's artistry than Bergvall's mispronunciation of his name (instead of "CHAR-dee" she reads "see-AR-dee").[2]

How is one to make sense of such an unusual work? A classicist might call it a cento, a poem stitched together out of other authors' writings. Bergvall, though, makes no attempt to suture her quotations into a single through-composed ut-terance in the manner of Ausonius's *Cento nuptialis* or Proba Falconia's *Cen-tones Virgiliani*. Her Dante tercets remain freestanding nuggets presented in a starkly paratactic fashion. A specialist in contemporary poetry might label "Via" a writing-through of preexisting texts, in other words, a piece akin to John Cage's "Mureau" (1971), Jackson Mac Low's *Words nd Ends from Ez* (1989), and Ronald Johnson's *Radi Os* (1976). "Via," though, is too formally uniform, syn-tactically conventional, and repetitive in content to sit well among such com-pany. Bergvall's turn-of-the-millennium impulse to look back to Dante's Chris-tian epic might please conservatives such as Geoffrey Hill and Harold Bloom, but her relative disinterest in publishing a written version of the work ("Via" did not appear in print until the Fall 2003 "Transluccinacion" special issue of the American journal *Chain*)—more closely resembles the cavalier attitude toward book culture that one encounters in a very different milieu, that is, among slam poets, dub poets, and spoken word artists.[3] In short, it can be difficult to find useful literary analogs.

"Via" is nonetheless worthy of academic attention because it represents a new phase in international English-language experimental writing. This emergent aesthetic combines the erudition, intertextuality, and conceptual complexity characteristic of Language Poetry and the Cambridge School together with the theatricality, dynamism, site-sensitivity, and emphasis on embodiment asso-ciated with neo-avant-garde sound poetry (as well as more populist forms of contemporary oral performance). Some of the relevant pieces, such as "Via" and Kenneth Goldsmith's *Fidget* (1998), initially took the form of recorded or live performances and only later appeared in print; others, such as Sawako Nakayasu's *And So We Have Been Given Time or* (2004), began on the page but subsequently became the basis for innovative performance poetry; still others, such as Christian Bök's beatbox-inspired work-in-progress *The Cyborg Opera*, have necessarily existed only in aural versions.

Regardless, these writers have shown themselves to be thoroughly at home in the new media ecology of the twenty-first century. They are adept at composing in multiple and mixed media. Indeed, they are so comfortable with "cross-platform" writing that they no longer seem to perceive any meaningful disciplinary boundaries between poetry, music, and the visual arts. Bergvall and her peers are as likely to put on a gallery show or put out an audio CD as they are to give a traditional poetry reading. While they gladly acknowledge poets as precursors—among them Bob Cobbing, Steve McCaffery, Maggie O'Sullivan, and Tom Raworth—they just as readily cite composers (Erik Satie, John Cage, Cornelius Cardew) and visual artists (Marcel Duchamp, Bruce Nauman, Yoko Ono). Goldsmith's popular internet site Ubu.com exemplifies this sensibility. It mixes cinema, radio dramas, concrete poetry, conceptual pieces, edgy music, and an array of other kinds of formally adventurous art. What else would one expect of writers coming of age during the digital era, when anyone with a laptop can be an author, musician, and film editor, and when anyone who buys a cell phone also acquires the tools to be a photographer and videographer?

A critic could try to analyze a piece such as "Via" solely within a literary-historical context. After all, the work is, from beginning to end, redolent of a print-based archive. It is easy to imagine Bergvall in the British Library, consulting card catalogs and bibliographies and calling up book after book from the stacks.[4] This mental image is highly suggestive. Instead of following Dante on his epic journey through hell, purgatory, and heaven, Bergvall gets no further than the opening lines. She remains mired in an archival wilderness that mirrors the "dark wood" in which the poem's speaker wanders.

One could look to another Dante-phile, Samuel Beckett, to help comprehend this Sisyphean scenario. It has obvious parallels in every Beckett novel from *Murphy* (1938) to *How It Is* (1961). And one could compare Bergvall's procedural mode of composition to Watt's mathematical thinking or Molloy's beachside stone-sucking. It is not clear, however, how far the Beckett analogy would be worth pursuing. The tone in "Via" is all wrong. Bergvall's delivery is level, unhurried, and Sidney Poitier-precise. She is a touch bureaucratic, or, perhaps more accurately, pedagogical, reminiscent of an instructor's voice on language-learning tapes. There is no bawdiness, dark comedy, melodrama, or despair, let alone anything approaching the mad pyrotechnics of Billie Whitelaw's performance in "Not I" (1973).

A better point of reference might be Gertrude Stein, many of whose compositional principles Bergvall appears to employ. Most obviously, "Via" begins again and again. It occupies a continuous present that could be extended in-

definitely by adding more and more translations. It is a showcase, too, for Steinian insistence, that is, her belief that repetition brings to light small but crucial
distinctions, the sort of tiny variations that, as Bergvall illustrates, render every translation of Dante a unique text that puts a slightly different spin on the
original. Finally, Stein would have appreciated the title's bilingual pun. It con-
flates a spatial reference—in Italian, *via* can mean "road," as in Via Appia or Via
Dolorosa—with a self-reflexive gesture, since *via* in English means "by means
of." An act of composition, an immersion in one's medium of communication,
creates a "path" for oneself and others to follow.

Traveling along such a "road" might lead nowhere, but that is not what matters. The point is to keep going, to keep the pen and the mind in motion as long
as possible. The resulting tone, not surprisingly, resembles a long-haul truck
driver's cheerful stoicism. And, significantly, the existing recordings reveal that
Stein even sounds a little like Bergvall when she reads aloud works such as "A
Valentine for Sherwood Anderson" (1922), "If I Told Him: A Completed Portrait of Picasso" (1923), and "Fifteenth of November" (1924).[5] Both are articulate, richly timbred altos with a measured, self-assured manner of delivery.

An integral aspect of Stein's self-presentation, however, is her idiosyncratic
virtuosity. Even her most permutational works, for example *The Making of the
Americans* (1925) and *Many Many Women* (1910), eschew collage. Her verbal
structures are invariably indubitably marked as hers, products of her pioneering
experimental forays into linguistic possibility. While Bergvall might call attention to her own writerly practice in a somewhat Stein-like manner, she also
downplays her ingenuity and craftsmanship, elusive qualities wherein the "genius" that Stein prized so highly might be said to reside.

Bergvall lets herself dwindle to what one might call a content provider, a cut-
and-paste language processor, and a rote reciter of others' words. She places the
spotlight not on herself but on the potentially interminable acts of translation
that constitute a poem's reception within linguistic communities other than the
one of its origin. Despite certain formal and tonal similarities between "Via" and
Stein's plays and poems, it would be astonishing to discover such an impersonal
work among Stein's papers at Beinecke Library.

To understand the contemporaneity of "Via," a critic cannot limit herself to
print archives and published texts. She has to supplement literary history with
interdisciplinary study, more specifically, research into the visual artists that
Bergvall habitually cites as influences. One of her favorites is the Cuban-born
American sculptor and installation artist Félix González-Torres (1957–1996).[6]
Of particular relevance are his candy spills, large frequently replenished mounds
of store-bought candy that museum-goers are encouraged to eat.

These spills might evoke minimalist and post-minimalist sculpture, but they function more like theatrical props. By displaying manufactured commodities in an unexpected way in an unaccustomed location, González-Torres transforms an empty room into a dramatic scenario in which his audience is asked to participate. A simple act, savoring a piece of hard candy, becomes a gesture of communion with the host institution, with the artist, with the other visitors, and, in the case of works such as *Untitled (Portrait of Ross in LA)* (1991), with an absent person being memorialized.

This invitation to an oddly physical intimacy lasts until a given show ends. González-Torres inaugurates a temporary utopian environment in which people are free to experience abundance, childlike pleasure, and fellowship. Visitors are prodded to reimagine "consumption" as a noncompetitive sensuous mode of relating to others (however much candy one might take, there always is or will soon be more).

Bergvall's stance toward her materials is instructively similar to González-Torres's. Granted, translations of *The Divine Comedy* are not exactly a common last minute grab in a grocery store checkout line, but she, too, arranges her found "objects" without in any way imposing her subjective judgment. This radically depersonalized attitude is rare in literature, even among the most diehard samplers and *collagistes*. When Charles Reznikoff, for example, assembled extracts from old court cases to create his landmark historical poem *Testimony: The United States (1885–1895), Recitative* (1965), he might not have added his own words, but he did introduce lineation, and he placed his reshaped texts under subject headings.

In contrast, in "Via," Bergvall, like many of today's visual artists, seems to consider the most important part of the creative process complete after deciding on a generative algorithm: "alphabetize the first tercets taken from every English translation of the *Inferno* present in the British Library as of May 2000" is her version of a González-Torres instruction such as "pour seven hundred pounds of black-rod licorice in a corner."[7] The artist's stamp—what makes an artwork "by" an individual—lies solely in this original concept. The final product can include any proportion of texts composed by others or things made elsewhere. Why hide that fact? Why not give credit where credit is due, and why alter perfectly good raw materials?

Does "Via," though, like a González-Torres candy spill, inaugurate a utopian space? The answer is not immediately apparent. As a recording, "Via" does not convey the sheer physical presence, let alone the odor, of a huge mass of candy plunked down in a gallery. One does not have to make a special trip to experience "Via," nor can it, as a largely intangible artwork, have the same sacramental (or sacrilegious) impact as a person-scale "body" on which audiences are invited to nosh.

It can, though, remove a time and space from the everyday course of life. A short discussion of a second of Bergvall's favored visual artists, the 2001 Turner Prize winner Martin Creed (b.1968), can help clarify this point.[8] Creed, like González-Torres, tends to make his art out of readymade items according to pre-determined instructions. His art, though, is often less obtrusive than González-Torres, indeed sometimes hardly detectable at all, as in *Work No. 88: a sheet of A4 paper crumpled into a ball* and *Work No. 79: some Blu-Tack kneaded, rolled into a ball and depressed against a wall* (1993).

Creed's most famous piece is *Work No. 227: the lights going on and off* (2000), which requires that the lights in a museum wing or gallery space be flicked on and off at five-second intervals. This intervention is minimal but its effects are unexpectedly far-reaching. One's eyes are constantly readjusting. Judging distances becomes dodgy. A person has to think a little more than customary during simple actions like reaching or walking. Conducting a conversation becomes difficult, since eye contact must constantly be reestablished.

Work No. 227 makes museum-goers acutely aware of how they perceive and occupy a space. Such an artwork cannot be viewed in the manner of a painting or a video. Rather, it demarcates a place and a slice of time as significant, and it shapes how people experience and remember what they witness while it is underway. Creed's creed, so to speak, is summed up by his *Work No. 232* (ongoing), a neon sign that reads "the whole world + the work = the whole world." An artist adds nothing new to the world. It is the same before and after she intervenes. She does, however, succeed in altering what and how people think about the world.

"Via" lasts roughly ten minutes. For its duration, Bergvall reads sentence after sentence about being "midway" through life and "astray" in a "dark wood." In other words, she is continually reasserting the fact that the world is always joined *in medias res,* in the middle of things. The divinely ordained right way forward has been lost—but it will always remain so, and ever has been. While alive everyone inhabits an incessant disorienting sequence of present-tense moments. The past and the future, especially postmortem reward or punishment (or oblivion), remain stubbornly offstage, except in a ghostly fashion, via inference, memory, or prediction.

Of course, no one needs a work of art to remind him or her of this fact. But, like Creed's lights flicking on and off, "Via," whenever and wherever it is played or performed, creates an acoustical environment that heightens a listener's awareness of the succession of never-returning precious instants that constitutes being-in-time. And if there is more than one listener, they all simultaneously undergo this heightened consciousness of being plunged in *medias res,* what Maurice Merleau-Ponty would call a thickening of perception. While not as dramatic a gesture of sharing as multiple people tasting candy from the same spill, this collective awareness of jointly occupying a place and time has ethical value. One affirms the existence of other minds and other bodies.

Such affirmation is also a subtle subtext of Bergvall's roll call of translators. So many people have recognized the importance of a foreign text, and a foreign writer. So many efforts have been made to give new readers access to a poem seven-tenths of a millennium old. Yes, these patient, persistent, and repeated efforts have failed to achieve a perfect translation that conveys every nuance of the original, but for two centuries certain individuals have nonetheless displayed a Beckettian pig-headedness and kept laboring away.

In an era more given to demonization than mutual regard, while "Via" might change nothing and give succor to none, it can nonetheless usefully call to mind the fact that everyone everywhere is *nel mezzo del cammin di nostra vita*, and while *la diritta via* might be unavailable, we do at least dwell in the same *selva oscura*. We must learn to make that wilderness our home, and we must learn to tolerate the others—even literary critics, even quixotic authors—as neighbors.

III
WRITERS READING

7
Hart Crane and the Challenge of Akron

In most textbooks the name of Hart Crane (1899–1932) is indelibly associated with New York City. There are good reasons for this connection. His epic poem *The Bridge* (1930) joyously celebrates Manhattan's skyscrapers, speakeasies, jazz clubs, and burlesque shows. One encounters, too, the city's diverse population, from subway commuters to sailors on leave, from "Crap-shooting gangs" to washerwomen (Crane 63). The book's title refers to Washington Roebling's cathedral-like Brooklyn Bridge, a recurrent motif that unifies the work and that stands for the glorious new artistry that Crane believed technological progress and mass urbanization had made possible. Not surprisingly, a series of later New York–based writers—among them Allen Ginsberg, Frank O'Hara, and Samuel Delany—have plundered *The Bridge* for rhetorical strategies capable of expressing the curious craziness of life in the Five Burroughs.

The tight association between Crane and New York City must, however, ultimately be judged something of an unfortunate distortion. In part, it stems from his early death. During his final years, he traveled widely, residing at different times in Paris, Mexico City, and Cuba. He left behind an unpublished manuscript of Caribbean-themed poetry titled *Key West: An Island Sheaf*, and, when he died, he was in the midst of researching and planning his next project, *Cortez: An Enactment*, a tragedy about Moctezuma II and the Spanish conquest of Tenochtitlan. Had he lived another half decade, he likely would have been memorialized not as a New Yorker but rather as a cosmopolitan poet who hymned the whole of the New World.

The overemphasis on New York in the secondary literature also stems from insufficient attention to Crane's early development as a writer. He grew up far from Gotham, in northeast Ohio, among the canals, factories, mills, and million-aires of the Midwestern economic boom of the early twentieth century. More-over, although he did escape to Manhattan at the first available opportunity—under the pretext of seeking entry to Columbia University—he was a callow adolescent in full flight from a home life so troubled that at the age of sixteen he tried to kill himself at least once, perhaps twice. His precocious plunge into Greenwich Village's avant-garde (1917–1919) produced little more than a scat-tering of derivative poems and short prose pieces. Typical of these years was his stint as business manager at the fabled *Little Review*: he succeeded in selling only two ads (one to his father). Afterward, out of money and unable to hold a job, he returned to Ohio and threw himself on Dad's mercy.

He spent the next three years living in Akron and Cleveland. During this pe-riod his verse matured by leaps and bounds. He wrote some of his best known short lyrics—"Black Tambourine," "My Grandmother's Love Letters," and "Praise for an Urn"—and began preliminary work on *The Bridge* and his celebrated poem sequence "Voyages." When he again attempted to crack New York's liter-ary establishment in 1924, he brought with him his first verifiable masterpiece, "For the Marriage of Faustus and Helen," a three-part urban-centered lyric writ-ten in the peculiar aureate ecstatic elusive idiom that would remain his trade-mark until the end of his life. The poet who wrote the oft-quoted lyric "The Broken Tower" (1932) in Mexico during his last days of life employed then a style first perfected while working in a store on Cleveland's Euclid Avenue. To appreciate fully the grand poems of Crane's maturity, one must figure out why 1920s' Ohio prompted him to "modernize" his verse.

How to Adapt?

Like most poets born in the United States during the nineteenth century, Crane began his career by imitating British models. More specifically, he fell under the spell of the Yellow Nineties. His earliest verse was anachronistic and lush, remi-niscent of Algernon Charles Swinburne and Ernest Dowson:

> The anxious milk-blood in the veins of the earth,
> That strives long and quiet to sever the girth
> Of greenery . . . . Below the roots, a quickening quiver
> Aroused by some light that had sensed,—ere the shiver
> of the first moth's descent,—day's predestiny. (94)

After moving to New York in 1917 he found himself surrounded by authors whose innovative modes of writing were better suited to the bustle, blare, and gabble of modern urban life, among them Djuna Barnes, Eugene O'Neill, Wallace

Stevens, Elsa von Freytag-Loringhoven, and William Carlos Williams. He was unsure how to respond. A lyric such as "In Shadow" (1917) might feature intensive inventive sound play, yet its Beardsley-esque posturing also appears *démodé* when compared to the chiseled free verse characteristic of such adventurous contemporary volumes as Ezra Pound's *Cathay* (1915) and H.D.'s *Sea Garden* (1916):

> Out in the late afternoon,
> Confused among chrysanthemums,
> Her parasol, a pale balloon,
> Like a waiting moon, in shadow swims. (10)

Pound himself so disliked "In Shadow" that he advised Margaret Anderson, the editor of the *Little Review*, not to publish Crane in the future (743).

How to adapt—or compete? A new note enters Crane's writing in 1919 in the months prior to his move back to northeast Ohio, most obviously in two book reviews published in the little magazine *The Pagan*. Here the decadent *manqué* unexpectedly begins to sound a little like a nineteenth-century French realist. In January, he publishes a positive review of Lola Ridge's *The Ghetto and Other Poems*. *The Ghetto*, he asserts, is a work "widely and minutely reflective of its time" in the manner of Balzac's *La Comédie humaine* whose value stems less from its aesthetic achievements than its "sincerity" and "social significance" (150). He quotes with approbation several lines from the second part of Ridge's "Frank Little at Calvary":

> Over the black bridge
> The line of lighted cars
> Creeps like a monstrous serpent
> Spooring gold. . . .
>
> Watchman, what of the track?
>
> Night. . . . silence. . . . stars. . . .
> All's well! (qtd. 149)

Although he does not specify what draws him to this passage, one can speculate. The image of automobiles passing over a bridge at night will reappear several years later in Crane's "To Brooklyn Bridge" ("Again the traffic lights . . . skim thy swift / Unfractioned idiom . . . Beading thy path" [34]), and he will recycle Ridge's odd use of "spoor" as a verb in his lyric "Cape Hatteras" ("Where spouting pillars spoor the evening sky" [55]). Likewise, Ridge's deliberate misquotation of Isaiah 22:11 ("Watchman, what of the night?") and near-mention of Shakespeare (*All's Well That Ends Well*) prefigure the jaunty jagged collage-texture of "The River" and "Cutty Sark." In short, she provides a poetic idiom that Crane will be able to draw on successfully as he moves from the symbolist dreamscapes that populate his first book, *White Buildings* (1926), to the modern industrial landscapes found in his second, *The Bridge*.

He wasn't there yet, however. Lola Ridge's lines would have to percolate in his poetic subconscious for several years before he would know how to respond to them. A second book review from 1919 shows him taking his first steps on that long path. It, too, illustrates a deepening interest in art "reflective of its time," and again Crane refers to Balzac as a touchstone (150). This time, though, he is positively effusive and unqualified in his praise. He has discovered a new literary hero:

> Beyond an expression of intense gratitude to the author, it is hard to say a word in regard to a book such as Sherwood Anderson's *Winesburg, Ohio*. The entire paraphernalia of criticism is insignificant, erected against the walls of such a living monument. (152)

Crane clearly identifies with Anderson's subject matter, "a certain period in the development of America's 'Middle West,' so called," and he finds impressive Anderson's ability to suggest "local garments and habits" with an "economy of detail" (152–53). But what most excites him in *Winesburg* is Anderson's ability to elevate everyday life in his home state into great art, the stuff of "epics, tragedies, and idylls." He conjures "everlasting beauty" as well as "ironic humor and richness" out of "windows, alleys, and lanes" of a small Ohio town (similar, perhaps, to Garrettsville, where the poet was born). The review's tone, a mix of awe and envy, is easily explained. One can almost hear Crane pondering whether he, too, might join the ranks of the immortals to which he compares Anderson—such writers as Lucretius and de Maupassant—by ceasing to copy British models and instead writing about what he knew best, the Cuyahoga Valley where he was raised. Could he, too, add "an important chapter in the Bible of [America's] consciousness" (153)?

The *Winesburg* review dates to September 1919. By mid-November the poet was back in Ohio working for the family business, the Crane Chocolate Company. His father assigned him "a position" in a "new store" in Akron, where he was supposed to sell candy during the holiday season (214). Crane *fils* described the setting to his old friend Gorham Munson in a letter:

> I was down there [at the new store] yesterday, and find that he has a wonderful establishment,—better than anything of its kind in New York. It's

too bad to waste it all on Akron, but there seems to be a lot of money there that the rubber tire people have made. The place is burgeoning with fresh growth. A hell of a place. The streets are full of the debris from old buildings that are being torn down to replace factories etc. It looks, I imagine, something like the western scenes of some of Bret Harte's stories. I saw about as many Slavs and jews [sic] on the streets as on [New York City's] Sixth Ave. Indeed the main and show street of the place looks something like Sixth ave. [sic] without the elevated. (214)

Akron—meaning "the high place" in Greek—had been important since the early nineteenth century due to its location at the highest point on a system of locks and canals linking Lake Erie and the Ohio River. In the later nineteenth century rubber companies began to open factories in the area because of the ease of access both to the Great Lakes and to the American heartland. The explosive growth that Crane observed, however, is a feature of one decade in particular, 1910 to 1920, when, piggy-backing on the success of Henry Ford's Model T, companies such as Goodyear and Firestone turned Akron into the biggest producer of rubber tires in the world. In just ten years, the town's population ballooned from 69,067 to 208,435, an increase of over two hundred percent. Moreover, almost twenty percent of the new inhabitants in Akron 1910–1920 were foreign-born.[1] When Crane arrived, the city was a frontier-like boomtown dominated by people from elsewhere, many from as far as Warsaw or Beirut. Encountering this newly sprouted metropolis, Crane gropes for an adequate way to depict it, resorting at last to paradox: the Wild West superimposed on Manhattan. For a nascent realist, this breakdown of straightforward description signals a serious problem, moreover, a problem that *Winesburg, Ohio*, with its focus on hothouse know-everyone small-town life, could not help resolve. What vocabulary, imagery, or symbolism could ever truthfully and precisely describe Akron's rapid drastic expansion and transformation? Any moment wrested from the flux would be like a snapshot, accurate for a day and outdated thereafter. Under such circumstances, what would constitute a "proper treatment" (153)?

The relative rootlessness of the Akron population added another complication. The city's factories and support businesses drew large numbers of unattached young men. Living in boarding houses far from kin and flush (at least once a pay period) with cash, these men were relatively free to act on their impulses, even to reinvent themselves completely. If they wished, they could interact across class, religious, ethnic, linguistic, and racial lines that would have been much less permeable "back home." For young gay men—like Crane—this social fluidity allowed rampant opportunities to meet potential romantic partners (or one-night stands). A poem that Crane never published, "Episode of

Hands," retells one such chance encounter between himself and an unnamed laborer in his father's factory. The man cuts his hand, presumably in a workplace accident, and the poet bandages the injury. One can almost hear a swell of schmaltzy B-movie music in the background:

> And as the fingers of the factory owner's son,
> That knew a grip for books and tennis
> As well as one for iron and leather,—
> As his taut, spare fingers wound the gauze
> Around the thick bed of the wound,
> His own hands seemed to him
> Like wings of butterflies
> Flickering in sunlight over summer fields . . . .
> And factory sounds and factory thoughts
> Were banished from him by that larger, quieter hand
> That lay in his with the sun upon it.
> And as the bandage knot was tightened
> The two men smiled into each other's eyes. (115)

During the last months of 1919, Crane gained the courage to come out to his friend Munson, and he refers repeatedly thereafter in their correspondence to an "affair," "the most intense and satisfactory one of my whole life" (220). This "affair" continued even after Crane's father pulls the plug on the Akron venture and the poet relocated to Cleveland. (Apparently, even with the rapidly increasing local population in the City of Rubber, the price of labor was still so "exorbitant" that his father C. A. Crane couldn't cover the costs of running a shop in a "poor" location [220].) The two lovebirds, though, were still able to be together on weekends: "I live from Saturday to Saturday. . . . [W]hatever might happen, I am sure of a wonderful pool of memories" (224).

This situation presented an obvious obstacle for a poet in the throes of a literary crush on Sherwood Anderson. While homosexuality had surfaced in American literature prior to 1919—it is, for example, hinted at in Anderson's short story "Hands"—not even Walt Whitman's notoriously homoerotic Calamus poems could provide many pointers when it came to celebrating a potentially long-term, unapologetically blissful gay male relationship. Writing about his current private life, even obliquely, would require him to enter uncharted territory. If Crane planned to break with the retro-1890s style of his early verse by forcing himself to attend to and accurately portray the modern world in which he lived, he had to solve the puzzle of Akron.

A Proper Treatment

One option Crane explored was to write short verse vignettes rich in psychological "suggestiveness" (153). "Episode of Hands" is one such poem; so too is "My Grandmother's Love Letters," in which an autobiographical speaker, on a rainy night, contemplates

> the letters of my mother's mother,
> Elizabeth,
> That have been pressed so long
> Into a corner of the roof
> That they are brown and soft,
> And liable to melt as snow. (5)

These poems show Anderson's influence. They take humble people in everyday circumstances and discover in them "epics, tragedies, and idylls" (153). He, like the short story writer, seeks to "elicit the sympathy, or at least, the understanding of his auditor toward each and every one of the characters" (152). True, Crane does not try to emulate the turns and twists of plot in *Winesburg*. His short lyrics give himself no room to experiment with narrative (or any other means of introducing and connecting multiple episodes or points of view). As a consequence, these poems come off as a bit static by comparison to the stories in *Winesburg*. They are closer to *tableaux vivants* than dynamic portraits.

"Garden Abstract" demonstrates why this "distilled Anderson" approach to writing lyrics ultimately proved limiting and therefore unsatisfactory. Originally written in first person, the poem audaciously attempts to present a gay man's sexual awakening (Woods 144). Instead of setting the poem in or near the crowded dirty streets of Akron, however, Crane places his speaker in a pastoral setting, beside a fruit-bearing tree. Anderson, again, seems to have been the inspiration. The poet admired "the simplicity of A[nderson]'s great power of suggestion" when treating scenes of "sex-awakening." Specifically, he employs organic metaphors such as "the sap is mounting into the tree," which Crane considers to be "most mocking to the analyst" because they identify eros with "Nature," moreover, a "Nature" to which "one so willing and happily surrender[s]" (236). Although the version of "Garden Abstract" that appeared in *White Buildings* substitutes "she" for "I"—the "phallic theme" proved too in-your-face for the 1920s literary world to accept without a heterosexual makeover (229)—a potent erotic undertow remains:

The apple on its bough is her desire,—
Shining suspension, mimic of the sun.
The bough has caught her breath up, and her voice,
Dumbly articulate in the slant and rise
Of branch on branch above her, blurs her eyes.
She is prisoner of the tree and its green fingers. (7)

What is lost when "I" becomes "she" is a sense of immediate intimate correspondence between body and external nature, the "Dumbly articulate . . . slant and rise" of an erection in unconscious "mimic" of phallic boughs and branches (7). Regardless, though, whether the speaker is male or female, the poem does effectively convey what it is like to become a "prisoner" of primal biological impulses that have nothing to do with higher brain functions. The rational, sentient part of a person seems to vanish altogether, leaving no sense of separation between oneself and nature's constant unthinking surge and flow of forces: "she comes to dream herself the tree, / The wind possessing her . . . Drowning the fever of her hands in sunlight." In such a rapturous state, an individual loses touch with everything except the here and now: "She has no memory, nor fear, nor hope / Beyond the grass and shadows at her feet" (8).

"Garden Abstract" both is and is not a success. It is an acute portrait of a young person verging on adulthood, akin to Cherubino's aria "Voi che sapete" from *The Marriage of Figaro* (1784). Compared to Crane's early poetry, its diction is simplified and vigorous, and it prefers the compression and vividness of metaphor to languid similes. The lyric does not, however, convey any clear connection between its tableau and the place and time of its composition. The scene it depicts could occur in many different locales or decades. While some poets prize precisely this kind of abstraction from the particularities that give rise to a poem—Wallace Stevens comes to mind—removing an instant from time's flow is a rhetorical operation not unlike writing an anachronistic poem, that is, one that appears to belong to a different era. In both cases, a poet strives to achieve ends other than fidelity to the present moment. "Garden Abstract" is a decisive advance on "In Shadow," the lyric Pound despised, insofar as Crane has learned to incorporate psychological realism into his verse. It is not much better, though, at suggesting a groundedness in the material reality of modern life, nor does it permit him more latitude in exploring how eros might fit into the amorphous mercurial society of the 1910s.

To become the bard of Akron-on-Cuyahoga, Crane had to start writing longer poems. That, in turn, also meant that he had to start writing lyrics that consisted of more than a single highly charged, introspective episode. Additionally, he had to find ways of letting the outside world more fully into his poems.

At this important crossroads, he could have stuck with Anderson and studied the narrative techniques characteristic of American realist fiction. This possibility might sound outrageous to anyone familiar with Crane's later work, especially *The Bridge*. Nevertheless, it was an option, and even if he did not seriously consider it, he recognized its viability. In December 1919 he writes Munson and expresses his "enthusiasm" for a long narrative poem by another eminent Midwesterner: Edgar Lee Master's "Spring Lake," from his collection *Starved Rock* (221). This rollicking strange eleven-part poem tells the story of a staid town gone suddenly inexplicably cuckoo, and it tracks the adventures of Alice the psychic and the cornet player "[w]ho enticed the wife of Starling Turner / And kidnapped Imogene" (134). Crane, even at age twenty, assuredly had the taste not to imitate Masters's skeltonics, but he could have committed to experimenting with continuous verse narratives. Eventually, he might have turned out a book comparable to such Pulitzer Prize–winning volumes as Stephen Vincent Benet's *John Brown's Body* (1928) and E. A. Robinson's *Tristram* (1927).

Providentially for literary history, Hart Crane was reading another poet, too, during December 1919. In the same letter that he praises Masters he goes on to say that "[m]ore and more" he is turning toward T. S. Eliot "for values" (221). At this point, of course, Eliot was not yet a New Critical god. He had published only one book, *Prufrock and Other Observations* (1917). The fragmentation and eccentric erudition of "The Waste Land" (1922) still lay in the future, as did *The Sacred Wood* (1920), which cemented his reputation as the *arbiter elegantiarum* of Anglo-American literary modernism. Eliot did, however, in "The Lovesong of J. Alfred Prufrock," offer an extraordinary and *très, très moderne* portrait of London. From the opening simile comparing the sky to "a patient etherised upon a table" to the closing image of Prufrock walking by the sea with "the bottoms of [his] trousers rolled," Eliot's poem serves up one *choc* after another (3–7). Along the way, he provides spot-on anecdotes and epigrams about English polite society and its hidden neuroses. Dramatic irony, apt allusions to Shakespeare, rampant feminine rhymes, and an array of other virtuosic techniques both deepen a reader's appreciation of Prufrock as a character and inflect in informative ways the poem's portrait of a wholly and identifiably twentieth-century metropolis. Finally—and for present purposes, most significantly—the poem's unity relies not on narrative but on tone, atmosphere, and repeated motifs, structural devices more often associated with music than fiction.

In mid-1920, Crane writes his first multi-part poem, a true breakthrough into a new style, which he calls his "Akron suite" (240). Its title alone—"Porphyro in Akron"—signals a shift in literary allegiances away from Anderson and toward Eliot. Porphyro is the name of the chief male character in John Keats's "The Eve of St. Agnes" (1820), a long poem in Spenserian stanzas that fancifully reworks the folk superstition that young women will dream about their future husbands the night before St. Agnes's feast day. Porphyro, in love with Madeline, sneaks into her chamber on the night of 20 January (the eve in question) and insures that, when she wakes, the first thing that she will see is him, in hopes that she will think that she is still dreaming and become convinced that he is her future spouse. Keats's tale of confusion between reality and fantasy is written in an intensely lyrical style forthrightly indebted to the medieval romance tradition. Plunking "Porphyro" down in "Akron" was a way of directly engaging what till now had remained implicit: What happens to a poet steeped in the masterpieces of British literature past who finds himself in a polyglot middle American insta-city? Could fey medievalisms be used to celebrate the Rubber Tire Capital? This scenario could be a tragic one—a reiteration of the alienated artist *topos* so common in modernism—but the title carries a hint of self-mockery. As an authorial stand-in, Porphyro is faintly ridiculous. No Michelangelo, his primary artistic gesture is to redecorate sleeping Madeline's bedroom by stacking "candied apple, quince, and plums, and gourd," and assorted other "spiced dainties" and "delicates" on "golden dishes and in baskets bright / Of wreathed silver" (274–75). And this artistry is not for the ages. It is to dupe Madeline, to make her think that she is still dreaming, and then to permit him to woo her under false pretenses. Porphyro the deceiver and Akron the get-rich-quick boomtown might, in fact, have more to offer one another than initially meets the eye. Crane's "Akron suite" contains subtle ironies foreign to the more straight-ahead, stoic style of *Winesburg*.

Indeed, Midwestern realism is one target for Crane's irony. Part 1 of "Porphyro in Akron" opens with a free verse passage that (except for the sly, slant-rhyme triplet in lines 1–3) sounds more like, say, Carl Sandburg's *Smoke and Steel* (1920) than Crane:

> Greeting the dawn,
> A shift of rubber workers presses down
> South Main.
> With the stubbornness of muddy water
> It dwindles at each cross-line
> Until you feel the weight of many cars
> North-bound, and East and West,
> Absorbing and conveying weariness,—
> Rumbling over the hills. (98)

In these streets given over to laboring men and the transportation of goods, there is no obvious place for Porphyro. In such a setting, what relevance might fancifully romantic nineteenth-century preoccupations have, whether it be William Morris's interest in Norse legends or Swinburne's Hellenic paganism? In Akron, references to the Old World are more likely to be literal than literary:

> The dark-skinned Greeks grin at each other
> In the streets and alleys.
> The Greek grins and fights with the Swede,—
> And the Fjords and the Aegean are remembered. (99)

The speaker tries to find an appropriate diction to celebrate the manly men of Akron. First he tries for a Biblical-prophetic register, but his echo of Isaiah 2:4 ("They will beat their swords into plowshares") veers quickly into the ridiculous: "The plough, the sword, / The trowel,—and the monkey wrench!" Then he tries for odic posturing, but again, the contemporary references undercut that stance, too: "O City, your axles need not the oil of song." In full pyrrhic retreat, he echoes the downbeat close of "Prufrock," consigning himself to irrelevance:

> I will whisper words to myself
> And put them in my pockets.
> I will go and pitch quoits with old men
> In the dust of the road. (99)

Crane knew his Eliot well: "dust," "old men," and "whisper" are a classic objective correlative for sterility, and "pitch[ing] quoits" is an Eliotic form of damnation. One gives up on higher things and shrinks into the meaningless roles and rituals of bourgeois life.

Do You Know the Country?

If "Porphyro in Akron" ended there, it would be no more than a somewhat depressing poem about the incompatibility of high art and twentieth-century commerce. Conventional orchestral suites, though, contain both slow and fast movements, a sarabande as well as a gigue, and Crane's "Akron suite" likewise changes its affect as it moves from the first to second part. This new section begins with a short bridge passage:

> And some of them "will be Americans,"
> Using the latest ice-box and buying Fords;
> And others,— (99)

The Akron folk desiring the "latest ice-box" and the newest model Ford belong to the gray world of part 1, the Akron of weary labor, competition, and oil-rinsed axles. Who are the "others," though? Part 2 takes up the topic of the easy sociability of strangers in a new land. The speaker is no longer a removed spectator of the city's comings and goings. He reminisces about spending a companionable afternoon with an immigrant family:

> I remember one Sunday noon,
> Harry and I, "the gentlemen",—seated around
> A table of raisin-jack and wine, our host
> Setting down a glass and saying,—

> "One month,—I go back rich.
> I ride black horse. . . . Have many sheep."
> And his wife, like a mountain, coming in
> With four tiny black-eyed girls around her
> Twinkling like little Christmas trees. (99)

The setting is Sunday, not a weekday. The mood is not resignation but *Gemütlichkeit*. Dialogue appears for the first time, as does fantasy ("I go back rich") and glimmers of beauty and transcendence ("Christmas trees"). The "fights" and "stubbornness" of Akron's unfettered capitalism in part 1 might be inimical to the poet and force him into self-defeating irony, but, paradoxically, that marketplace also gives rise in part 2 to new, if transient, forms of community where poetry and art do find a welcome home (98–99):

> some Sunday fiddlers,
> Roumanian business men,
> Played ragtime and dances before the door,
> And we overpayed them because we felt like it. (99)

This kind of music, "Sunday fiddl[ing]," is a "business" perhaps, but it takes place in ephemeral spaces of joy and camaraderie ("ragtime and dances"), and money is an impoverished inadequate measure of what performers give the audience ("we overpayed them because we felt like it"). Part 2 does not so much contradict as supplement part 1. The role of objective chronicler of the city might be barred to the poet in an era when verse is like "quoits," a game played only by men too old or unskilled to be part of the work force. Activities deemed profitless entertainment by bean counters, though, do have their place when judged by different standards, and poets as scribes and purveyors of dreams can thrive interstitially and opportunistically wherever people come together to forget the importunate demands of the Protestant work ethic.

Part 3 provides yet another perspective, a more private and reflective one. It also adds a feeling of balance and completion to the work by tightening the poem's focus yet further, from outdoor and public spaces (part 1) to shared domestic spaces (part 2) to the privacy of the speaker's hotel bedroom (part 3). (Narrative, as Crane was quickly discovering, is not the only way to create momentum and logical coherence in a multi-part work.) One might expect this final section to resemble the Anderson-ish character studies that he had been writing in the months previous, since the speaker is now alone in a room into which the *realia* of Akron life do not visibly intrude. It would fit Crane's recent pattern if part 3 launched into another abstracted portrait of a mental state, whether arousal ("Garden Abstract") or loss ("My Grandmother's Love Letters") or otherwise. Instead, the speaker's privacy is unexpectedly porous and populous, decisively shaped by his experiences with books, popular culture, and other people.

Right off, the diction is emphatically, even parodically American: "Pull down the hotel counterpane / And hitch yourself up to a book." Then, another text and mind intrude. Crane quotes the first three lines of a stanza from Keats's "Eve of St. Agnes," which in its entirety reads:

> Full on this casement shown the wintry moon,
> And threw warm gules on Madeline's fair breast,
> As down she knelt for heaven's grace and boon;
> Rose-bloom fell on her hands, together prest,
> And on her silver cross soft amethyst,
> And on her hair a glory, like a saint:
> She seem'd a splendid angel, newly drest,
> Save wings, for heaven:—Porphyro grew faint:
> She knelt, so pure a thing, so free from mortal taint. (272)

At this point in the story, Porphyro has crept into Madeline's room, and he is watching her pray for a vision of her future husband. This stanza by itself can sound rather chaste, and Crane does end his quotation after the words "heaven's grace and boon." But anyone who obeys the poet's order and "hitch[es]" herself to Keats's *Lamia, Isabella, the Eve of St. Agnes and Other Poems* (1820) will discover that the next stanza turns into a strip tease:

> Anon his heart revives: her vespers done,
> Of all its wreathed pearls her hair she frees;

Unclasps her warmed jewels one by one;
Loosens her fragrant boddice; by degrees
Her rich attire creeps rustling to her knees:
Half-hidden, like a mermaid in sea-weed,
Pensive awhile she dreams awake, and sees,
In fancy, fair St. Agnes in her bed,
But dares not look behind, or all the charm is fled. (272–73)

Crane's speaker turns right to the "good part" of the poem, so to speak. What draws him to this semi-salacious scene? This variety of verse might be canonical but is neither prophetic nor rhapsodic (masks the speaker had tried out, unsuccessfully, in part 1). It is a poetry of gorgeous surfaces that titillates both the ear and inner sight. While Keats might not be everyone's favorite *livre de chevet*, he, too, like part 2's Romanian fiddlers, is shown to be capable of playing a joyful role in the world of Akron 1920.

Suddenly, the poem takes a wildly disorienting free associative leap. After spying on the "warm gules" of Madeline's "fair breast," abruptly and without transition a reader encounters a new quotation, this time in French: "Connais tu [sic] le pays . . . ?" (100). True, in 1920 the reference would have been much more obvious than it is today—a little like interjecting "It's been a hard day's night" into a 2007 poem—but why it appears would have been just as mysterious to audiences then as now. "Connais-tu le pays" was a popular aria from Ambroise Thomas's opera *Mignon* (1866) that would have been a standard part of any American amateur singer's repertoire well into the twentieth century. In the opera, after Wilhelm frees Mignon from the band of gypsies that kidnapped her as a child, she shares what she dimly remembers of the land where she was born:

Connais-tu le pays où fleurit l'oranger,
Le pays des fruits d'or et des roses vermeilles,
Où la brise est plus douce et l'oiseau plus léger,
Où dans toute saison butinent les abeilles,
Où rayonne et sourit, comme un bienfait de Dieu,
Un éternel printemps sous un ciel toujours bleu?
Hélas! que ne pis-je te suivre
Vers ce rivage heureux d'où le sort m'exila!
C'est là, c'est là que je voudrais vire,
Aimer, aimer et mourir!
C'est là que je voudrais vivre, c'est là! oui, c'est là!

Do you know the country where the orange tree flowers,
The country of golden fruit and vermillion roses,
Where the breeze is sweeter and the birds lighter
Where the bees gather nectar in every season
Where it glows and smiles, like a kindness from God,
An eternal spring under a blue sky?
Alas! that I cannot follow you
To the happy coast from which fate has exiled me!
It's there, it's there that I wish to live,
To love, to love and die!
It's there that I wish to live, it's there! yes, it's there! [2]

What if anything explains the speaker's non sequitur introduction of this song after only three lines of Keats? While the themes of love and longing connect "Eve of St. Agnes" and "Connais-tu le pays," Crane could easily have chosen any number of other texts (or arias) that share as much or more. The leap from Keats to *Mignon* seems calculated to register as a puzzle, a sequence of statements that invites readers better to understand the speaker's interior life. One certainly has the impression that there might be an inaccessibly private, missing term that could link A and B in a rationale manner. An ensuing flashback contains a crucial clue:

Your mother sang that in a stuffy parlour
One summer day in a little town
Where you had started to grow.
And you were outside as soon as you
Could get away from the company
To find the only rose on the bush
In the front yard (100)

The speaker recalls a time when, as a boy, he slipped away from one of those interminable "stuffy" adult occasions to which grown ups are forever subjecting their offspring. This escape "outside" offers a surprise, however. He finds a single "rose on the bush." Inside, his mother, pretending to be enslaved Mignon, had been singing about her ardent desire for "le pays des fruits d'or et des roses vermeilles," the land of golden fruits and vermillion roses. Her son has escaped captivity of a kind, only to discover . . . what, one of the roses his mother was singing about? Art uncannily, unexpectedly mirrors life. What counts as truth under such circumstances, what as dream? There's another twist, too. Thinking that he would be by himself, the boy instead finds a flower that has become indelibly associated with his mother and with art. When and where can one be truly alone if symbols stumbled on accidentally so easily recall to us our intimates? Out of such introspective moments poets are born.

Significantly, the rose in the yard explains the earlier leap from Keats to "Connais-tu le pays." The line immediately after Crane stops quoting "Eve of St. Agnes" mentions roses—"Rose-bloom fell on her hands, together prest" (272)—as does the second line of the aria, again, one line after Crane ceases quoting. The speaker has suppressed the image linking the two, though not irretrievably so. It emerges full-flower, as it were, only on the third occasion, creating in retrospect a coherence that the poem had lacked until this point. The poem thereby dramatizes how random thoughts, disparate texts, and stray memories can crystallize into form.

Of course, in a poem about art and the perpetually changing modern city such moments of crystallization do not last. The drift of the speaker's thoughts is rudely interrupted:

> But look up, Porphyro,—your toes
> Are ridiculously tapping
> The spindles at the foot of the bed. (100)

Memory's tricks give way to solid reality as the speaker's wandering mind is recalled to the body ("toes . . . ridiculously tapping"). Or so it would appear, at least at first. This awakening, however, like the young boy's escape from the "stuffy parlor," in fact runs smack into a symbol, this time the phallic "spindles at the foot of the bed" instead of the feminine rose. It's as if the speaker's restless feet complete another three-act movement: from purely textual and hetero-erotic (Porphyro gazing at Madeline) to past tense Oedipal (mother and son) to prospectively homoerotic (spindles in bed). "Porphyro in Akron" captures the quicksilver mobility, and inseparability, of thought, fantasy, and desire, what Sigmund Freud in another context would describe as the amazing malleability of the libido.

The poem draws to a close by making explicit what had been implicit throughout: Crane's quest to redefine the vocation of poet in response to Akron's challenge. Leaving Balzac and Anderson far behind, he seeks a fluid transgressive voice for himself to rival what Eliot achieves in *Prufrock and Other Observations*:

> And a hash of noises is slung up from the street.
> You ought, really, to try to sleep,

Even though, in this town, poetry's a
Bedroom occupation. (100)

The speaker first returns to exaggeratedly American diction ("hash . . . slung up"). Crane underlines that this poem, unlike his earliest verse, is not subservient to the British tradition. One can read Keats without writing like him. One can even borrow his seeming-paradoxes, such as the proximity and interpenetration of truth ("really") and dream ("sleep"), and renew them to be relevant to "this town," where poetry, instead of the balm that Keats wished it to be, is a "Bedroom occupation." These last two words are richly ambiguous. On the face of it, they would appear to repeat the note of alienation and isolation that occurred at the end of part 1. Yet part 2 demonstrated that the artist's "business" exceeds and eludes the logic of the market—thus making "occupation" a similarly unsettled term. In addition, part 3 has shown that a "bedroom" is hardly a retreat from questions of nationality, power, and identity. Bedrooms, as Crane knew well, were places where "affairs" that violate the norms and expectations of society at large take place. And this poem—a missive to the outside world—ends in the bedroom, with the poet listening to the "noises . . . slung up from the street" and responding with a display of his most private thoughts and feelings. Poetry as a bedroom occupation overcomes any separation between privacy and publicity, and it insists on active links between economics, community, psychology, and self-fashioning. Moreover, instead of representing a refinement on realism à la Balzac or Anderson, poetry as a bedroom occupation breaks with it, recognizing that "the real" is a slippery mutable concept. One person's reality is another's dream (or nightmare).

When he finished "Porphyro in Akron," Crane had fully modernized his poetry. He had fought through the fundamentally nineteenth-century modes of representation that had attracted him earlier in his career and embarked on the project that would preoccupy him until the day of his suicide: Can one write poetry as endlessly variegated, as protean, as modern life itself? What rhetoric, what language, what forms are capable of accomplishing such a titanic task? In an important sense, every major lyric that Crane wrote after 1920 amounts to a revision of, or coda to, the breakthrough that was "Porphyro in Akron."

8

Robert Duncan and Gertrude Stein

On 24 February 1973, Robert Duncan published the following quatrain as a broadside from Ārif Press:

> Time to return to Gertrude Stein
> to the hesitating glitter of the stone
> that breaks
> along the line of ancient fault[1]

Throughout, he plays with the fact that "Stein" is German for "stone." He suggests that her violations of English grammar might have been considered a "fault" during her lifetime, but decades later the fault "line[s]" that crisscross the "hesitating glitter" of her writings prove not a hindrance but an inspiration to a poet such as himself intent on mastering the "breaks" within language—the slippages and ruptures that inevitably occur as one strives to make meaning in a postlapsarian world still reeling from the "ancient fault" that was the Fall.

This broadside is a surprising document. In "Late Duncan: From Poetry to Scripture" (2005), Norman Finkelstein repeats received wisdom when he claims that Duncan's engagement with Stein extended "from the late thirties to the early fifties," a period that "culminate[d] in the volume *Writing Writing* (1952–53)" (345). He also asserts that after a subsequent transitional volume—*Letters* (1958)—Duncan's "apprenticeship with Stein" ended. He then embarked on the "major phase in his work," which includes the collections *The Opening of the Field* (1960), *Bending the Bow* (1968), *Ground Work: Before the War* (1984), and *Ground Work II: In the Dark* (1988) (347). Existing treatments of the Duncan-

Stein relationship tend to adhere to this plotline and concentrate on the 1940s and 1950s.[2] Few critics would expect to find Duncan advocating a "return to Gertrude Stein" in a year that he was also working on such late sequences as "A Seventeenth Century Suite" and "Dante Études."

One could argue that Duncan's renewed interest in Stein was ephemeral and superficial. A good supporting piece of evidence would be "Constructing the Course of a River in the Pyrenees," a lyric from *Ground Work II* dedicated to Stein. More precisely, Duncan declares that it is written "For G.M.P. by Grtde Stein" (*Ground* 230).[3] Since he singles out one book for special attention—*GMP: Matisse Picasso and Gertrude Stein with Two Shorter Stories* (1933)—he could be pointing toward a substantive intertextual dialogue.[4] The intended connections, however, are far from obvious. *GMP* is repetitious and abstract. It avoids nouns and active verbs and instead prefers pronouns, articles, prepositions, infinitives, and participles:

> That one had been that one. The one that one had been was one who was not needing anything for being that one. The one that one had been was one not winning everything in being that one. The one that one had been was one doing everything and completing these things and not needing being that one (*Gertrude* 140).[5]

The writing here is permutational, testing the sense, value, and sonority of a small set of words variously recombined. "Constructing the Course of a River" exhibits a different sensibility:

> The city I dreamt about was not O.
> I was not among the weepers at Puivert.
> I was not among the quiet ones.
>
> Yet the door was open,
> Time passt
> and the light was queer I saw.
>
> This is the way over the water
> where I am arrested in the lady's presence (*Ground* 230)

Ezra Pound, not Stein, seems the presiding genius. Duncan employs *Cantos*-like abstruse allusions: *Plan of the City of O* (1971) is the first collection of verse by his protégé Michael Palmer, and Puivert is a castle in Southern France associated with the gnostic heresy of Catharism. Moreover, Duncan's bent is less mathematical than mystical. Reminiscent of Pound's encounter with a "new subtlety of eyes" in Canto 81, his speaker travels through a mysterious "door" and over a body of "water" where he is "arrested" by the appearance of a numinous "lady." In short, Duncan's poem might mention *GMP*, but it appears to require no familiarity with that work.

One should not, however, permit stylistic differences between Stein's and Duncan's writings to inhibit appreciation of his long-term investment in her poetics. The 1968 preface to *Bending the Bow* announces that his goal is the creation of "a poetry of all poetries" and a "grand collage" (vii), and Michael Palmer has rightly called the *Ground Work* volumes "an echo chamber" in which "[h]omages, derivations, imitations" pay "tribute to the many voices that constitute his own" (x). While authors such as Baudelaire, Dante, Mallarmé, and Zukofsky might feature more recognizably in this choral poetics, Stein, too—as this chapter will show—remains a key presence. From the 1950s to the 1980s, she provides Duncan with compositional techniques that enable him to use a flawed, time-bound medium, language, to gesture toward eternal truths.

To some readers, this take on Stein might appear counterintuitive. Duncan's Stein does not resemble the secular experimentalist promoted by the Language movement since the 1970s.[6] Nor does she much resemble the playful pragmatist presented in milestone studies such as Ulla Dydo's *The Language That Rises* (2003) and Steven Meyer's *Irresistible Dictation* (2003). Learning to distinguish Stein as one of "the many voices that constitute [Duncan's] own" (Palmer x) requires a degree of skepticism toward his customary self-effacing "insistence upon calling himself a derivative poet" (Mackey 95). Duncan was in fact an interventionist reader who often recast his favorite authors in line with his own sensibilities. (He once wrote, for instance, that he saw Stein as "conveying soul and spirit" regardless of her "avowals of intent" [Duncan and Levertov 582]. Another time he talked of "Bending Stein . . . to my own weaving, like a chair maker bending the wicker-work" [389].) His "grand collage" is less a collage in the strict sense—a paste-up of excerpts from found documents—than an alchemical fusion of carefully selected ingredients. When critiquing authorial agency or expounding on his passive participation in a "community of language" (*Fictive* 231), Duncan might sound like a poststructuralist *avant la lettre,* but in practice he had a habit of interpreting his sources such that his "arrow flies from its bow with exact aim" toward targets already in his sites (79).

Ingenue Ingenuity

Duncan was first introduced to Stein around 1938 by his mentors Robert Haas and Louise Antoinette Kraus, married graduate students whom he met at Berkeley.[7] His interest became intense in 1950–53, a stretch when he sought models that could help him move beyond the mannered style used in *Heavenly City*

Earthly City (1947) and *Medieval Scenes* (1950).[8] He spent "over a year writing in imitation of Gertrude Stein to change my metabolism." He studied the ins and outs of the writing process: "the Stein period isolated me in my workbook" (Duncan and Levertov 204). He came out the other side with a catholic appreciation of her *oeuvre*. In his early correspondence with Levertov (1953–55), he recommends works in a variety of genres from different points in Stein's career: *How to Write* (1931), *The World Is Round* (1939), *The First Reader* (1946), and *Bee Time Vine and Other Pieces 1913–1927* (1953).[9]

Significantly, he endorses this last work—*Bee Time Vine*—as an example of "neglected contemporary poetry" (28). On the face of it, "contemporary" might seem a peculiar label for pieces written three to four decades previously. *Bee Time Vine* was, however, a new text, volume three in Yale University Press's *Unpublished Writings of Gertrude Stein* (1951–58). While Stein was alive only a small fraction of her work saw print. Most of that appeared in small press editions with limited circulation. Now, for the first time, writers looking for inspiration outside the circle of poets favored in university settings (Eliot, Yeats, Auden) had access to the full range of her experiments. For young poets such as Ashbery, Creeley, and O'Hara, this delayed reception made Stein feel more a "contemporary" than a forbear; after all, for most of the 1950s, a new book appeared every year.

In 1955 Duncan concedes to Levertov that Stein has become a literary "fad." He insists, though, that he is drawn to her for his own unique and compelling reasons (21). Unfortunately, these reasons remain unstated. A reader is left wondering what specifically might have led him to devote "over a year" of his life to studying and copying Stein's writings (204). Unfortunately, during his early career, Duncan made few explicit public attempts to explain his enthusiasm.[10] The best resource turns out to be the imitations themselves.

The chief literary record of his early 1950s involvement with Stein—*Writing Writing* (1964)—shows that he primarily looked to two stages in Stein's development as departure points for his own investigations. First, as the title indicates, he was intrigued by her heavy reliance on gerunds and participles in works composed in 1911–13 such as *The Making of Americans* and *GMP*. Duncan's book tirelessly repeats such words as "beginning," "speaking," "including," "pretending," "describing," and "writing." Like Stein, he limits the number of concrete nouns in order to direct attention to these essential actions and their primordial interrelations.

But *Writing Writing* is less concerned than early Stein with such airy abstractions as "living being." He, like Stein in the late 1920s, more narrowly inquires into the act of composition and corollary problems of identity and representation. He works from the premise that "ideas" and "the self" are not independent entities that an author can mirror in a poem. Instead, they come into being in the very process of "writing writing." Duncan's chief formal model for this kind of self-reflexive inquiry is Stein's *How to Write*, which exemplifies "composition as explanation," her tenet that only through employing language can its essence become apprehensible. No amount of talk about language's potential can substitute for what becomes manifest as a writer inductively explores the limits of his or her medium.

How to Write and *Writing Writing*, then, can be said to pursue similar ends by comparable means. Nevertheless, Duncan's act of "imitation" is not slavish (Duncan and Levertov 204). In practice he diverges significantly from Stein's precedent. Comparing two passages will illustrate that in 1952–53, the years when his work sounds most derivative, he is already learning to incorporate aspects of her poetics without violating the integrity of his own.

In "Sentences," a 1928 essay published in *How to Write*, Stein investigates fundamental problems in literature and language by posing the same question repeatedly:

> What is a sentence. A sentence is an imagined master piece [sic]. A sentence is an imagined frontispiece. In looking up from her embroidery she looks at me. She lifts up the tapestry it is partly.
> What is a sentence. A sentence furnishes while they will draw. (123)

Such prose resists straightforward logical development. Stein interrupts herself in the middle of sentences ("it is partly") and returns to her starting point ("What is a sentence"). As she would put it, she "begins again and again." This assault on forward progress extends to syntax itself, as in the violation of the sequence of tenses in the final part of this passage ("furnishes" and "will draw"). Such solecisms encourage an audience to set aside its conventional means of sense-making and consider how else Stein might be relating her statements.

Here as elsewhere Stein offers rhyme as a possible alternative means of word-association. This selection is tied together through two rhymes: "master piece" / "frontispiece" and "embroidery" / "look at me" / "tapestry" / "partly." Such sound play, though, approaches doggerel. When reading Milton, say, or Auden, a reader might expect rhymed words to be paired for semantic as well as aural reasons, but Stein's indiscriminate chiming inspires no such confidence. As usual, she both suggests a connection, here via sound, while simultaneously undercutting it. Her use of anaphora ("A sentence is a . . .") and simple repetition ("What is a sentence") operate similarly. She lays bare the devices that structure discourse in order to highlight how arbitrary, how willed, they often are, even when we wish to assume otherwise. She teaches that the structures on which we depend to organize language in fact guarantee little in regards to truth or meaning.

One cannot, however, condemn sight unseen everything she writes as mean-

ingless gibberish. To lack a guarantee of meaning does not license one to presume its absence. It is possible, for instance, to make a tentative reading of this
extract from "Sentences." The first two key words in the first paragraph, "master
piece" and "frontispiece," seem to proffer an opposition between a sentence as
something complete and self-sufficient and as something prefatory and incomplete. Perhaps Stein, after proposing these alternatives, decides to comment on
the idea of the "master piece" by countering this phallic form of creation with
"embroidery," a female art. The thought of feminine artistry, combined with the
idea that every work of art is somehow incomplete ("frontispiece"), may in turn
lead to "tapestry" by way of that archetypal woman artist, Penelope. A comparison between Penelope the weaver and Stein the writer would indeed be apt.
Stein, like Penelope, "begins again and again" and insists that the act of creation
is never-ending, dependent on partial execution, erasure, and repetition.

However satisfying such a reading might be, it must be conceded that Stein
never allows her meanings to become quite so definite. "Tapestry" might imply
Penelope. This passage might endorse Penelope's artistry as superior to Homer's
"master pieces." But Stein could also be describing a scene in a friend's home in
rural France. *How to Write* is full of references to domestic spaces and things,
but one must hesitate before rashly attributing allusive or allegorical purposes
to such objects. There is usually insufficient textual support. Stein teases her
readers with elusive profundities because such ambiguities further her global
investigation into the fundamentals of language and art.

Writing Writing does not accompany Stein to the brink of a deconstructive
abyss. Duncan might want "writing" to reveal itself through the act of writing—
to write so that "it says what it does" (Stein 71)—but he wants mystical revelation, not disconnected insights into linguistic possibility. The following excerpt
from "Imagining in Writing" clarifies this distinction:

> It is the measure of the crippled sentence. It is the pleasure of the poetry
> rotting its words until the flesh of the language falls away from its bone.
> It is the beautiful senseless tone in the language crippling the sentence.
>
> The poetry. The stink of the real to the imaginary nose.
> The skull is the rose. A face like all other faces unlike.
> A finality. A betrayal.
>
> The rows of uneven teeth like the measure of the sentence. (*Selected* 31)

Formally, the similarities between Duncan and Stein are legion. Instead of relying on explicit logical or narrative connections, Duncan employs parallelisms,
such as anaphora ("It is the . . .") and rhyme (measure / pleasure, bone / tone,

nose / rose / rows) to link his statements. Instead of active verbs he uses linking verbs and sentence fragments made of noun phrases. The only punctuation is the period. All utterances seem declarative, as if the speaker were trying to explain "the measure of the sentence" by naming, by pointing, to things. Nevertheless, the comparisons that the speaker makes between these things are anything but clear. What is the "it" in the first three sentences? Can "it" be the same in each case? In the next to last line, what is "final" and who "betrays" whom or what? The passage also works hard to produce similes and metaphors, but the way in which they are stated generally leaves a reader uncertain of their force or meaning. "A face like all other faces unlike" paradoxically advances and retracts a possible similarity. The statement "The skull is the rose" is so abrupt and so gnomic that it lacks the impact of, say, T. S. Eliot's "the fire and rose are one," a metaphor toward which the whole of *Four Quartets* builds. Duncan demonstrates that he has mastered many of Stein's techniques for simultaneously asserting and undermining connections between words.

Ultimately, though, "Imagining in Writing" is less disjunctive than "Sentences." In this passage he recycles a cluster of associations that would have been familiar to Middleton and Webster. The human body ("nose," "teeth," "face," "flesh") is as mortal and subject to corruption ("rot," "stink," "cripple") as the fairest summer "rose." We all face "betrayal" by time, and in the end we will be reduced to that "finality," our skeletons ("bone"). And, no matter how "unlike" our faces be in life, in death our skulls are hideously "alike." Duncan, in other words, imports a variety of melodramatic Jacobean props, everything but a ghost, while also prodding readers to consider the Big Questions: life, death, and poetry. He does not share Stein's focus on what she calls the "commonplace," that is, everyday words and household implements. Duncan aims for something grander through his "imagining in writing" than Stein seeks via her "imagined frontispiece."

Moreover, one can speak with greater confidence about his intended message. He implies that the poetic can function as a "rot" in the flesh of language that "stinks" of the real and functions not as an escape from time but as a *memento mori*. It is not so much humanity that is sick unto death as it is language, our "crippled sentence." Poetry is the agent by which one can return to bare "bones" and start over. Significantly, the last line—"The rows of uneven teeth like the measure of the sentence"—not only refers to the earlier "skull" but also contains an allusion to Cadmus seeding the fields with a dragon's teeth. In this myth, the warrior Myrmidons spring from "rows of uneven teeth," fight among themselves, and then, the survivors having made a truce, build the city of Thebes. So too, Duncan seems to propose, the "uneven teeth" of his poem— its bone-like fragments—can sprout, vie, and renew the language.

He thus successfully integrates Stein's disruptive techniques into his own poetry without allowing them to become an end in themselves. Stein's "Sentences" permits different ways of approaching her work: either as a coherent statement on her position as a woman poet or as an experiment in exploding every possible means of reading through her prose in a linear fashion. A reader can, of course, choose to emphasize one or the other dimension of her project. In "Artifice of Absorption," for example, the Language poet Charles Bernstein favors Stein the decomposer of language. He praises Stein's "great achievement in anti-absorptive writing" and singles out *How to Write* for its remarkable ability to impose a "word-by-word halting" on a reader (*Poetics* 56). Duncan tilts the balance in the other direction. He tends to read Stein as embedding myths and archetypes within arcane prose that, to be deciphered, requires the same devotion as esoteric scripture. Duncan would happily pair Stein with Penelope; Bernstein would more likely align her with Derrida or Wittgenstein.

In *How to Write* Stein comments that "It is impossible to avoid meaning" (71). As the context makes clear, she is meditating on two things. First, she ponders the mind's amazing ability to infer meaning when any two words, however arbitrary, are placed together. Second, she mulls the way reference always inheres in language, no matter how hard one tries to exclude it. Asked to explicate her statement, Bernstein would probably emphasize that meaning is always present when one starts to write. A poet might even be obligated to produce poetry as opaque as possible to introduce new meanings into the world and into the language. Since readers are guaranteed to "make meaning" out of any poem, there can be no failure to communicate.[11]

Duncan, in contrast, would likely expound on Stein's insight that language always points beyond itself, into the world. As he writes in "Towards an Open Universe," "the order man may . . . impose . . . upon his own language is trivial beside the divine order or natural order he may discover in [it]" (*Fictive* 81–82). For him, reading Stein is almost a kabalistic exercise, a search among the broken vessels for the remnants of the primal influx of Light. As Duncan asks Levertov in 1955, "¿but if the poet makes the fragment clear, the Reader can see?" (32). Teaching the reader to see—such would always remain Duncan's aim.

Amuse-Bouche

Duncan knew that he was choosing to read Stein in a particular way. He was also aware that her methods require a writer to grapple with problems concerning the interplay between form, content, and technique. Composed soon after *Writing Writing*, the poetry in *Letters* demonstrates that he rapidly developed a keen sense of how she could and could not help him achieve his goal, the poetic manifestation of truth and mystery. His lyric "For a Muse Meant" is worth special attention in this regard. It clarifies his stand toward Stein on philosophical grounds. He rejects purely linguistic experimentation as an inadequate solution to solipsism.

A reader could easily miss his subtlety in "For a Muse Meant." The poem exhibits a number of stylistic debts to Stein that could be mistaken for an unqualified declaration of allegiance. Most obviously, the poem "begins again and again" with great fanfare. Three times colons appear flush left, interrupting the flow and signaling new departures. Just as Stein repeats "what is a sentence" to allow herself to reinitiate her thinking about language *de novo*, here Duncan uses the phrase "specialization, yes" (*Letters* 1–2). He also interpolates a list counting from the number one, varies mode from prose to verse and back, adds a footnote, and, near the end of the piece, bizarrely seems to announce a new poem altogether by interjecting a second title, "For a Song of the Languagers" (2–4).

"For a Muse Meant" exploits a second Steinian device to generate its material: repetition. The first fifteen lines mull over the word "inspired" and play out a variety of chains of association based on the Latin root, *spir-*, which means "to breathe." A Platonic "aspirant" "aspires" to "essences"; to "aspirate" is to "breathe out" "vowels"; a "familiar spirit" hovers nearby even as words threaten to give up the "ghost" (1). Another, later passage repeats words derived from the Latin verb *trahere*, to drag: "abstract," "tract," "distract," and "traction" (2). Throughout, the poem recycles a small set of words such as "sign," "design," "ritual," "words," and "memorize."

Finally, Duncan ruptures logical and grammatical syntax in a recognizably Steinian fashion, as in the following prose paragraph: "List of imaginary sounds I mean sound signs I mean things designd in themselves I mean boundary marks I mean a bounding memorizations I mean a memorial rising I mean" (3). Duncan claims to offer a "list" but instead presents a sequence of phrases that cancel each other out. He discards the phrases "imaginary sounds," "sound signs," and "things designd in themselves" one after another because none of them seems quite right. Instead of advancing, he sputters. Each of these unacceptable alternatives is linked to the others via wordplay. "Imaginary sounds" proposes a contradiction between eye ("the image") and ear, which "sound signs" attempts to rectify, but the mention of a "sign" begs the question of a "designer," so Duncan's speaker abruptly confronts the issue of a creator.

Fixated on "I," not on God, he rejects this train of thought and, appropriately, switches to problems of "boundaries," the limits of the known or sayable. He then promptly mires himself in grammatical troubles. The phrase "a bounding memorizations" echoes both the preceding phrase, "boundary marks," and the following one, "a memorial rising," thus providing a provisional unity among his words, yet "I mean a bounding memorizations" is also a confusion of singular and plural forms. This error functions as something of a speed bump. A reader has to stop and reconsider. Could there be another way to parse this unpunctuated stream of thoughts? One could wrench them into a grammatically correct arrangement such as:

> List of imaginary sounds : I mean sound signs : I mean things designd in themselves : I mean boundary marks : I mean a bounding : memorizations I mean : a memorial rising I mean.

Midway through this reconstruction, "I mean" must awkwardly switch from the beginning to the end of the constituent clauses. There are other possible ways to reorder the syntax, but they are equally unsatisfactory. Moreover, once one begins to consider such possibilities, the number of grammatical confusions requiring clarification becomes almost overwhelming. Should "rising" refer to "memorial" or "I" or both? Should the final "I mean" be construed with "a memorial" or with the next words in the poem, "a con glomerations," which nevertheless repeat the singular/plural error of "a bounding memorization" and thus have some claim to association?

After these sorts of fissures start occurring to readers, they are apt to reconsider even the most basic of initial assumptions. For example, in all likelihood "sound" in "I mean sound signs" is intended to be an adjective, though it could also be a verb in the imperative. This stuttering voice that insists that it knows what "I mean" yet consistently fails to deliver could be demanding that we, its auditors, "sound signs" ourselves, that is, read aloud. Listen to the words, attend to them, speak them, and make them your own, it pleads, even though the "signs" we are to "memorize" remain inscrutable "things."

In the final analysis, then, is this knotty passage a heartfelt cry or a torrent of babble? The dilemma is Steinian, but the tone is not. Instead of her equanimity we encounter self-doubt. The poem seems to be describing itself when it declares,

> to hesitate, retract.
> Step by
>   / to be idiot-awkward
>   step (4)

Like *How to Write*, "For a Muse Meant" hesitates over its utterances and moves forward step by halting step. But unlike Stein, who was never given to self-deprecation, Duncan concedes that such a method may amount to being "idiot-awkward." He calls his own discourse into question not only on linguistic grounds but also on aesthetic, perhaps even ethical, grounds. Is it "awkward" for Duncan to abandon the fluency of his early poetry? Has he become an "idiot"?

True, there is no necessary reason to identify the speaker here too closely with Duncan himself. The poem's "idiotic" persona could be offered up as a model of what not to do. To puzzle out the relation between poet and speaker in "For a Muse Meant" requires careful thought. One has to discern why "idiocy" might appeal to Duncan as a mask or as subject matter. What advantages does such a persona grant him?

Etymologically, "idiot" means an ignorant or unskilled person. Moreover, as Socrates claims, only the truly ignorant man is wise because he has the curiosity to probe matters that more sophisticated men take for granted. "Idiotic" behavior may be the only path available to reach truth. On its first page, the poem concisely states that to "hesitate" leads to "clearing old greym attar." In this convoluted pun, Duncan seems to suggest that "hesitation" is capable of banishing the "grim attar" of tradition, clearing off the "grim altar" of worship and de-fogging the "gray matter" of the brain. To "hesitate" might make one "idiot-awkward," but it might also yield spectacularly beneficial results.

Moreover, the "idiocy" of the speaker seems a prerequisite for the poem's most outstanding feature, its exaltation in wordplay. If the speaker knew what "I mean," if he did not "hesitate" over what to say, there would be no reason to spin out lists, pick apart words, and reorder them. He could simply write a memo. The title "For a Muse Meant" invokes a "muse" for the purpose of pleasure, and the poem proceeds to exhibit an almost child-like exuberance for language. By indulging in free association and whimsical connections, Duncan likely has in mind the argument of romantics such as Wordsworth and Emerson that children experience the world and language freshly and immediately; hence they directly apprehend truths that their elders forget. He does not, though, display a sentimental attachment to lost innocence. On the contrary, his ideal poet more closely resembles a maenad than Little Orphan Annie. The "inspiration" that the poem seeks turns out to instigate violence: "take care / by the throat & throttle it." The "magic" that "bottled genius" (genie?) provides not a simple "vacation" but instead "intoxic/vacations," a blend of poison, purgation (*vacuo*), and ecstasy. Accordingly, even as the speaker affirms "the breath, the pulse, / the constant / sluffing off of old stuff," he is simultaneously "a-wailing / the failing" in his "morning lang / wage," a language that mourns despite the dawn (3–4).

Life, death, poetry, innocence, and experience: the poem's speaker grapples with a heady blend of themes. No wonder he eventually feels compelled to declare his incapacity! His quest begins auspiciously, though, as an attempt to attain higher knowledge. On the poem's first page, he orders himself to "still thy brathe" to hear "them" speak, "them" standing ambivalently for "voices," "images," "essences," "vowels," and "meaning." In a marginal comment, Duncan comments on the route that the speaker has chosen to take toward truth. He presents this decision as an act of introspection, a looking within: "as if the bone-cranium-helmet in-hearing." The speaker peers into the dark of his skull and strains to "in-hear" "them speak." To disclose the "spirit," the "ghost" at the heart of the "word," he opts to plumb his interior depths (1).

What the speaker discovers "inside" is three-fold. First, he encounters "lists" and "con glomerations" of words. Second, he perceives his power to combine those words as he sees fit. Third, he experiences the "boundaries" that "mark" out the limits of language and self. Has his quest to "in-hear" essences failed? At the poem's close, the speaker directly addresses this question. Just as in "Imagining in Writing," he resorts to a favorite Jacobean image—the skull—to crystallize his sense of the agonized interplay between the artist, eros, and thanatos. He opposes the "intoxic/vacations" of the inspired genius to the fate of the "sober" man:

> It is sober he stumbles
>   on truth? Hell, no—
> this he sober gnaws
> the inconsequential
>   eternity of his skull. (4)

This passage alludes to two scenes in *Inferno* XXXII. First, Dante trips over the head of a soul sunk in the ice of Cocytus (ll. 76ff). Soon afterwards, Dante happens upon Count Ugolino, who is gnawing another man's skull (ll. 124ff). The speaker, however, indicates that his Dante-figure, also in search of revelation, does not "stumble" across spiritual "truth." He does not even meet another spirit. Whereas Ugolino at least succeeds in revenging himself on the man who starved him to death, Duncan's man, also starved, is trapped inside himself, able only to gnaw the "eternity" of his own skull. Notice the pun on "gnaws"—not only does it substitute for "knows," but it also hints at gnosis, the religious insight that he craves. "Sober," man is self-enclosed, lost in a private hell. The hopeful turning inwards, the "in-hearing" that the poem initially proposes, here gives way to bleak solipsism.

But is "in-hearing" altogether repudiated? The poem's close emphasizes sobriety as the danger, not the quest for higher knowledge. "He" fails, not "I." The speaker distances himself from the plight of the "sober" man. Inspiration, intoxication, ecstasy—these are routes out of the round of the skull. Duncan in

"For a Muse Meant" dramatizes the gradual advance of a lyric voice toward a new depth of understanding about art, the self, and the world.

Once elucidated, the final line of the poem becomes a powerful statement of this poetic stance: "His appetite is not experimental." In a poem so conscious of words and their histories, these words should carry the full resonance of their etymologies: "appetite," from *appeto*, to ask for, to petition; "experimental," from *experior*, to put to the test, to know by experience. The solipsist does not hunger for "the experimental," that is, knowledge arrived at through personal experience. Discoveries arrived at through "experimentation" cannot satisfy the drive to exceed the self. For a poet's word to become manna in the wilderness it must partake of power that originates outside him- or herself. In making such a statement, Duncan is clearly in dialogue with Gertrude Stein. Her tenet of "composition as explanation" enjoins an inductive testing of language's boundaries. He replies that such a method, unaccompanied by a petition to Dionysius, amounts to "gnawing on one's skull." The title of *Letters* says it all. Its poems are "letters," both letters on the page and epistles intended for others to read. Poetry reaches into itself, into language, at the same time as it also reaches outward, toward others, toward the Other.

Critics' tendency to overlook Stein's presence in Duncan's verse from 1960 onward should now be much easier to understand. Without grasping the idiosyncrasy of his engagement with her writings in the 1950s, one cannot appreciate the sea-changes that her techniques undergo as he incorporates them more fully into his poetics. Duncan's "Often I Am Permitted to Return to a Meadow," from *The Opening of the Field* (1960), can concisely illustrate this point. Many writers have taken inspiration from the lyric's vision of a "made place" that is transcendent, central, and endlessly productive. No one, however, has thought to associate it with Duncan's Stein imitations. Its mythopoetic clarity seems to represent a radically new departure. Nevertheless, Duncan began writing "Often I Am Permitted" in 1956, the same year that he compiled and revised the poems that appear in *Letters*. He then sent the 1956 draft along with a revised 1958 version to Levertov in August 1958; the proofs of *Letters* arrived on his desk in October.[12] "Often I Am Permitted" deserves to be read alongside the earlier book. The poem exhibits the same turning and "re-turning" of words observable in "For a Muse Meant":

Often I Am Permitted to Return to a Meadow

as if it were a scene made-up by the mind,
that is not mine, but is a made place,

that is mine (*Selected* 44)

The sound cluster "m" plus "d" predominates. "Meadow" becomes "mind" becomes "made-up" becomes "made place." "Mind" blurs into "mine." Duncan first asserts that the "scene . . . is not mine" only then to retract his statement: "a made place / / that is mine." He almost loses his reader in what the poem calls its "disturbance of words within words" (7).

Just as Stein's repetitions and word-play find their distant echo here, so too does her dictum "beginning again and again." For her to begin again is primarily a rhetorical or narrative technique; for Duncan it becomes a metaphysical proposition. One must return again and again to the "meadow" at the heart of things, "Wherefrom fall all architectures I am," in order to restore the boundaries that "hold against chaos." Returning to the "place of first permission" offsets entropy and allows the poet to perceive again the "omen of what is," the generative ordering principles that underpin a universe that only appears to be in constant flux (7). Duncan has overhauled Stein's Penelope-poetics to accord with his gnostic worldview.

Yet he continues to recognize her importance as a sage. He encrypts homage to her work in one of the poem's most striking images, a circle of children playing ring-around-the-rosy. Here ring-around-the-rosy becomes "a children's game / of ring around the roses told" (7). The phrase is an awkward one. The final word, "told," seems out of place. Does it modify "game," "ring," or "roses"? Who tells whom what? Why make "rose" plural? Are the children circling up around several rose bushes? As one turns and "returns" the words in an attempt to make sense of them, they began to lose definition. "Told" perhaps suggests "tolled"—one "rings" bells, after all. The words "roses told" shade over into "rose is told." What might "telling a rose," though, have to do with children playing? Words circle and resound, and their connection to the image that they describe becomes progressively less certain.

Duncan almost certainly has in mind another instance of "telling" and "circling" roses, Stein's china set, on which Toklas had the tag line "a rose is a rose is a rose is a rose" printed in a circle—quite literally, "around the rose is told." What evidence is there for this allusion? In 1969, Duncan published a pamphlet called *Play Time Pseudo Stein*, which includes several of his notebook entries from 1953. Between the 1969 preface and the book proper appears an instructive drawing. Duncan here is forthrightly playing off Stein's china pattern. "A rose" becomes "arrows." He explores the tension between circularity and linearity latent in her move from a sentence with a beginning and end ("A rose is . . . a rose.") to its new Ouroboros-like visual form. Time's "arrow" rounds upon itself, and "straight as an arrow" gives way to a paradox, "a round of arrows told." The "arrow" of life-as-we-live-it simultaneously participates in the "round" of eternity, a circle in which martial "arrows" are transfigured by "Eros."

In Stein, Duncan thus finds a concise expression of loving harmony between the human and the superhuman. Her dinner plates, on which "around the rose is told," become in his eyes "an everlasting omen of what is." A contemporary critic might be tempted to read "a rose is a rose is a rose" as an emptying-out of meaning, a reduction of "rose" to its bare quidity as a word; he instead discovers an affirmation of the Rose of Dante and Yeats. Her tag line might be simple as a "children's game," but when read aright, "the rose is told," the Rose is manifest.

Moreover, the issues addressed in "Often I Am Permitted" recall Duncan's earlier explorations of Stein's techniques. Death, life, and art remain his chief subjects, and he again examines how child-like play can reach toward eternal verities. Just as the "amusement" in "For a Muse Meant" is anything but light entertainment, so too the game in "Often I Am Permitted" is quite serious. Ring-around-the-rosy is traditionally thought to commemorate death by Black Plague ("ashes ashes we all fall down"). In Duncan's poem, we discover children centuries after the great plagues still dancing in celebration of their inevitable doom, a morbid illustration of his earlier contention in "Imagining in Writing" that "the skull" and "the rose" are one. The lesson here, though, is hopeful. Language enables an escape from mortality and solipsism. Though death is the end of any one life, the human race as a whole transcends it by making it the occasion of songs and games passed on from generation to generation. Participating in this collective endeavor, the "arrow" of the individual life finds its place in nature's "round," the perpetual cycle of growth, rot, and renewal.

After 1960, although other authors moved to the forefront of Duncan's attention, he nonetheless continued to accord Stein a central place in his poetic pantheon. In 1962, he ordered *An Acquaintance with Description* and three other hard-to-find Stein texts from the bookseller Henry Wenning.[13] In 1964, he acquired and read the unabridged *The Making of Americans* (Duncan and Levertov 620). He also assiduously placed his 1950s Stein imitations with various publishers under different titles. Not only did New York's The Tenth Muse Press put out *Play Time Pseudo Stein* in 1969 but *Writing Writing* also came out from Albuquerque's Sumbooks in 1964, *Names of People* from Los Angeles's

Black Sparrow Press in 1968, and a second edition of *Writing Writing* from Trask House Press in Portland, Oregon, in 1971. And he continues to cite her as an authority in his correspondence with Levertov. He holds forth about her "discovery of new formal possibilities" (Duncan and Levertov 374) and her sense of herself as a "word-worker" akin to a modern painter for whom "the paint is the thing in the painting" (582). So closely does he associate himself with Stein that, during the rancorous 1971 exchange of letters that leads to their rupture, Levertov targets her as well: "Most of Gertrude Stein bores me—she's nice for tea but I wouldn't want her for my dinner" (679). When, in his 1973 broadside, he announces that it is "Time to return to Gertrude Stein," he invites other poets to join him where he had long stood, in an "in-group of a Master personality— Stein" (Duncan and Levertov 396).

Cherchez La Femme

An awareness of Stein's ongoing importance in Duncan's later poetry can help readers appreciate material that might otherwise escape notice. A prime example is the neglected poetic sequence "Sets of Syllables, Sets of Words, Sets of Lines, Sets of Poems Addressing: Veil, Turbine, Cord, & Bird." This piece was the outcome of "a workshop at the Naropa Institute" led by Duncan in 1976. Apparently, he felt obligated to produce his own response to an assignment that he had given his students.[14] The "fortuitous result" was first published as a chapbook in 1979 from Davies Press and then later included in the collection *Ground Work II* (Palmer xiii). "Veil, Turbine, Cord, & Bird" looks somewhat out of place, however, when grouped with Duncan's better-known late works. It contains no obvious autobiographical content (unlike "Santa Cruz Propositions," "Circulations of the Song," and "After a Long Illness"); it contributes no installments to a Poundian life poem (unlike "Before the Judgment," "In Wonder," and "The Dignities"); and it does not take the form of commentary on previous texts (unlike "Poems from Margins of Thom Gunn's *Moly*," "A Seventeenth-Century Suite," "Dante Études," and "To Master Baudelaire"). Readers unfamiliar with Duncan's variant on Stein's "composition as explanation" will likely find it thoroughly perplexing. Nevertheless, it arguably represents an aesthetic achievement at least on par with these other works.

"Veil, Turbine, Cord, & Bird" opens with a section titled "*PRELIMINARY EXERCISE*":

What does a turbine veil? a bird avail what chord?
I heard a bird whir no word, felt
a turbine shadow turning from the floods of time

electric currents the darkness stirrd,
and trees in blaze of light arose
casting shadows of speech, seductive, musical, abroad. (*Ground* 208)

The first line repeats three of the four words of the sequence's subtitle—"turbine,"
"veil," "bird"—but it also initiates a process of variation, replacing "cord" with
"chord" and "veil" with "avail." Then the words begin "turning" and returning in
earnest. Both "bird" and "cord" lead by consonance and assonance to "heard,"
"whir," "word," "currents," "darkness," and "stirrd." The "exercise" announced by
the section heading turns out to be another in-hearing of the "hosts" that are "a
disturbance of words within words" (*Selected* 44).

The grammar and sense, too, begin to go off track in familiar fashion. How
does one "feel" a "shadow"? What is a "turbine shadow" anyway? One cast by a
turbine? Or a shadow that somehow resembles a turbine? Does "turning from
the floods of time" imply a turning away from the floods, or does "from the
floods of time" indicate the location where the turning is taking place? How
does one parse the line "electric currents the darkness stirrd"? Does Duncan
intend—despite the lack of a comma between "floods of time" and "electric"—
that we should read the line as an independent clause, the equivalent of either
"electric currents stirrd the darkness" or "the darkness stirrd electric currents"?
Or is the phrase a defective noun absolute: "I . . . felt / the shadow turbine . . . /
[upon its having] stirrd electric currents [and] the darkness"? The next few lines
muddy matters further:

It was a single tree. It was a word of many trees that filld the vale.
It was a store of the unspoken in the bird
that whirrd the air, that every occasion of the word overawed. (*Ground* 208)

Duncan uses anaphora ("It was a") to provide local structure to his verse, but the
referent of the "It" is unclear. How can "It" be a "tree," a "word," and a "store"?
Then there are the two confusing clauses beginning "that." The statement "that
every occasion of the word overawed" could be modifying adjectivally the "store
of the unspoken" or it could be describing adverbially the consequences of the
"whirr[ing] of the air," depending on which conjunction has been omitted:

It was a store . . . that whirred the air, [and] that every occasion overawed
It was a store . . . that whirred the air, [so] that every occasion overawed

(Duncan could, of course, also be using inversion, in which case "the store"
should be understood as overawing the "occasion," and not vice versa . . . .)

"PRELIMINARY EXERCISE" fulfills Duncan's Steinian tenet that "the dynamics of the making needs as much incoherence . . . as it needs coherence" ("Ten Letters"). His writing suggests not forecloses possibilities.

The second section of the poem sequence is titled *"NOTES DURING A LECTURE ON MATHEMATICS,"* and, predictably, it repeats but varies what has come before:

> And now I know it. The irrational is trying.
> Prove it as permissible speech.
> SET talk. No one has it. We are going into it.
> IT received a name. Name it.
> We are in the mystery of the name. (208)

The pronoun "it" recurs. "It" still remains a "mystery," however. "It" is like a "name" insofar as it is used as if it pointed to something or someone, yet "it" continues to lack a stable referent. A pronoun without an antecedent is certainly "trying": it taxes one's patience. But here "it" also is "trying" to intimate the "irrational," that is, truths that exceed or defy scientific logic ("mathematics") yet still encompass and enfold us ("We are in the mystery").

The wordplay here might feel belabored. Why keep repeating "it"? Why not declare once and for all that the ineffable has no name—and move on? The proliferation of ways of saying the same (no)thing is, however, a common device in Duncan's later writings. The sequence's peculiarly long title is apropos. A poet generates "sets of syllables, sets of words, sets of lines, sets of poems" by rearranging a small number of elements, in this case "veil," "turbine," "cord," "bird." Such a task no longer appears "idiot-awkward," as he feared in "For a Muse Meant." In his word weaving he now intends to illustrate the power of *"hwyll,"* a Welsh word that appears twice in the poem sequence (209, 211). Hwyll refers to an "emotional quality that inspires and sustains impassioned eloquence" (OED). As we have seen, he believes that the poet's duty is always everywhere the same, to body forth truth. There is an unfortunate corollary, of course: in our fallen world that task's failure is preordained. "Veil, Turbine, Cord, & Bird" proposes that *hwyll* and its component attributes—among them ingenuity, wit, and enthusiasm—prevent despair and carry the poet and audience through yet more rounds of this perpetual cycle.

Accordingly, the sequence proceeds to begin again and again by testing new structures and word-configurations. The third section—"THE RECALL OF THE STAR *MIRAFLOR*"—is subdivided into five numbered parts (209). Previously, the verse was printed flush left; now it appears centered beneath Arabic numerals. The fourth section—"THE NAMING OF THE TIME *EVER*"—contains five "songs" with odd titles:

FIRST: SONG TWO
SECOND: SONG FIVE
THIRD: SONG ONE
FOURTH: SONG THREE
FIFTH: SONG FOUR (209–10)

Here Duncan reprises one of Stein's favorite techniques, a mismatch between the ordinal number assigned to pieces of writing and the order in which they are presented. (Scenes I and II come after III and IV in act V of Stein's play "At Present" [1932], for example, and the chapter numbers in *A Novel of Thank You* [1958] are thoroughly scrambled.) After all, if one always begins from the same point and continually re-arrives there ("often one is permitted to return"), why keep track of what comes after what? Why not put "song three" fourth, or "song two" first?

The next two poems, "I POUR FORTH MY LIFE FROM THIS BOUGH" and "THE TURBINE," switch to left justification. They continue to try out new permutations of and variants on the words "veil," "turbine," "cord," and "bird." The sequence then concludes with "WHAT THE SONNET MEANS THE SONNET MEANS." This heading is the first in the work to be followed by a punctuation mark—a colon—which naturally leads one to expect that a summary, list, or other kind of illustrative material will immediately follow. No sonnet ensues, however. For four sentences, Duncan switches to writing prose. Moreover, he mentions neither sonnets nor any other verse form. Like Stein in *Useful Knowledge* (1928)—a collection he once paired with the *Cantos* and *Finnegans Wake* as featuring "beauties, individual and bold" (*Fictive* 67)—Duncan uses a title to raise a question only then to defer giving a definite answer. A reader who expects to find "what the sonnet means" delivered in polished paraphrase will be as frustrated as one who presumes Stein will ever pinpoint "Wherein Iowa Differs from Kansas and Indiana" or explain "American Biography and Why Waste It." Steinian poetry does not move decisively toward a destination. It travels in rings and rounds and tells the already told.

To refuse to travel in a straight line, though, is not to deny an answer altogether. By never making explicit "Wherein Iowa Differs from Kansas and Indiana," Stein insinuates that there is no essential difference between these two Midwestern states, whatever their inhabitants might think. Similarly, by mentioning sonnets and then producing prose, Duncan shows his disinterest in arbitrary rules governing preset forms. Octave, sestet, Shakespearean, Spenserian: such terms refer to merely accidental features of a poem. He is interested instead in the essence of the sonnet tradition, that is, the force that motivates poets to pen them in the first place. More specifically, he endorses the neo-Platonism associated with the sonnet since the Italian Trecento. Like Petrarch and Michelangelo, he espouses "belief in the possibility of approaching [the divine] through identification with the beloved" (Francese 20).

Indeed, he embraces this "Way of Romance" as his rightful path. He acknowledges other goals (a paradisal "crown" or the attainment of *nirvana*) but presents them as subsidiary. He asserts an essential "I" that will continue to seek "what I love" regardless of the fate of that part of himself organized religions might call a "spirit" or "soul": "Tho the turbine hum with power and the source of enlightenment would crown the spirit, I would leave my spirit, if it so chose, to their play and go still on my way; and if my soul craved the currents of Buddha compassion, give up my soul-suffering to whatever washing away from being it seek, for I go swiftly and even alone to what I love." The way "I" have chosen is not the way of the monk or *sadhu*, that is, the way of renunciation. Instead, this path requires involvement in a world fervently loved and "gladly" experienced: "I follow the Way of Romance, a mere story of loving and the household we found in the design of the veil. I am entirely a creature of the veil, there my life cord, there my bird song of scents and colors. I go gladly into stages of pain, of aging, of loss, of death, that belong to the passionate and, if the wheel so return me, I shall embrace again birth cord and pang of this animal being and come into whatever desires and delusions in memory of you and this passing time in your care" (212). The world might be no more than a "veil," a place of "delusions." Nevertheless, "the design of the veil" includes a "household" wherein "I" can persist in the "story of loving." "I" will be able to dwell "in memory of you" while also "passing time in your care." This "you," this addressee introduced so abruptly, is, of course, his partner Jess Collins, but it is simultaneously and without contradiction also what "Often I Am Permitted" terms the "First Beloved," the first cause "Wherefrom fall all architectures I am" (*Selected* 44). Significantly, this profession of neo-Platonic love means resigning himself once more to a Steinian beginning again—this time, *samsara,* the cycle of birth and rebirth ("if the wheel so return me"). As before, time's arrow rounds on itself in the service of eros.

"WHAT THE SONNET MEANS" ends with an exchange between the speaker and the First Beloved in her guise as "She Who Will One Day Recall Me." Approached via the "Way of Romance," she disavows the need for esoteric knowledge: "*No initiation, you are right, dear boy, / Just the simple facts of life / including death / rocks goats and herbs*" (*Ground* 212). She also perceives "life" as "including death"; in other words, immortal and eternal, she sees all of time all at once. Temporal divisions—now alive, now dead—are irrelevant. Appropriately, then, the speaker replies by naming himself "Sundown's herald, Dawn's answerer, / Night's companion in Day's realm," a bard for all hours. He announces, too, why he has selected this vocation: "For *this* ever am I Love's good beast and dancer" (212). But what does "*this*" refer to? To the poem sequence just read? To the Beloved, to the world, to the wheel of time?

Ultimately, "*this*" refers to everything and to nothing, to an "it" that escapes the bounds of human language and knowledge. No other moral-to-the-story seems possible within the "design of the veil," that is, in an unredeemed cosmos unable to endure the full force of the Light. To aver such a thing is not to lapse into pessimism. As Stein teaches, properly speaking "there is no such thing as repetition," an exact recurrence of the same. In saying the same thing more than once, authors do not repeat. They "insist" (*Lectures* 166–67). Reiterating divinity's ineffability does not lead to tedium. It prolongs, elaborates, and passes on the hymn of thanks to the "Queen Under the Hill" whom true poets serve (*Selected* 44).

Tout S'Explique

Would Stein recognize herself in "Veil, Turbine, Cord, & Bird"? Probably not. She never wrote resonantly romantic lines such as "This veil of flowering now / weaves itself before tomorrow morning / cords potential of our returning / ring beyond ring" (*Ground* 210). She prefered a leaner, less lyrical presentation: "she passes she surpasses, she passes and passes and she surpasses the folded roses. They fold roses and she surpasses them" (*Gertrude* 279). A poet can, though, study a precursor without falling into pastiche. Duncan might claim that "'originality' is NOT either interesting or available to me," yet his Stein, a master of shamanic word-magic, is in fact quite original, utterly unlike the Steins promoted by his contemporaries (Duncan and Levertov 5). She resembles, for instance, neither the barricade-stormer imitated by Ashbery in *The Tennis Court Oath* (1962) nor the charming *salonnière* who appears in Merrill's *Changing Light of Sandover* (1982).

As critics learn to discern Stein's influence on Duncan's verse, many received notions are sure to receive renewed scrutiny. If *Passages*, for example, puts Penelope at her loom in the second installment and thereafter becomes an exercise in tearing down and beginning again, does the work deserve the label "Steinian epic"? Duncan, after all, eventually ceased numbering *Passages'* individual sections, a gesture which suggests a Steinian indifference toward ordinal numbering. The point of such provocations is not to reassess how much of which precursor goes into the "beloved coffee pot" of his compositional process (Duncan and Levertov 5). The goal is to savor more fully the "grand design" of the finished product (*Ground* 272).

9

Reginald Shepherd at Hart Crane's Grave

In September 2008 the poet Reginald Shepherd passed away after a battle with cancer. He was only forty-five years old and at the height of his career. He had just published his fifth volume of verse, *Fata Morgana* (2007); a collection of essays, *Orpheus in the Bronx: Essays on Identity, Politics, and the Freedom of Poetry* (2008); and a compilation titled *Lyric Postmodernisms: An Anthology of Contemporary Innovative Poetries* (2008). A stint as a blogger at Poetryfoundation .org also made him a prominent, if controversial, figure across the many divisive camps that make up the current American poetry scene.[1] It is too soon, of course, to speak with any confidence about Shepherd's prospects for a lasting place in the literary canon. Little has yet to be written about him in scholarly venues.[2] He was, however, a poet who had thought a great deal about his relation to poetic tradition:

My poetry operates within a literary tradition and a literary language to which I owe my formation as a writer, yet which is not "mine" (as a black gay man raised in Bronx housing projects). . . . This language, the language of Yeats and Stevens, Eliot and Hart Crane, has both made me possible as a writer and made being a writer an asymptote. It is a language to which I aspire in the act of writing it and being written by it (every writer is as much the tool of language as its wielder). Thus my relationship to my own language (simultaneously mine and not mine at all) is ambivalent, constantly haunted by the questions, "Can I truly speak this language? Can this language speak through me?" . . . It's my intention to inscribe my presence into that language and that tradition, not to "subvert" it but to produce a place of possibility within it.[3]

Shepherd's reference here to "Yeats and Stevens, Eliot and Hart Crane" is telling: he chooses four famous white male modernists to serve as a synecdoche for the much longer list of English-language canonical poets to which he aspires to add his own name. Indeed, in his last years, Shepherd repeatedly turned to these Anglo-American high modernists—his "primary forbears" (*Orpheus* 3)—to provide standards of value against which he measured (and generally found wanting) both the "aimless noodling" of the "self-identified avant-garde" (76) and the "self-righteous" reaffirmation of social divisions in "identity poetics" (42). Coming from a "black gay man raised in Bronx housing projects," such arguments can sound peculiar. Why prefer a body of writing infamous for its hermeticism and elitism to poetry openly committed to utopian or other radical progressive causes?

Such a question is overhasty. It prejudges how aesthetics and politics intertwine, and it underestimates, too, Shepherd's reservations concerning modernism's excesses. As a first step toward thinking through his place in (and challenge to) American literary history, this essay explores his involvement with one of his favored precursors, Hart Crane, a poet whose "extravagances of language and vision . . . enthralled" him from adolescence onward (*Orpheus* 21). While perhaps not the greatest influence on Shepherd's writings—Yeats, Stevens, and Eliot do all have equal or better claim to that distinction—Crane undeniably left a profound mark on his poetry, especially on his third and fourth books, *Wrong* (1999) and *Otherhood* (2003). By analyzing and contextualizing his most overt expression of filiation—the elegy "At the Grave of Hart Crane"—this essay will, however, show that Shepherd is anything but a complacent mouthpiece for tradition. In fact, he believes that "being written by . . . language" is a perilous process. While he agrees that writing good verse might require poets to channel predecessors and to let language play as it will, he also maintains that one's very survival as an autonomous individual demands that submission to outside agents never becomes total. "My aim," he once said, "is to rescue some portion of the drowned and drowning, always including myself" (*Orpheus* 188).

Beneath the Wave

In 1997 Shepherd published "At the Grave of Hart Crane," in the *Indiana Review*. Two years later, it appeared in his collection *Wrong*. The lyric opens on the shore of Lake Michigan, and its first quatrain testifies to Shepherd's intimacy with the notoriously ecstatic-clotted style of the poet he has chosen to honor:

Mobile light paints me an undertow, trailing
a northeasterly hand through day, riptide
scattering coins of noon: silvers
surface currents to the key of water foaming (88)

Here one encounters many of Crane's characteristic mannerisms: a loose trailing syntax, a jostling crowd of metaphors, rampant consonance, and a penchant for trochees. Shepherd echoes the baroque intricacies of such celebrated lyrics as "Voyages," "Atlantis," and "For the Marriage of Faustus and Helen." His most immediate precedent, however, as his title alerts us, is "At Melville's Tomb." That homage, too, begins at the boundary between land and water and makes similarly resonant if elusive pronouncements: "Often beneath the wave, wide from this ledge / The dice of drowned men's bones he saw bequeath / An embassy" (*Complete* 33).

Shepherd's lyric participates in a venerable poetic tradition. Like John Berryman in "Dante's Tomb," Allen Ginsberg in "At Apollinaire's Grave," and Stanley Kunitz in "At the Tomb of Walt Whitman," he is announcing his vocation and stature by affiliating himself with an august precursor. His title, however, alerts readers that they are about to encounter a most unusual version of this topos. Strictly speaking, Crane has no grave. Nor is his body buried near the Chicago coast. In 1932, after a drunken night and amidst a deep depression, he leaped off the cruise ship *Orizaba* and drowned in the Caribbean Sea. At the time, he was *en route* from Mexico to New York City and nearly three hundred miles out from Havana. His body was never recovered. Shepherd's slipperiness here is not mere whimsy. The motif of "sea burial" in African American writing is almost by definition fraught, linked to the Middle Passage that is both "origin" and "vanishing point" of Black America (Nielsen, *Integral* xiii). How is one to interpret an African American writer's invocation-by-misdirection of a white poet's suicidal embrace of a Middle Passage–like death? Why does he locate his speaker on the edge of an inland fresh water sea thousands of miles from Crane's grave-that-is-not?

Answering these questions is no simple task. From the mid-1990s onward, Shepherd's writing became, on the one hand, increasingly sensuous and sonorous even as, on the other hand, his language became more enigmatic and his ideas more sophisticated. He is a prime example of what Charles Henry Rowell calls the "third post-1960s wave" of African American poets, that is, a third, distinct cohort of writers to emerge in the wake of the Black Arts Movement (viii).[4] This newest wave is marked by three traits. First, it has come to prominence "in the wake of the ascendancy of critical theory." "[T]hese poets have learned, and they teach their readers, to take nothing for granted," including the most basic, commonsensical ideas about writing, politics, and social interaction. Second, these contemporary poets are suspicious of rigid identity-based subdivisions of the literary field. They hope to "build a tradition as hybrid as that which the jazz masters created," one that is not limited by "geography, race, culture, [or] class." Finally, they exhibit an unparalleled writerly boldness: "each of these poets is prepared to use whatever he/she finds and deems appropriate to create a poem" (Rowell ix). This combination of a thoroughgoing self-awareness with a penchant for reinventing poetic tradition means that one cannot rely unreflectively on old maps for reading verse. One has to be ready to grapple with unprecedented means and modes of expression.[5]

Kevin Young, perhaps the best known of Rowell's "third wave" poets, reprinted "At the Grave of Hart Crane" in his pioneering anthology *Giant Steps: The New Generation of African American Writers* (2000). While this elegy is not representative—stylistically, thematically, or philosophically—of that collection, let alone of "third wave" poetry more generally, nonetheless it offers a starting point for assessing the challenge that contemporary African American verse often presents to literary historical commonplaces. To read Shepherd, one must learn to set aside the genealogical and reproductive metaphors so common in literary criticism—father/son, generations, family, tribe, and inheritance—and instead imagine the poem as a space of highly charged erotic encounter. Here as always "eros" is shorthand for a tangled weave of fantasy, fact, and language, a weave, moreover, in which the intimately personal is inseparably, intricately bound up in the shared and social. Suddenly, before blithely discussing a topic such as "intertextuality," a critic must start drawing on psychology, sociology, and the study of sexuality. Untangling Shepherd's poetics, one discovers "what makes this wave of poets different from their predecessors": a "vision of the world" that "challenges the old verities and renders them uncertainties" (Rowell ix).

The first problem that Shepherd's elegy poses is—why Hart Crane? Why might he interest a twenty-first-century African American poet? The answer is not immediately apparent. The author of only two books—*White Buildings* (1926) and *The Bridge* (1930)—Crane has conventionally been considered something of a second-tier modernist, eminent, perhaps, but ranking in prestige and accomplishment below the likes of T. S. Eliot, Langston Hughes, Gertrude Stein, Wallace Stevens, and William Carlos Williams. In particular, his archaic aureate diction, showy elusive rhetoric, densely knotted tropes, and proclivity for abstraction have long frustrated readers in search of substance beneath the flash. (Eric Sundquist, for one, has declared that Crane's poetry offers "a drunken candy world . . . poisonous at the center" [377].)

Moreover, as a Midwesterner whose candy magnate father invented Life Sav-

ers, Crane was a white son of privilege who rarely questioned his era's racial politics. He had no objection to forming friendships that crossed racialized lines—
his correspondents included the Harlem Renaissance writer Jean Toomer and
the Jewish critic and novelist Waldo Frank—but such ties did not stop him from
penning basely racist limericks (Crane, *O My* 317). His published verse might
be less overtly offensive but nonetheless also exhibits a troublesome romantic
racialism. He typically equates Blackness, raw sensuality, and jazz performance
("For the Marriage of Faustus and Helen" II, "The River"), and, insofar as he
acknowledges African American history, he tends to present it as a pleasurably
melancholic spectacle of abjection ("The interests of the black man in a cellar /
Mark tardy judgment on the world's closed door" [*Complete* 4]). Native Americans fare even worse. Crane intended his long poem *The Bridge* to offer "a mystical synthesis of 'America'" (*O My* 131). That synthesis, though, is founded upon
an act of repression. He consigns the continent's indigenous peoples to the forgotten, mythic past: "Papooses crying on the wind's long mane / Screamed red-
skin dynasties that fled the brain, / —Dead echoes!" (*Complete* 59). This vanishing apparently leaves their lands available for settlement by white Europeans,
a miracle that leaves these settlers with "no Indian blood" on their hands or in
their veins (Gardner 25). Unsurprisingly, a number of African American poets,
among them Bob Kaufman, Melvin Tolson, and Jay Wright, have felt compelled
to talk back to Crane and offer alternative ways of thinking through the relation
between race, nation, land, and colonialism.[6]

Readers familiar with Shepherd's early verse might be tempted to read "At
the Grave of Hart Crane" as an expression of solidarity founded on a shared
sexual orientation (and a consequent shared experience of homophobia). Oft-
anthologized lyrics such as "Eros in His Striped Blue Shirt," "The Gods at 3 A.M.,"
and "Skin Trade" document the thrill, pain, and wonder of Shepherd's life in
the Boston, Chicago, and New York City gay communities. A paean to Crane
might seem a logical, literary-historical extension of this project. The modernist's homosexuality has been the subject of frank literary-critical debate since the
1930s.[7] Indeed, from Thomas Yingling's *Hart Crane and the Homosexual Text*
(1990) onwards, the subject has come close to monopolizing academic writing on the poet. A number of contemporary scholars have explored connections between Crane's formal innovations, thematic preoccupations, erotic self-
understanding, and participation in queer communities in the United States,
France, and Cuba.[8] Like John Ashbery, Mark Doty, Allen Ginsberg, Stephen
Jonas, James Merrill, and many other post–World War II American gay male poets, Shepherd could be looking to Crane as a queer literary ancestor, an author
of passionate homoerotic love poetry ("Voyages") who also obliquely depicted
scenes such as a gay-bar pick up ("Cutty Sark") and sex in public restrooms

("The Tunnel"). Crane, in other words, could be serving as an empowering father figure who suggests the possibility of a successful, ongoing gay male literary tradition.

This explanation, while not entirely wrong, remains rudimentary. Shepherd's
writings rarely if ever exhibit an uncritical affirmation of homosexual identity.
His autobiographical essay "Coloring Outside the Lines" explains why. After
graduating from Bennington College, Vermont, he discovered that East Coast
gay urban enclaves were:

> not as welcoming of their oppressed darker brothers as I had been led
> to believe. . . by the gay liberation tracts that were already outdated by
> the time I got my hands on them in 1976 or so. . . . [T]he main thing I
> learned was that white gay men were a lot like other white people, and as
> my mother told me some time ago, white people stick together. In Bos-
> ton and Chicago and New York, when you go out to gay clubs and gay
> youth groups and gay political meetings and gay social groups, what you
> mainly meet are white gay men, and what they're mainly looking to meet
> are other white gay men. . . . Your average white gay man, whatever his
> political identifications or inclinations, is white and a man long before he's
> gay, certainly when it comes to his allegiances to or disavowals of other
> gays who might not be sufficiently either. (136–37)

His isolation was heightened because of his self-described "bad object choice,"
an erotic fixation on these very white men:

> [T]o what "home" could I expect to return (for the first time, no less) as
> a snow queen?[9] There are certainly enough black gay people (or is it gay
> black people?) out there willing to inform me in no uncertain terms that
> *that* is the true white man's disease, and I've got a bad case. . . . If I expect
> to come to *that* home, the House of Gay-Men-of-Suitably-Proud-African-
> Descent, it had better be with an adequately revolutionary black loved one
> in tow. (138; emphasis in original)

He began to feel as if he occupied an unstable nowhere:

> For me, to be black and to be gay have been two radically discrete subject
> positions, which to a large extent have contradicted one another, except
> to increase my sense of the lack of any position called *mine,* much less
> *me.* (134; emphasis in original)

This "lack of any position," he goes on to assert, has prompted him to embrace a poststructuralist and psychoanalytic account of subject formation. More specifically, following Jacques Lacan, he believes that identity is "a compensation for a lack" and that the chains of signification that traverse the subject lead it ever onwards in pursuit of impossible fulfillment of this inaugural absence (134).

This understanding of subject formation clarifies why, when discussing Crane in a 1998 interview published in *Callaloo*, Shepherd eschews essentializing rhetoric. He cannot effusively, unreservedly praise Crane as a pioneering out gay writer. Such a scenario would reify, that is, render solid and overly simple, a shifting web of fantasy, identification, and aversion. Instead he speaks abstractly about language, "experience," and the new "worlds" that verse creates:

> I'm not interested in the poem as a record of experience; I'm interested in the poem as an experience in itself. Many of the poets I love, Hart Crane for example, write poems which are little worlds which one can explore, in which one can lose oneself. I'm interested in the poem as an object in the world, or even a miniature world itself, and not just as a statement, however eloquent, about other objects. Obviously, a lot of my poems have a very apparent subject matter. But I've always felt that if subject matter were the only thing, then there'd be no reason to write a poem. If life is your primary interest, just live. (306)

Here race and sexuality seem to enter the picture, if at all, as mere "subject matter" or as kinds of "experience" that the poem "record[s]." One might construe this argument as a dream of escape, of deracination and desexing, except that he provides a very specific literary context for this position while also clarifying how he sees poetry related to identity:

> I've been reading . . . a lot of poets in the vicinity of language poetry, people like Ann Lauterbach, Kathleen Fraser, Mei-mei Berssenbrugge, Jorie Graham, Aaron Shurin, and Michael Palmer. I think of my recent work as moving closer to the poem as a self-generating linguistic occasion, the poem as an event occurring in language and nowhere else. . . . Part of what poetry does is remind us that things, including language, including ourselves, aren't what we think they are, aren't as accessible or apprehensible as we think they are. (305)

Shepherd values poetry as a genre that highlights the obduracy of "things, including ourselves," their resistance to easy apprehension or definition. Sex and race, presumably, number among these "things" difficult of access, difficult, that is, because we apprehend and wrestle with them in language, a medium that is, at base, very far indeed from providing transparent or immediate access to some exterior, extra-linguistic material reality. He credits "poets in the vicinity of language poetry" for this insight—a statement that puts an unexpected spin on his interest in Crane's "little worlds" and his espousal of "the poem as an experience in itself."

Language Poetry was a 1970s and 1980s avant-garde literary movement centered in San Francisco and New York City. It preached a poetics thoroughly informed by French poststructuralism and Marxist political philosophy.[10] Shepherd's list of figures "in the vicinity of" the Language movement are poets who share its theoretical bent as well as its delight in disjunctive formal experimentation while simultaneously distancing themselves from its more strident side, especially its ascetic antilyricism. Shepherd also implicitly signals his dissent from the macho posturing that is common in Language polemic.[11] His list begins with four women (Lauterbach, Fraser, Berssenbrugge, Graham), mentions an out gay man (Shurin), and then adds, almost as an afterthought, a lone but lushly lyrical heterosexual male, Michael Palmer. Equally significant is Shepherd's inclusion of Berssenbrugge, one of the few Asian Americans to have achieved prominence in American experimental poetry circles prior to the 1990s (the other poets he lists are white).[12] The literary landscape in which Shepherd situates himself is not beyond or removed from considerations of nationality, race, sex, and gender. Rather, they are inflected through and by a range of theoretical positions and compositional practices that have their own genealogies, conflicts, and particularities.

When Shepherd explains his interest in Crane by distinguishing between "the poem as a record of experience" and "the poem as an experience in itself," he is not trying to dismiss the importance of identity categories *per se*. Rather, he is shifting the discussion toward a larger statement on the nature and function of language, a theoretical precondition to an informed discussion of how race and sexuality are discursively constituted, experienced, reproduced, and policed. In the 1998 *Callaloo* interview he avoids pursuing this logic rigorously, almost certainly because of generic constraints. His astute invocations of Jacques Lacan, Fritz Fanon, and Homi Bhabha in other contexts illustrate that he is entirely capable of articulating and defending his ideas in academy-speak.[13] On this occasion, however, he defers explaining "the direction of linguistic investigation" that he is currently pursuing, stating simply that a new manuscript of his is going "further" in this direction than he has ever gone before (305). The resulting book, published in 2003 as *Otherhood*, offers, as its title suggests, a sustained meditation on otherness, othering, fraternity ([br]otherhood), and community among outsiders (the 'hood where others live). The lyrics in this collection, written hard on the heels of "At the Grave of Hart Crane," can provide for us an imaginative and theoretical context in which to revisit, and rethink, the importance of Shepherd's affinity to Crane. After investigating *Otherhood*, we will be prepared to return to that elegy and discover that, while he does feel sympathy with Crane as a precursor poet of queer desire, he has a bolder end in view than homage. He aspires to use a retooled variant of Crane's poetry of homoerotic-masochistic transport to jolt readers into a recognition of language's primary role in subject formation.

In Pairs

Otherhood contains forty-two free-verse lyrics divided into four sections. Throughout, these lyrics display the cluster of attributes that Stephen Burt has enumerated as characteristic of the present "elliptical" phase in American versecraft: a decentered speaker; oblique, mannered, or otherwise thickened language; abrupt or no transitions; and attenuated, wrenched, or broken syntax.[14] What distinguishes *Otherhood* from other volumes in a stylistically comparable vein—for example, Peter Gizzi's *Some Values of Landscape and Weather* (2003), Harryette Mullen's *Sleeping with the Dictionary* (2002), and Cole Swensen's *Goest* (2004)— is its anachronistic, homoerotic paganism. The poems are populated by "gods" and "boys" who love, hate, and make love in archetypal, unstable landscapes: parched desert, wintry waste, dead-leaf autumn, and heaving sea. This mythic realm crazes the poetry like cracks in opal. A reader jumps, bewildered, back and forth between rundown Chicago industrial lakefront and the arcadia of Hyacinth and Apollo. In the process brutal fact and idealized fantasy so interpenetrate that they create bitter-beautiful verse:

> Eros
> goes shaking the bushes
> for sex . . . .
>   men fall from
> ripe branches: apples, quinces,
> pomegranates, pears. In
> pairs, legs intertwined (50)

Shepherd here introduces moralizing Christian theology ("men fall," "apples"); venerable slurs (men who have sex with men are "fruits"); and the state polic-

ing of venues for public sex ("shaking the bushes" to flush out the perverts).
(For a taste of the outrage and helplessness that this last image connotes for an
American gay male audience, consult John Rechy's *The Sexual Outlaw* [1977].)
Shepherd takes these homophobic materials and cross-grains them with homoerotic lyricism. The god Eros, not a policeman, rousts the "fruits." The men so
exposed are neither cuffed nor jailed but instead prance a lyrical pageant, metrical and alliterative:

/ ^   / ^   / ^ / ^   /
apples, quinces, pomegranates, pears

These men, too, are not vulnerable individuals abandoned to their fates. They
are couples coupling openly (pears / In pairs). Overall, this passage is torn between anger and camp, critique and Busby Berkley. Shepherd's is not a post-
Stonewall poetry of joyous liberation. Rather, here as throughout *Otherhood*,
sexuality, poetics, and history—official and subcultural—collide, producing a
mash-up in which utopia and dystopia, actuality and imagination, are as "intertwined" as the "legs" of this passage's copulating men.

Among the "gods" in the collection are two recurrent characters. One, more
or less an authorial alter ego, is a fire god, associated with deserts, the sun, and
the color black ("Apollo is black, wolf to / the moon, *Sol* burnt" [*Otherhood* 49,
his emphasis]). The other is a sea god, associated with winter, ice, the moon,
and the color white ("He's . . . untethered oceans . . . next time he is the snow"
[30–31]). Their romance is Orphic in its extremity ("No teeth draw blood like
his kiss" [16]), so much so, in fact, that in the gruesome lyric "Hygiene," Shepherd invokes Jeffrey Dahmer, the 1990s serial killer who murdered and ate his
tricks, many of them "hot black numbers" picked up at "the unfashionable /
Club 219": "Every white man on my bus home looks / like him, what I'd want
to be destroyed / by, want to be" (52). The fractured tale of the two gods reads
like oblique confessionalism. *Otherhood*'s face-off between Black Apollo and the
God of Snow appears to transpose Shepherd's fantasies, fears, and frustrations—
especially his alienation from the "so-called gay community"—into a mythic key
("Coloring" 137). Just as in the "Eros . . . shaking the bushes" passage, he seeks
to take images and signifiers with a hurtful history and, if not redeem them,
counter them with an aestheticizing imagination.

Otherhood does not, however, remain balked at the level of complaint. Even
as it establishes a powerfully, if violently, homoerotic binary between racially
marked figures, it also deconstructs that vision. "Coloring Outside the Lines"
provides an introduction to the requisite principles. Shepherd echoes Jean Baudrillard in defining race as the interplay of power, desire, and absence:

Both blackness and whiteness are simulacra of what has never existed, but both for blacks and whites, to achieve the simulacrum of whiteness (a simulacrum of a simulacrum) is the mark of personhood, always erased before *I* get to make *my* mark. It is at least possible for "whites" to *believe* they have attained to whiteness, while for "blacks" the impossibility of such an attainment gnaws at one night and day. (139; emphasis in original)

This approach to race licenses a remarkably self-aware statement on his lust for "privileged, pretty white boys":

I hate *and* love those boys, hate them precisely because they have never reciprocated my love, have perhaps never even recognized it as such; I've hidden it so well. I tell myself I hate them *because* of their whiteness (a mantle so unthinkingly assumed), their arbitrary power over my world. But . . . I can't avoid wondering whether these things are actually the same, other than in my racialized imagination, my blocked identifications with an impossible . . . object of desire. Is whiteness really beauty? Is beauty really power? . . . Lucas and Jeremy, Jonathan and Todd and their lovely brothers . . . are the *not-me* to whom I have delegated the power to justify or negate me, a power for which they never asked. . . . It's hardly fair to ask them to bear the burden of my image repertoire. I've known those men for years, slept with many of them. . . . They're neither muses, myths, nor nightmares, just young Caucasian males with good cheekbones and large clothing budgets. My projections are only ghost bodies . . . somewhat like mine, the after-effects of desire and deprivation. (138–39; his emphasis)

Race and sexuality are, from this point of view, a ghostly theater of "desire and deprivation," in which bodies, thoughts, values, and acts are never only themselves but are always implicated in chains of substitution, stand-ins for "an impossible . . . object of desire." Given this Lacanian argument, any assertion of identity is misguided. To claim to "be" such-and-such a person obfuscates the regress involved, the way in which "black," "white," "gay," or any other identity category is in fact a signifier that points to other signifiers that in turn point to others in a dissemination of desire and significance that has no end.

Otherhood repeatedly models this process, most obviously through its treatment of color. "Reasons for Living," for example, portrays, slantwise, two people nude sunbathing on a lakefront. The speaker mentions their "awkward skin / on green towels," a phrase which brings color (green) and human skin into proximity without permitting a reader to draw conclusions about the race (or sex) of the sunbathers (4). Throughout the lyric, the introduction of "color" causes the poem's central subject matter—the two sunbathers and their actions—to blur or drop from sight, the language instead moving rapidly outwards and other-where:

> Mold-colored water dulled
> by use (pastel, muddled
> nephrite, more common
> than true jade, less highly prized,
> its luster oily rather than vitreous,
> a scum spilled across perspective) (3)

Shepherd here begins by setting the scene ("Mold-colored water"), only then to seek out a more accurate, abstract, or poetic way of capturing the exact shade of the water: "pastel, muddled / nephrite." This first substitution licenses further slippage. Having mentioned a gemstone, Shepherd launches into the language of mineralogy for several lines. This digression is, admittedly, quickly contained; the speaker returns to the landscape, renaming the "Mold-colored water" as "a scum spilled across perspective," and the closing parenthesis suggests the side-excursion is over. A reader might expect the lyric's underlying narrative to re-assert itself now. Last we heard from the sunbathers, they were "tak[ing] off" their "pants"; isn't it time for a skin shot, so to speak? The speaker readies him-self, and—we have more gemstones:

> with a turquoise line to build horizon
> out of: prehnite, andradite,
> alkali tourmaline, a seam of
> semiprecious chrysoprase: anything
> but true emerald, a grass-green beryl,
> *smaragdos,* prized for medicinal
> virtues: uvarovite even rarer
> among garnets, its crystals typically
> too small to cut. (3; his emphasis)

Parentheses, which imply interjection or subordination, give way here to colons, which signal a running ahead to a new topic. Shepherd moves a reader swiftly along a chain of associations, demonstrating that the desire to attribute value, utility, or pleasure to "color" can let loose a welter of prized objects, each dis-placing another, and each located farther and farther afield from one's original intent. This centrifugality is, as another poem in the collection puts it, a "re-invention of the fruit of race" via "fine verdant particulars // dispensed" to the reader's "retina" (70).

This strategy of semantic slippage occurs, too, in poems devoted specifically to the gods of fire and ice. The second of the "Three Songs about Snow," for example, illustrates the way that "black" and "white" behave metonymically, that is, refuse to remain fixed to racialized bodies and instead migrate outward onto other objects:

I hide myself, but am
no one, come into view
the same white

overpass, cars tossed
underhand across the lane
divider, line dividing gray

-brown field and gray
-white afternoon:
I am a dark (38)

This "I" that is "no one"—a Lacanian speaker conscious of his lack of an essential self, an Invisible Man for the twenty-first century—sees race and its politics dispersed onto—and thus legible in—the very landscape of the contemporary United States. A highway "overpass" that is "white" stands for the elevated status and the ease of movement accorded to European Americans in American society. These privileges are paradoxically in plain view ("overpass") and yet covert and illicit ("underhand"-ed). The "white / overpass" is also, without contradiction, an instantiation of Du Bois's color line. It is a "line dividing gray // -*brown* field and gray / -*white* afternoon." Brown is associated with earth and agriculture. White, in contrast, describes the sky ("white afternoon"), the dwelling-place of celestial wisdom, higher virtues, and inscrutable law. The color line forcibly divides the lowly, funky, and bodily "brown" from its imputed antithesis and superior, the transcendent, godly, and spiritual "white."

Crucially, the poem's racial allegory is something superadded to the scene it portrays. Instead of Imagist-fashion purporting to offer us the *Ding-an-Sich*, the speaker, in describing a scene, racially marks it for us. He emphasizes key words by placing them at the beginning or end of lines: "white," "brown," "dark." Repetition draws attention to the imputed color line: "divider, line dividing." This process of marking is, in turn, a self-aware one. The off-rhyme "lane" / "line" prompts one to ponder the poem itself as lineated, a thing of lines, that offer us a "line," a particular point of view, and gives a particular itinerary of connections and thoughts to follow (a "lane"). The speaker implicitly acknowledges that his language projects racialized tropes onto base matter. This self-reflexive dimension to the poem culminates in its abrupt non-ending. The speaker gives us no noun, no substantive, to complete the phrase "I am a dark." We are left hanging. Furthermore, "I am a dark" comes after a colon, which, as we saw above, serves Shepherd as a signal of rapid movement along chains of desire. This lyric dramatizes for us the way in which a subject does not possess an identity but instead identifies, vainly, with a series of inadequate, unstable simulacra ("dark" things that, if possessed once and for all, would give an essential content to "being black"). The sentence ends partway through in order to suggest that *any* word that the speaker might supply after "I am a dark" would do equally well (or equally badly) as a substitute for the never-attainable true object of desire. "I am a dark _____": fill in the blank however you will, but it will remain a blank.

Is this moral fatalistic? Shepherd would probably characterize it as usefully disillusioning. A single further syllable, after all, could end part two of "Three Songs about Snow" with a self-contained assertion of identity: "I am a darkie." Though there might be political or literary circumstances in which such a racist epithet could be reclaimed, it nonetheless indicates a willingness to be scripted, however provisionally, into a hellishly demeaning role. Shepherd contrasts the vertigo of the never-autonomous self to the horror of race as it has been constructed by the history and language of the United States. Granted, he concedes, the social circulation of racialized and racist fantasies has occurred and will continue to occur in and through the speaking subject, regardless of conscious individual intent. "White" and "black" will continue their discursive creep. Such circulation is an inevitable feature of what Lacan calls the "symbolic" modality of the ego, its impersonal, transpersonal traversal by chains of desire.[15] But one can try to do something in response. One can become self-reflexively aware of this process and use this knowledge to interrupt or impede the movement along these chains in the course of specific speech acts. One can stop after "I am a dark"; there is no need to complete that thought, to allow identification to vanish into the falsity of identity.

Of course, nothing about race is quite that simple to derail. When *Otherhood* is at its best—in such mysterious compelling lyrics as "Frame" and "A Little Bitter Commentary"—it communicates the Gordian knottiness of the chains of signification (the symbolic) that the ego must parse before being able to take any meaningful action or make any meaningful gesture. Moreover, merely thinking about the psyche in these terms endangers the cherished integrity and autonomy of the ego. "I" am no longer a monad; "I" designates a crossing-point of fantasies and energies that do not belong to "me" in any proprietary sense. "*I* seems / a ceremony of sums," as Shepherd puts it (*Otherhood* 6; emphasis in original). The Orphism of the fire god/ice god relationship illustrates the dangers of Lacanian self-analysis. The two men risk any sureness of selfhood as the passionate erotic intensity of their mutual scrutiny exposes racial difference as a (no)thing: impossible, on one hand, to fix and define and impossible, on the other hand, to elude and escape. Their bodies, as they have known and experienced them, prove mediated by a language (the symbolic) whose origins, ends, and purpose exceed individual reason. Psychic borders prove permeable, burst, or are absent; who am I, where am I, am I you? Amidst this vertigo, how can one verify when a particular intervention ("I am a dark") has consequences for the socio-linguistic conventions that it seeks to counter? Won't such aberrant language use be interpreted as a symptom of illness, potentially of psychosis? Shepherd is willing to take that risk. He sees no alternative.

Divider Line

"At the Grave of Hart Crane" represents a preliminary version of *Otherhood*'s recurrent, potentially disastrous, potentially salvific encounters between a "black" lover and "white" beloved. It opens, as we have seen, with the speaker associated with sunlight ("Mobile light paints me"), hence a forerunner of *Otherhood*'s fire gods. He walks alongside Lake Michigan and observes how "lakewater pours up into, overflowing" rocks on the shoreline. In this liminal space, the attributes of *Otherhood*'s ice god begin to accumulate: "White-shining autumn, early, wave crest, / silver-tipped." The elegy, however, suddenly takes a turn toward the self-reflexive, which heads off the erotic fantasies that ensue in later, comparable lyrics, such as "Wing Under Construction" and "Photogram: Submerged Rocks." Instead of illustrating the course and consequences of desire, he explores its textuality, how language instigates it only to block the possibility of its fulfillment:

> I'm tired of the ocean
> metaphors, old sea in me and thee:
>
> a skeleton of sea, shape left behind
> by what is left, just this idea of water. Someone
> floating, someone sinking just out of sight,
> drowning in earnest one more time. I believed
>
> in his unsheltered sea, made my way
> to cold fresh water, then lost heart. (*Wrong* 88–89)

First Shepherd acknowledges that he is writing in figurative language ("ocean / metaphors"), and he concedes that tropes are the merest tracery of actuality ("a skeleton . . . shape left behind"). He proceeds to replay Crane's famous suicide, a seemingly futile reenactment of a self-destructive act. In the trope-theater of the poem "Someone / . . . drown[s] in earnest one more time." This repetition, however, is also a variation. Crane, who jumped off a cruise ship *en route* from Veracruz to New York in 1932, has no gravesite, at least in the usual sense. Shepherd now provides him with one, the elegy itself.

Yes, this new grave is utterly, self-confessedly fictional, propped by popped "ocean / metaphors," and hence a sham replacement. And yet, wouldn't any gravesite be a sham? A glance at Shepherd's intertext "At Melville's Tomb" shows that Crane, for one, seems to have thought so. He ignores the incontrovertible fact that Melville lies beside his wife in a Brooklyn cemetery. Instead, he blithely writes as if the author of *Moby Dick* were buried at sea ("High in the azure steeps / Monody shall not wake the mariner. / This fabulous shadow only the sea keeps" *Complete* 33). Crane suggests that a tombstone and a corpse are inadequate tropes dispensed with in the search for higher truth. Or, to put it differently, they are simply signifiers, pointing to the writerly absence that is "Melville" (his "fabulous shadow"). The true object of desire—the beloved in his ineffability—will never be found. It is always already beyond grasp, lost to the sea. The lyric as a call to a departed beloved is fated to nonresponse, the frustration of "silent answers" no matter how many "altars" one might build (33). In visiting the tombs of poets—indeed, in striving to make any contact with deceased writers, whether by reading their collected works or imaginatively resurrecting them—one embarks perilously on the open ocean, the "rimless floods, of unfettered leewardings" of desire and its ceaseless, centrifugal pulsions (35). One chances becoming lost among traces, echoes, and false substitutions ("A scattered chapter, livid hieroglyph / The portend wound in corridors of shells" [33]).

Shepherd nonetheless pursues Crane out into these "azure steeps," where "The dice of drowned men's bones . . . bequeath / An embassy" (33). As he puts it: "I believed / in his unsheltered sea, made my way / to cold fresh water" (*Wrong* 89). He hazards Crane's "sea plains where the sky / Resigns a breast that every wave enthrones" and where, "Past whirling pillars and lithe pediments," the psyche begins to undergo a "death" that is "no carnage" but instead a "silken skilled transmemberment of song," a dismembering that is also a transfiguration (*Complete* 36).[16] Shepherd will repeat his Cranean foray into sublimity in *Otherhood* albeit in a different register, as his study of the labyrinthine circulations of social (symbolic) fantasy threaten his integral ego. In both cases, as literary critic Susan Stewart would describe it, Shepherd suspends his "propositional will" and opens himself up to "lyric possession" by vectors, texts, symbols, and language that originate elsewhere.[17] Crane's precedent is invaluable to Shepherd because Crane's poetry moves outward from the discrete, bounded self (Lacan's "imaginary" modality of the ego) into the realm of the symbolic and its transpersonal, impersonal tides of language and desire.[18]

The two poets differ, however, in how to interpret that movement. For Crane, it is a masochistic being-overcome that represents a devoutly sought breaking-through of the divine, a transmemberment that grants access to God's "Ever-presence, beyond time" (*Complete* 107). Shepherd, though, does not share Crane's rhapsodic mysticism. While not entirely opposed to glimmers and surges of the transcendental—"Occasionally a god speaks to you," as he puts it in "Syntax" (*Otherhood* 34)—his gods, as we have seen, are always countermanded and contained by brutal reassertions of the fallen world of linear time, the reality principle, and history's burdens. Crane, in contrast, wished to push past the compromised, compromising world of everyday reality and sail, once and for all, into the "azure" in search of ecstatic self-immolation in the "radiance" outside "time's realm" (*Complete* 107–8). Shepherd, testing the waters there, finds neither home nor harbor; indeed, he finds he has "lost heart" (*Wrong* 89). That is, he finds that he begins to lose the specificity of his body, will, and passion. He threatens to give up not simply a stable identity but personhood altogether, becoming intermingled with and indistinguishable from the "scattered chapter" of "death's bounty" (*Complete* 33). If he were to follow Crane fully and forever into the "unsheltered sea," the result would be another suicide, a "drowning in earnest one more time" (*Wrong* 89). The elegy's final Hart/heart pun signals Shepherd's move back onto land and out of danger. To prevent himself from "losing heart," Shepherd is willing to "lose Hart," that is, let the other poet swim onward alone into self-cancellation. Paradoxically, though, by re-anchoring himself firmly at the edge of land and lake in "At the Grave of Hart Crane," Shepherd is able, after a fashion, to find Hart again. He keeps writing, and in so doing, provides Crane with the gravesite, inscribed name, and memorial that he would otherwise lack.

"At the Grave of Hart Crane" is ultimately much less concerned with canonicity *per se*—a contemporary queer of color declaring himself son of a white gay ancestor—than it is with alterity, memory, versecraft, and the limits of selfhood. What are the grounds of my identification with this other poet, and where must identification cease? Crane is a seductive figure, a Snow God, who threatens to lure Shepherd into transgressing writerly and psychic taboos essential for continued living. Shepherd might imitate and revel in Crane's homoerotic-masochistic poetics in certain respects, but only to the point when the self ceases to serve as a locus for action. As he sees it, without individual agency, there remains no possibility, however remote, of distinguishing and then interrupting or blocking the chains of signification that constitute the symbolic. Crane—the only son of a factory-owning Ohio businessman—has the privilege of associating egolessness with blissful release. For him, selfhood was apparently "a mantle so unthinkingly assumed" that chucking it equals being relieved of a burden

("Coloring" 138). A contemporary black gay poet like Shepherd, however, for whom "the lack of any position called *mine*, much less *me*" is not a utopian dream but a pressing inescapable problem, cannot quite so readily or enthusiastically embrace oblivion (134; emphasis in original).

Shepherd's deep albeit qualified engagement with Crane's verse has obviously left a profound impression. Anyone who turns from *White Buildings* to *Otherhood* will find a surprising degree of overlap. Both books feature impossible symbolist landscapes, intense sound play, arcane anachronistic vocabulary, and tortured or incomplete syntax. The ocean recurs insistently, from poem to poem, as do moments of sadomasochistic erotic transport ("I, turning, turning on smoked forking spires . . . . Tossed on these horns, who bleeding dies" (Crane, *Complete* 18). While *Otherhood* is also clearly in dialogue with other writers— "In the City of Elagabal" and "Periplus," for instance, recall Kathleen Fraser's *When New Time Folds Up* (1993), and "Apollo Steps in Daphne's Footprints" provides a welcome, queer-inflected response to Jorie Graham's "Self-Portrait as Apollo and Daphne," one of the most influential lyrics of the 1980s—the aftermath of Shepherd's encounter with Crane in "At the Grave of Hart Crane" ramifies throughout the volume. That encounter seems to have prepared Shepherd to grapple in an extended fashion with "otherhood" in the multiracial but white-dominated gay subculture whose dynamics of identity, identification, difference, and desire he seeks to comprehend. Shepherd discovered in Crane a dangerous but compelling interlocutor whose total eroticized submission to lyric possession both tempts and repels him. The tension between those responses has been productive; it has prompted him to embark on a sophisticated and demystifying poetic inquiry into race, sexuality, and community (de)formation.

Tethered

In the late 1980s and early 1990s, anthologies such as *In the Life* (1986, ed. Joseph Beam) and *Brother to Brother* (1991, ed. Essex Hemphill) and such films as Isaac Julien's *Looking for Langston* (1989) and Marlon Riggs's *Tongues Untied* (1989) confidently announced an emergent, politically conscious community— gay, male, African diasporic—and joyously endorsed its literary traditions old and new. Hemphill's preface to *Brother to Brother* is typical in its denunciation of 1980s mainstream gay culture and in its call for a particularist response:

> We must begin to identify what a black gay sensibility is; identify its esthetic qualities and components; identify specific constructions and uses of language suitable for the task of presenting our experience in the con-

text of literature; and then determine how this sensibility and esthetic relates to and differs from African American literature as a whole. Ours should be a vision willing to exceed all that attempts to confine and intimidate us. We must be willing to embrace and explore the duality of community that we exist in as black *and* gay men. We would be wise to develop strong, powerful voices that can range over the entire landscape of human experience. (xxvii)

The generally optimistic, affirmative tone of these works that date from circa 1990 stems from a sense of participating immediately and substantially in the creation of "black *and* gay" as a socially recognized identity category with its own unique "qualities and components." Both in the academy and at large, this message has generated tremendous excitement.[19]

Re-viewed through the lens of *Otherhood*, however, it can appear woefully idealistic. From Shepherd's point of view, a polemic such as Hemphill's overestimates the ability of individual (imaginary) actions to transform collective (symbolic) fantasies. It presents identification with essences ("sensibility," "qualities") as a solution to oppression, not as the root problem. Finally, it artificially separates off "black" and "gay" from the other half of the relevant, migrating binaries that govern and guide desire's circulations. The fire god and ice god are mutually (de)constructing: "a sinking / water table leaves behind / its salt: the man I made of him" (*Otherhood* 36). How far and fast the rhetoric has shifted in a decade! "At the Grave of Hart Crane" could in fact be interpreted as an elegy not only for a modernist precursor but also for the viability of the very process of transhistorical, interpersonal identification that enables one to talk about discrete, unitary "sensibilities"—gay, black, or "gay *and* black"—in the first place. That loss is all the more painful insofar as Shepherd would surely agree that, despite a pervasive rhetoric of inclusiveness, the "so-called gay community" has advanced depressingly little since the late 1980s, when Marlon Riggs wrote of San Francisco's Castro neighborhood, "In this great gay mecca, I was an invisible man, still. . . . I was an alien, unseen, and seen, unwanted. . . . I was a nigga, still" (203).[20] To combat this ongoing injustice, instead of a nationalist or libratory politics *Otherhood* promotes *faute de mieux* a strategy of selective elucidation, interruption, evasion, and rejection of racial and sexual interpellation.

One does not have to see eye to eye with Shepherd on every point. He concentrates so intently on linguistic and psychological questions, for example, that he fails to investigate any role that institutions might play in actively and prospectively shaping desire's flows and hence potentially creating, regulating, and grounding new identity positions. His particular slant on poststructuralists such as Baudrillard and Lacan also leads him to adopt a baroque fractured style, an introspective melancholy tone, and a radical racial antiessentialism that are far from universally shared among today's black queer writers, as a glance at *Callaloo*'s "In the Family" special issue (Winter 2000) will demonstrate. Finally, his decision to foreground interracial homoerotics has left him particularly vulnerable to hostile criticism.[21] There would likely be strenuous resistance to any attempt to hold him up as somehow representative or illustrative of a "generational shift" since the days of *Tongues Untied*.

Such reservations do not detract, however, from the theoretical and aesthetic importance of Shepherd's poetry. A visionary volume such as *Otherhood* differs in so many respects from the writings of such other prominent African American queer male poets as Hemphill, Melvin Dixon, Carl Phillips, and Assoto Saint that, in its wake, all existing, unreflective generalizations about "black gay poetics" in the secondary literature will have to be revisited and reevaluated. Also, insofar as Shepherd looks to Crane, he is engaged in a literary activity, a poetic interchange across racial lines, that scholars such as Rachel Blau DuPlessis, Aldon Lynn Nielsen, and Michael North have argued ranks among the most important subjects for contemporary study of American literature.[22] More specifically, Shepherd's intertextual relationship with Crane highlights the value of bringing together two academic conversations: (1) the ongoing inquiry within critical race studies into the contingency, multiplicity, and mutability of subject formation and (2) queer theoretical commentary on literary form, as pursued from Roland Barthes's *Fragments d'un discours amoureux* (1975) to Carla Freccero's *Queer/Early/Modern* (2006). Poetry, Shepherd reveals, can serve as a privileged space for elucidating the circulations of desire—its "shoots / down into bloom, relays and intermittencies"—that (re)produce race and sex (*Otherhood* 59).

Finally, "At the Grave of Hart Crane" and *Otherhood* support Christopher Beach's 1999 prediction that one of the "most encouraging signs that there is a future for poetry in North America" is the trend toward the "combination of the linguistic and formal energies of the avant-garde or experimental tradition with the transcultural and interpersonal energies of an expanded racial and ethnic context" (185). Picking up Shepherd's work, one discovers a potent, importunate fusion of thought, passion, and lyricism that is highly unusual in the present era of "retrenchment," which, according to Beach, "lack[s] a strong critical and poetic direction" (183):

> Remembered limbs as a because,
> swan box of tethered monodies,
> rope and pulley, winch of extinct

gods: saw me deserting my grief's
oligarchy of referential skin,
abraded by the glacier for the greater

good. (*Otherhood* 40)

Struggling against the "oligarchy of referential skin," hierarchies based on skin color, and the violence directed toward a black man in a white-dominated society ("abraded by the glacier"), Shepherd questions—here via an ironizing throat-clearing pause between stanzas—where "the greater // good" truly resides. Spurred by embodied desire ("Remembered limbs as a because"), he uses his writerly craft ("rope and pulley") and his lyrical gifts ("swan box of tethered monodies") to stand witness ("saw me") to his dissent. Shepherd's is a poetry of mission, not retrenchment, and its critical and poetic direction are not merely "strong" but inspired, leading readers into unforeseen vistas of dream, thought, and word.

IV

ASSOCIATIVE READING

10
Rosmarie Waldrop
Renews Collage

In *Leaving Lines of Gender* (2000), Ann Vickery announces an ambitious project, a cartography of women's experimental poetry that attends first and foremost to its "practice," that is, the specific modes, means, and occasions of its production. For Vickery, elucidating poetic practice does not imply a retreat into ahistorical formalism. On the contrary, it "involves reframing many aspects of . . . poetic practice in order to link text with context." Vickery continues:

> Aspects that must be addressed include the multiple text (its written or performed versions), the text-in-process (drafting, editing, and reprinting), the relationship between readers and the text, the use of particular poetic forms, the structure of small-press culture and its marketplace, and the social politics of poetry (as manifested in how poetic communities relate to one another and the individuals). These may be further contextualized in larger social and cultural structures, including the media and pedagogic institutions. (15)

For Vickery, exploring "the shifting 'mess' that encapsulates actual poetic practice" serves a dual function. On the one hand, it "maps out interweaving, multiple lines of affiliation" in all their complexity, thereby forestalling falsely reductive or atomistic treatment of experimental writing by women. On the other hand, it charts "the debates arising out of difference, whether these be regional, aesthetic, cultural, or ideological." Highlighting "difference" in this manner exposes the partiality or strategic blind spots in totalizing accounts of contemporary innovative verse (13).

Inspired by Vickery's turn to "practice" as a means of clarifying recent literary history, this essay extends her cartographic enterprise into new territory. It closely examines the writerly practice of Rosmarie Waldrop, who has not only enjoyed three decades' prominence as an American experimental poet but who has also actively promoted avant-garde literature as a publisher (Burning Deck Press), as a teacher (Brown University), and as a translator (of Elke Erb, Helmut Heissenbütttel, Edmond Jabès, and many other post–World War II Continental writers).[1] Moreover, a German immigrant to the United States, Waldrop has proved throughout her career to be exceptionally sensitive to the displacements, imbalances, and transpositions instigated by movement between nations, cultures, and languages. Her poetry is resolutely hybrid—"between," as she would say—as well as thoroughly secular and skeptical, preferring wit to ecstasy, insight to murkiness, and precision to evocative vagueness. An inquiry into Waldrop's compositional practice exposes the degree to which American innovative writing remains implicated in the trans-Atlantic crossings, collisions, and dispossessions that mark and mar so much of the country's past. Waldrop seeks through her writing a means of dwelling creatively, sustainingly in this chaotic, contested terrain.

This essay follows Vickery in its preference for thick descriptions of the specifics of poetic practice—in this case, of "text-in-process," "the relationship between readers and the text," and "the use of particular poetic forms" as well as the "larger social and cultural structures" that constitute their horizon. Collage, one of Waldrop's favorite writerly devices, is well known for its ability to destabilize textual boundaries, unsettle authorship, transgress generic distinctions, and otherwise dramatize writing's refusal to buttress any system of knowledge univocally and unequivocally. By exploring how, when, and why Waldrop adopted a collage-based aesthetic, one begins to perceive the "affiliations" and "differences" that demarcate the consequent purpose, value, and function of the technique in her verse. Moreover, as Vickery predicts, this close scrutiny of poetic practice exposes both "unpredictable relationships" and "hidden or elided" distinctions within the field of present-day experimental writing. Although a complete picture of how Waldrop's use of collage situates her in relation to her contemporaries—and how this network of relations has in turn manifested itself in what Vickery calls the "social politics of poetry"—will have to await further study and elaboration, this essay makes it possible to discern key pieces of that future account (15). Unlike, say, Susan Howe, whose use of collage signals her qualified participation in the Pound-Olson tradition, Waldrop looks to alternative, Central European sources to give her the confidence to move through and beyond the ideogrammic method of *The Cantos*. She employs collage less for its ability to introduce the raw stuff of history into a poem than as a means of encouraging her readers to compare, contrast, and otherwise interrogate the strategies and assumptions at play in different discourses. Collage enables her to transform "betweenness" from marginality to a mode of intervention and critique.

Take It to Them

In 2001, Northwestern University Press reissued Rosmarie Waldrop's experimental fictions *The Hanky of Pippin's Daughter* and *A Form / of Taking / It All*. In an introduction titled "Between, Always," Waldrop reports that these two novels represent more than an interlude in a writing career devoted primarily to poetry. In fact, she explains, they played indispensable roles in the development of her principle art form. *The Hanky of Pippin's Daughter* marks the end of a phase in her career as a poet insofar as it enabled her to escape a compositional rut. More specifically, it provided her with a capacious form that made it possible for her to explore viable alternatives to the fast-moving, short-line, syntactically ambiguous mode that had come to predominate in her verse in the later 1970s and early 1980s (viii).[2] In contrast, Waldrop attributes to *A Form / of Taking / It All* the status of a new beginning. In this mixed-genre piece she chose to make "Collage, juxtaposition . . . the heart of the book" to a degree unparalleled in her earlier work. Although she had "used collage before," while writing *A Form* in the years 1983–1985 she hit upon an "art of separation and fusion, of displacement and connection" that has served as the "main procedure" of her subsequent poetry, down to the present day (xvi–xvii).[3]

Waldrop's claim that the novel *A Form / of Taking / It All* records an artistic turning point is rather surprising. A jagged, four-part, prose-and-verse retelling of an impossible "mystical marriage" between Amy Lowell and Alexander von Humboldt, *A Form / of Taking / It All* is an exceptional, even peculiar work within Waldrop's *oeuvre* that has received scant attention from reviewers, critics, and other poets.[4] Its melodramatic treatment of Lowell's and von Humboldt's "more or less suppressed homosexuality" yokes together sections written in such disparate styles as stream of consciousness, commonplace book, metafictional commentary, and free verse (xv). This rather unnerving formal heterogeneity is matched by the incongruity of the book's contents. The concluding bibliography of sources lists textbooks on astronomy, chemistry, and ballet; biographies of Beethoven and Napoleon; American avant-garde poetry; Austrian avant-garde novels; histories of the Spanish conquest of Mexico; the *WPA Guide to Washington, D.C.*; and a technical manual for undertakers (*A Form* 248). Reading *A Form / of Taking / It All* at the time of its completion, one would have been hard pressed to guess that Waldrop would soon turn to writing the elegant, witty, erudite prose poetry that characterizes *Reproduction of Profiles* (1987), *Shorter American Memory* (1988), *Lawn of the Excluded Middle* (1993), and *Reluctant Gravities* (1999).

As Kornelia Freitag has pointed out, however, by the time that Waldrop wrote "Unpredicted Particles," the fourth part of *A Form / of Taking / It All,* she was already engaged in the practice that would become a hallmark of these later writings: selectively (mis)quoting Ludwig Wittgenstein's writings.[5] The first page of "Unpredicted Particles" includes the lines:

> "the grammar of the word 'knows'
> is closely related to that of
> 'mastery'" (237)

As Freitag informs us, these lines derive from *Philosophical Investigations* # 150: "'The grammar of the word 'knows' is evidently closely related to that of 'can,' 'is able to'. But also closely related to that of 'understands'. ('Mastery' of a technique)" ("Rosmarie Waldrop's Language Games" 257). By omitting the softening "evidently" and all but one word after "closely related to," Waldrop transforms Wittgenstein's original, rather abstract statement into a Michel Foucault-like observation concerning the imbrication of knowledge and power. The next few lines—"the difference / in a window / in Genoa"—rapid-fire connects the Wittgenstein misquotation to several of the key themes in *A Form / of Taking / It All*: representation ("in a window"), otherness ("difference"), and the confrontation between European colonizers and New World colonized ("Genoa," an oblique reference to Columbus, who will emerge as the protagonist of "Unpredicted Particles") (237). In short, Waldrop offers us a staccato reprise of the basics of postcolonial theory as articulated by Fritz Fanon, Gayatri Spivak, and an array of other thinkers. While not as subtle or sophisticated as the responses to Wittgenstein that would soon appear in Waldrop's *Reproduction of Profiles*, we can nonetheless observe here in germ the same general methods of composition and commentary.

A Form / of Taking / It All thus deserves scrutiny as a transitional work, prefiguring the philosophical and formal preoccupations that mark Waldrop's writings of the subsequent fifteen years. Moreover, it is uniquely appropriate to examine the process of "transition" in Waldrop's writing—especially when that examination necessitates closer scrutiny of an aberrantly mixed-genre work. As she reminds us in "Between, Always," she "feel[s] a strong affinity for this word, 'between'" (which in fact served as the "title of one of [her] first poems in English")(vii).[6] This sense of occupying an indefinite, intermediary zone became particularly acute in the aftermath of writing *The Hanky of Pippin's Daughter*, which was initially received as "too ornate, too metaphorical," in short, too poetic to qualify as a straight-ahead novel.

> I found myself in . . . [a] place between genres. Between poem and novel. Between verse and prose.
>
> Between two stools. A bad spot. Supposedly. Close to the middle excluded by the law. But does a door have to be open or closed? All words are ajar. Could I not settle in the between? Like most truly contemporary writing? And could I not, like Luce Irigaray, make it not only a third term between binaries but also a locus of desire? Of encounter? Dynamic and dynamite?
>
> I went on to another novel—which, if we count the title, begins and ends in verse. (xv)

In other words, *A Form / of Taking / It All*—the novel she alludes to at the end of this passage—might be through-and-through a jumbled, contradictory text. Even its title perplexes, as Waldrop notes. Its combination of italics and virgules mixes codes by suggesting, on the one hand, that "A Form of Taking It All" is the name of a work of literature and, on the other hand, that the phrase is a quotation from a lineated poem.[7] The book's resolute refusal to resolve, its straining at cross-currents, in short, its in-betweenness: these characteristics are the very stuff of Waldrop's poetics.

Dance of Veils

In "Between, Always" Waldrop reveals that the proximate inspiration for her turn to collage in *A Form / of Taking / It All* was an innovative Austrian prose piece, Konrad Bayer's *Der Kopf des Vitus Bering* (1965) (xv–xvi). This choice seems to have been dictated by her desire to find a mode of writing that would permit a healthier balance between critical distance and passionate personal investment than she was able to achieve while writing *The Hanky of Pippin's Daughter*. In that earlier case, too, she looked to Central European precedents: Wittgenstein's *Tractatus Logico-Philosophicus* (1921) and Johannes Bobrowski's *Levin's Mill: 34 Sentences About My Grandfather* (1964). But her topic—"the Nazi Germany into which I was born"—proved to be a "subject so overwhelming, a knot of connections so complex" that these models turned out to be wholly inadequate (ix). She resorted to an improvisational, gap-filled narration that required her to "put [her] trust in language" and concentrate on the "rhythm" of delivery instead of the shape of the work as a whole (xii). While she is satisfied with the results, it nonetheless took her eight frustrating years to bring the novel to completion (ix).

Konrad Bayer's *Der Kopf des Vitus Bering* seems to have offered a tempting, alternative mode of writing: the deployment of collage to create an absorbing narrative without having to agonize over how to put into words one's deepest thoughts and emotions. The work's thirty-odd pages recount the adventures of its eponymous hero, the eighteenth-century explorer responsible for charting the waters off Kamchatka and Alaska. Organized into short sections with italicized, headline-like titles, the story consists almost entirely of passages excerpted from other texts, chiefly memoirs, histories, and imaginative literature. (An appendix conscientiously lists every source.) Many of the passages that have been stitched together are digressive, whimsical, or recalcitrantly unrelated to what comes before or after. As Bayer explains in a preface, his goal in assembling *Der Kopf* was not to produce a faithful reconstruction of actual events and personages. Indeed, Bering the historical figure interests him far less than the opportunities Bering affords for launching into other, juicy subjects: he is "only a location . . . from which to establish relations, like a fisherman casting a net in hopes of catching something" (168).[8]

The resulting crazy quilt is openly indebted to pre–World War II European avant-garde practice. Bayer prominently cites the Surrealist André Breton as an authority in his preface, and the texture of the book's disjointed construction distinctly recalls *cadavre exquis* (168). Indeed, if one takes Waldrop at her word and reads Bayer in an attempt to understand why it prompted a change in her fundamental method of composition, one can begin to suspect whether this particular collage text ultimately differs enough from its antecedents for its form alone to explain its potent appeal. Other, earlier texts could also have served Waldrop as synecdoches for the ongoing Dada and Surrealist tradition of juxtaposing found materials—for instance, Max Ernst's *La femme 100 têtes* and *Une semaine de bonté*. Well known for her expertise regarding avant-garde French and German literature, she presumably had an array of comparable examples from which to choose.

Der Kopf, I believe, helped catalyze an artistic breakthrough because of its compelling fusion of content—repeated voyages of discovery into the unknown—and form—serial juxtaposition of prose by different writers. Bayer's narrative, like Waldrop's earlier *The Hanky of Pippin's Daughter*, is a variant on the old tradition of the quest narrative, and again like *The Hanky*, the itinerary that the work traces requires that it enter unexplored country. There is one crucial difference, however. Bayer's text does not mire itself in compulsive authorial self-reflexivity. Agency is distributed among a cohort of writers. Any truths to be found, fostered, or created are a joint, even a communal, responsibility.

Decentering "authorship" in this manner is not, of course, the same thing as excluding the personal altogether. Waldrop knew that collage by itself could not prevent autobiographical content from finding its way into *A Form / of Taking / It All*. The novel's prospective theme—the "enormous migration from Europe to America, wave after wave of explorers, conquerors, immigrants"—was too intimately related to her own experience of moving from Germany to the United States; this "change of world . . . surfaces again and again" in her writing ("Between" xv). In addition, she had already learned that, although collage involves recycling others' words and hence nominally absolves the writer of "authoring" them, self-expression nonetheless stubbornly reinserts itself in the very acts of selecting and arranging one's found materials:

> I had used collage before. . . . I had turned to collage as a way of getting away from writing about my mother. I would take one or two words from every page of a novel, say. The poems were still about my mother. This taught me that one does not need to worry about contents: our preoccupations will get into our writing no matter what. (xvi)[9]

For Waldrop, then, *Der Kopf des Vitus Bering* would not have held out the promise of a straightforward, ecstatic release from either subjectivity or the burden of the past. She would not have been drawn to it because it advertised impossible escapes into the unconscious, surreality, or other, higher, egoless states of consciousness. Rather, she seems to have chosen Bayer's narrative because it implicitly extols the power of heteroglossia to reframe an author's contributions as only one aspect of an ongoing, collaborative, intertextual excursion. A casting of the net, a forging of a network of relations.[10] This paradigm for understanding writing as fundamentally intersubjective, processual, and investigative is evident in her comments regarding the indispensability of collage in her writing since *A Form / of Taking / It All*: "No text has one single author. Whether we are conscious of it or not, we always write on top of a palimpsest. To foreground this awareness as technique. A dialogue with a whole net of previous and concurrent texts" (xvii).[11] In short, *Der Kopf des Vitus Bering* provided Waldrop with a set of premises regarding language, craft, and literature that permitted her to sublime both the "betweenness" of her dual nationality and the troublesome generic hybridity of her first novel into a potent, persuasive compositional methodology: "An art of separation and fusion, of displacement and connection. For without our connecting them into a picture the dots are not even visible. An art of betweens" (xvii).

Memories

Although in the finished text it appears as the second section of *A Form / of Taking / It All*, "A Form of Memory" was in fact the first part to be written, and in it the influence of Konrad Bayer's *Der Kopf des Vitus Bering* is at its height (xv–xvi). Most obviously, "A Form of Memory" echoes *Der Kopf* in its layout, short blocks of prose grouped under such fanciful rubrics as "A Physical Description of Sexual Intercourse," "Illustration," "Eyewitness Report," and "Elegy." Again as in *Der Kopf*, its passages all read as if they have been excerpted from disparate other texts. A list of sources in the back of the book confirms this impression, and, like Bayer's appendix, it seems to be both reliable and comprehensive. Bayer's precedent permits Waldrop to make drastic alterations in the affect and the style of her prose. In contrast to *The Hanky of Pippin's Daughter*—recounted by a mischievously biased narrator in a nominally epistolary format—"A Form of Memory" aspires to a thoroughgoing impersonality in its manner of construction and presentation. Nowhere in "A Form of Memory" does Waldrop speak *propria persona*. Assembly-line fashion, we are delivered what can initially appear to be no more than raw boluses of fact, definition, and observation.

Whereas Bayer mitigated the abruptness of this plunge into unadorned collage by providing a preface to explain his methodology and intent, Waldrop opts for another, albeit comparably pedagogical, means of easing a reader into the welter. The opening section of "A Form of Memory," titled "Physical Description of Motion," self-consciously and gradually establishes the pattern for the remainder of the chapter. Its first four prose blocks serve as a concise introduction to the sorts of materials its readers will be encountering as well as suggesting the kinds of reading skills that they will require in response. Additionally, Waldrop evokes only then to dismiss a possible American precedent for her embarkation on a career as a *collagiste*:

Alexander von Humboldt shipped out on the mail boat "Pizarro" with sextants, quadrants, scales, compasses, telescopes, microscopes, hygrometer, barometer, eudimeter, thermometer, chronometer, magnetometer, a Leiden bottle, *lunettes d'épreuves* and a botanist, Aimé Bonpland.

Before him, using the newly improved astrolabe to determine the ship's position, Columbus had thrown his coin not as a mere adventurer, but with a plan.

The mistress drew the switch through her left hand and smiled at each of us in turn.

"Stress" is used for metrical stress whereas "accent" is reserved for the emphasis demanded by language. (185)

The first paragraph's catalog foreshadows the radically paratactic construction of "A Form of Memory" as a whole. It also alerts readers that they are responsible for inferring what connections—if any—exist among its oddly juxtaposed passages of text. The last item in this catalog, the "botanist," is a calculated non sequitur insofar as he is a living being and everything else in the catalog is a non-animate scientific instrument. Waldrop hints broadly that von Humboldt looks upon his traveling companion as just another tool, to be employed dispassionately in the process of scientific inquiry. That she only *hints* at this is telling; a reader must make a leap him- or herself to reach this conclusion.

Faced with these odd, paratactic juxtapositions that invite inferential interpretation, an experienced reader of twentieth-century American literature might reasonably conclude that Waldrop has tacitly declared her allegiance to the tradition of Ezra Pound's *Cantos,* which are built throughout on precisely this basis. The next paragraph, the one beginning "Before him," appears to confirm this intuition. It unexpectedly switches location and dramatis personae, though it retains the same general subject, a maritime journey to the New World. Hugh Kenner, writing about the *Cantos,* has called this kind of associative leap a "subject rhyme," that is, a juxtaposition of disparate historical personages that is also an assertion of family resemblance.[12] We are almost certainly supposed to read von Humboldt as a latter-day avatar of Columbus—just as in the *Cantos* we are expected to read Eleanor of Aquitaine as a medieval beauty who parallels Helen of Troy and see Mussolini as a munificent patron akin to the Renaissance *condottiere* Sigismundo Malatesta.

The third and fourth paragraphs of "A Form of Memory" accelerate the vertiginous transitions to new scenes and topics. First, we are given an italicized passage about a cheerful-yet-threatening "mistress" with a "switch," presumably a teacher of some kind. Then we are supplied with what sounds like a quotation from a textbook on prosodics that distinguishes the technical meanings of "stress" and "accent." These abrupt changes in discursive register again recall Pound's *Cantos,* more specifically its ideogrammic method, in which fragmentary verse and found texts are strung together to create cumulative statements about an implied subject matter. Considered together, the first four paragraphs serve as a Poundian ideogram for "discipline": scientists, like teachers, arrange and order the world and language, a process that overtly or covertly involves force. Waldrop is reiterating a theme that we have already seen, namely that the European encounter with the New World, even in its outwardly benign guise of the search to discover new knowledge, involves the impulse to "discipline" its unruly otherness.

So far there is little to distinguish Waldrop's Bayer-derived compositional method from the paratactic mode of Pound and his progeny. "A Form of Memory" initially seems to position itself as yet another masterful example of post–World War II, *Cantos*-inspired prose in the tradition of Charles Olson's *Call Me Ishmael* (1947) and Susan Howe's *My Emily Dickinson* (1985). Waldrop's first measurable swerve from the Poundian variant of collage occurs in paragraph 9 of "Physical Description of Motion": "Alexander von Humboldt knew that Columbus's inspiration 'from the heart' had been a flock of parrots flying toward the southwest, a word with level stress where the accent falls with equal emphasis on both syllables. Birds, said Alexander von Humboldt. All land his discovered by birds. He lifted his field glasses, but could see nothing but an expanse of water apparently boundless" (185). While remaining within the thematic orbit of the opening paragraphs, this passage does not display the same internal integrity. Yes, "southwest" can be scanned as indicated, but it is extremely difficult to imagine a source text that would interject this piece of information in the midst of reporting von Humboldt's ruminations on his predecessor. Waldrop has intrusively treated one kind of text—presumably the biography of von Humboldt by Douglas Botting that appears in the "List of Sources" at the book's back (248)—as an occasion to illustrate the definitions of "stress" and "accent" earlier introduced. While the *Cantos* do selectively edit, (mis)translate, reconfigure, and otherwise alter their source texts, the deadpan wit here is foreign to the tone of Pound's epic, which aggressively pursues the *directio voluntatis*, the thrust of his will, through eons of historical and archaeological evidence.[13] Nor does Waldrop's impersonal intervention dovetail well with the prophetic posturing common in the prose collages of such Poundian heirs as Olson and Howe. Her cheery digressiveness serves not to overawe a reader with superior, transcendental insight into the timeless order of things but instead seeks to distance him or her, however briefly, from the "discipline" ideogram and to provoke her or him to attend to the limits and assumptions that inform any given act of writing.

By eschewing the authority of the archivalist, Waldrop aligns herself with Bayer, who dismisses any claim that "A mosaic of facts" can "be treated as irrefutable knowledge [*gewissheiten*]." One must adopt a skeptical attitude, he explains, toward "so-called historical fact [*tatsachen*]" in the name of "what cannot be proved [*überprüfen*]," namely, "the sum of possibilities." He selected Vitus Bering's story, recorded in scattered and biased records, for his departure point not because he wishes to resurrect a wronged, neglected hero (such as Pound's Malatesta or Howe's Anne Hutchinson) but "because [Vitus's story] leaves things sufficiently open, because it is unclear, because it is contradictory, because one can falsify (or correct) it without losing the historical backdrop" (*Der Kopf*

168). Falsifying, correcting, contradicting, prizing open, obfuscating—these are boldly interventionist activities, hardly evincing the documentary fidelity to the historical record that is the (ostensible) guiding principle of such Poundian, collage-based works as Olson's *Maximus Poems* (1983), Howe's *The Birth-mark* (1993), William Carlos Williams's *Paterson* (1963), and Charles Reznikoff's *Testimony* (1965). Waldrop, like Bayer, makes the discourses of history subject to open, crass, and ludic manipulation so as to free her readers from their aura of immediate, privileged access to historical truth.

Waldrop, in fact, goes a step further than Bayer in this regard. His rhetoric remains transcendentalist in one crucial respect. While evincing scorn for an archival art, his critical attitude toward "so-called historical fact" nonetheless coexists with longing for mystical revelation, an entrance into a temporality in which "past and future . . . are bound into a single point" (168). As far back as 1971, in her study *Against Language?*, Waldrop registered her distaste for all traces of vatic self-presentation in mid-twentieth-century European avant-garde art, a category to which Bayer unmistakably belongs. In *Against Language?* she argued that the solution is for a writer to redirect a reader's attention from airy flights of speculation to the nuts and bolts of language's functioning (122–23). We find this same tactic at work more than a decade later. Waldrop comments that "I flatter myself that [in "A Form of Memory"] I pushed the juxtaposition of heterogeneous materials farther than [Bayer] had, even into the sentence" ("Between" xvi). That last qualification—"even into the sentence"—is no mere throwaway line. Bayer exposes the contingency of the discursive production of history, but he also leaves open the possibility of banishing history altogether as false artifice in order to inhabit a messianic Now. Waldrop, by pushing her inquiry into history further, by operating at the sentence level and below, focuses more narrowly on the *language* of history. She begins to speculate less about what transcends the historical record than about the rules of selection (semantics) and combination (syntax) by which that record is assembled.

The third grouping in "A Form of Memory," titled "Physical Description of Motion, Continued," contains an early, illustrative instance of the splicing internal to a sentence that would soon come to distinguish her variant of collage. First, there appears a statement that reads as if were lifted from an introductory medical textbook: "The action of a muscle is to contract, or to shorten in length, and thus the two structures to which it is attached are brought closer together." Four prose blocks later occurs a drastically reworked version of this statement: "Metaphor implies a relationship between two terms which are thus brought together in the muscle" (186). Waldrop has hybridized the diction of two disciplines, literary criticism and gross anatomy. She implies that they are comparable, perhaps equally invasive forms of knowledge. Obviously, this connection again relates to her overarching theme that "to know = to master." It also likely accounts for the recurrent interest in ballet in *A Form / of Taking / It All*. For Waldrop, dance, as an emphatically embodied art, serves as an analogue for fiction ,writing insofar as both are means of disciplining flesh (of bodies, of language) and function as alternatives to the more instrumentalized languages of the academy (medicine, poetics).

First producing a Pound-like collage-quotation, and then soon afterward misquoting it, Waldrop provides readers with an object lesson in how collage will operate in her work. She informs them that they will encounter skewed, ill-sutured, and whimsical reinscriptions of other writings. A statement such as "A vast twilight zone, nearly 1500 miles wide, was slipping around the earth as the latter turned on its axis"—which first appears in a section titled "Eye-witness Report" in "A Form of Memory"—is liable to reappear without notice in another permutation, whether it be simply paraphrased ("The vast twilight zone slips around the earth as the latter turns on its axis" [226]) or radically re-worked in a spliced sentence ("A later meaning of elegy was a poem in what-ever meter in which a twilight zone slips around the globe" [190]). These later near-repetitions, in turn, destabilize our confidence in the original statement. Can we trust that Waldrop has indeed lifted it intact from a source in the bibli-ography, such as von Humboldt's *Kosmos* or David Todd's *Professor Todd's New Astronomy*? The Poundian promise of direct treatment of the thing gives way to a discomfiting, Derrida-like display that all citation is always already poten-tially miscitation.

One need not, though, jump to Derrida or poststructuralism to help us under-stand Waldrop's take on collage. Such a rhetorical move would falsely suggest that there is something uniquely "postmodern" about it. Instead, we can return to the technique's ur-scene, the *avant-guerre* years when Georges Braque and Pablo Picasso first elevated *papier collé* from a kitschy popular art into a cutting-edge avant-garde strategy for Making It New.

Poundian collage is akin to the newsprint that Picasso frequently pasted to his Cubist canvases during the movement's founding "analytic" phase. Both Pound's and Picasso's incorporations of borrowed text purport to offer a direct, indexical relationship between the artwork and the social world from which these materials have been drawn. The finished work partakes in the ephemeral and the social with non-literary bluntness. Any attempts to praise it as a her-metic or autonomous text will founder on its unlovely incorporation of mun-dane, often journalistic writing. As Peter Bürger would put it, such collage fur-thers the avant-garde project of breaking down the baleful distinction between art and "life praxis" that prevails in late capitalism.[14]

Waldrop's version of collage—linked, via Bayer, with a non-Poundian, Continental descent line—also recalls Cubist collage, albeit in a very different manner. It aspires to emulate the *whole* of a Cubist painting. In the years 1912–13, Picasso typically included not only found materials (chair caning, wallpaper, etc.) but also painted patches, stenciled letters, *trompe l'oeil* wood grain, and other traces of the artist's hand. In works such as *Violon et partition, Tête d'homme au chapeau,* and *Bouteille et verre sur un guéridon,* Picasso seeks not simply to undermine aesthetic autonomy but to issue a radical challenge to a complacent viewer's presumptions about how painting signifies. He quite literally deconstructs his art: he employs shading that does not indicate depth, lines that do not suggest edges, superimposition that does not convey protension, and so forth, as Rosalind Krauss has richly detailed.[15] The mixture of found objects, *faux* found objects (wood grain), and free painterly expression functions within this more general semiotic project of reeducating the eye to perceive the conventionality of illusionism, that is, the "painting = window" metaphor fundamental to the art since the Renaissance. Similarly, in "A Form of Memory" Waldrop suggests that her borrowings have nothing naïve about them. She promises to manipulate, violate, crosscut, and otherwise render their unspoken assumptions overt. Pound's collage is evidentiary. Waldrop's is forensic.

Shutters Shut

After completing "A Form of Memory," Waldrop proceeded to write the three other sections that make up the remainder of *A Form / of Taking / It All.* Throughout, she chose to employ as a structural scaffolding a technique internal to "A Form of Memory": the appearance of quotations that recur in partially or drastically revised forms. She made two changes, however. First, the prose passages in "A Form of Memory" serve as her primary source for this game of repetition and variation. Second, by positioning "A Form of Memory" as part II, she insures that a reader first encounters these source texts in part I ("A Form of Vertigo") in their occulted, spliced forms. As a consequence, part I is full of unpredictable, fanciful moments that at first refuse easy assimilation into plausible explanatory frames, causal chains, or dramatic scenarios. Much of the narrative's appeal lies in this uneven, surreal surface. For example, in "Vertigo," in the midst of a stream-of-consciousness passage, one encounters, "A fork in the road. Henry. What a disaster if they had married. Curing stingray bites by having a prostitute urinate into the wound. It leads to a particularly virulent form of syphilis. Does forgetting count as forgiveness or just being forty, holding her face up to the sun?" (162) The thoughts about Henry, marriage, turning forty, and making choices ("fork in the road") fit the immediate context. Amy Lowell is vacationing in Mexico and musing about the course that her life has taken. The stingrays, prostitutes and syphilis though—these are vivid, intrusive subjects that are less easy to square with the setting and point of view. Is Lowell reaching for a suitable metaphor for the imagined "disaster" wedding? Does she feel prostituted? Diseased? These grotesque metaphors—if they indeed *are* metaphors—leave a reader guessing at possible constructions that would accommodate their jolting interruption of the story's course.

Forty pages later, "A Form of Memory" provides a short passage offering a possible yet oddly tardy answer to the conundrum:

> To cure injuries caused by the sting-ray, you must find a woman willing to strip and urinate into the wound. For the sake of completeness it must be stated that, as there are hardly any women here except peasant prostitutes, this cure more often than not leads to a particularly virulent kind of syphilis. (207)

Here we are presented with the bemused, condescending tone of a travel writer presenting, and debunking, a folk remedy for the audience back home.[16] Perhaps, in the earlier stream-of-consciousness passage, we witness Lowell's fleeting, condensed memory of what she had read in this same travel book. Her thoughts about Mexico, as she lies in bed with the shades down, arbitrarily commingle "original" thoughts with words and images lifted from her reading. One is not free of other authors' voices even in the privacy of one's skull.[17]

A Form / of Taking / It All gradually takes on the air of a funhouse in which things recur unexpectedly in new, often distorted guises. Sometimes the changes of context and content provide ambiguously supplementary information, as in the example of the stingray cure. Other times the repetition-with-variation estranges the material more drastically. The two narrative sections—part I, recounted from Lowell's perspective, and part III, written first-person from a novelist's viewpoint as she struggles to round off the tale of von Humboldt and Lowell—are pocked with these odd moments. Ada, Lowell's love interest, is forever being described in stilted, inappropriate terms that "A Form of Memory" makes one suspect have been purloined from Aggrippina Vaganova's *Basic Principles of Ballet*. John, Ada's son, spouts awkward statements about Beethoven and Montezuma that reappear verbatim in part II. Astronomical and poetological passages from part II reoccur in the novelist's stories about Washington, D.C. In each of these cases, verisimilitude suffers badly. Would any real person ever spontaneously repeat the bland, fact-choked language of a textbook with such uncanny fidelity?

Even the most vivid, seeming-profound moments of Waldrop's story are susceptible to demystification. At the end of part I, Lowell has a dreamlike vision of herself struggling, physically acrobatically contorting, to escape the burdens and embarrassments of childhood:

> [A]s her lids go shut again, a flock of birds, is it geese? parrots? lifts off, beating the air with a thunder of cries, and here is again the ceiling under which childhood waits to be left behind. This is why she must learn to walk on her hands. Two older girls take hold of her legs. Her hair is hanging down to the floor, her skirt falls over her belt down over her neck. Thus, legs high in the air, she walks across the stone floor, a moving island surfacing from the music that has spread all over the ground. Again and again, till the teachers turn away: "Her thighs are too fat," she hears, "and she already has pubic hair." (180)

A couple of these details will recur prominently in part II—the parrots (185) and the thundering (193)—but the bare essentials will reappear in a single narrative outtake, again likely derived from Vaganova's *Basic Principles of Ballet*:

> In my new class I was made to walk on my hands. Two older girls took hold of my legs. My hair hung down to the floor, my skirt fell over the belt down over my neck. Thus, legs high in the air, I walked across the stone floor. (203)

The first iteration of this incident conveys the intense shame involved in the process of publicly disciplining a vulnerable body. One sympathizes acutely and viscerally with Lowell's discomfort in her own skin. When, however, one comes across another version of the same story twenty pages later, the anecdote ceases to be Lowell's unique "property." Now an extract from a textbook, it loses what had been a florid, revelatory particularity. Also, the scene with Lowell established a set of expectations—about her psychology, biography, and place in society—that are thrown into doubt when the same words ("Two older girls," "hair . . . down to the floor," "legs high in the air") pop up again to describe a different-yet-similar action, another girl walking on her hands. We are forced to go back and attend to the specific words and turns of phrase that gave rise to our first, powerful impressions; we thus look anew at the earlier passage with an eye less to its content than to the details of its composition. Recurrence in *A Form / of Taking / It All* undermines a reader's faith that fictions, window-like, grants us transparent access to other worlds. We discover repeatedly that a given "window" is in fact a carefully constructed tableaux of words susceptible to artful rearrangement and re-presentation. Collage decisively enters Waldrop's *oeuvre* in a work dedicated to rigorously exposing the troubling power relations that inform every act of communication, even (or especially) the act of creating literature.

After *A Form / of Taking / It All*, Waldrop made rapid advances in the use of collage. In her hands, the technique has become increasingly supple and expressive, especially as she has gained more confidence in manipulating her found material. At her best, Waldrop is able to keep a reader deliciously off balance, unsure what is original, what borrowed. Incongruity alone is no guarantee that one has encountered a seam between discourses. Indeed, one of her goals in a book such as *Reproduction of Profiles* is to expose the gaps and slippages *within* the language of her source texts (in that case, Wittgenstein's *Philosophical Investigations*). Although she has had frequent recourse to the metaphor of the palimpsest to describe this vertigo-inducing writerly surface (e.g., "Between" xvii and "Form and Discontent" 61), a better analogy might be a word processor file that consists of cuts, pastes, deletions, and rearrangements of text originating elsewhere. Unlike a palimpsest, such a file would contain no optical indication of depth that would enable an easy sorting out of past and present, original and copy.

A sample of Waldrop's more recent use of collage can usefully conclude this essay by demonstrating the continuities (and discontinuities) in her practice as she returned to her principle vocation, writing verse. A good choice is "Shorter American Memory of Salem," a piece brief enough to examine in its entirety that also evinces important thematic connections to *A Form / of Taking / It All*, namely the ugly, murderous power politics involved in the European colonization of North America.

Shorter American Memory (1988), in which "Shorter American Memory of Salem" appears, is a collection of twenty-two pieces that, as Waldrop explains on the obverse of the title page, "are derived from sources collected in Henry Beston's *American Memory* (New York: Farrar & Rinehart, 1937)." Beston's *American Memory* turns out to be an anthology of diary entries, letters, court transcripts, official pronouncements, and other historical documents intended to offer a reader "a mirror of the stirring and picturesque past of Americans and the American Nation," as the title page puts it. In the book's preface, Beston states the none-too-covert nationalist thesis informing the anthology's implicit narrative:

> From its beginning, America has been writing about itself, and writing well. Indeed, it is not in the literary imitation of European models that American literature has its deepest roots but in the vigorous narrative prose of the native-born generation who left us their seventeenth century accounts of Indian captivity. . . . [Using] immediate experience still sharp

with emotion wherever I found it, I have put together this memory of the adventure of the Republic, now as then in the making. (xix)

In other words, *American Memory* celebrates "native-born" Americans who are neither Native Americans nor Europeans. It retells their exciting "adventure" in "vigorous prose" so that we, their patriotic descendents, can relish their "memory." Intent on establishing (white) American identity as the product of racial and national conflict, *American Memory* devotes the bulk of its attention to subjects such as the colonization of the Eastern seaboard, war with Indian tribes, war with Britain, and the development of a self-sufficient indigenous culture and economy.

In short, the "memory" enshrined in Beston is archival but also highly selective, adjusting the historical record to serve as a record of the trials, tribulations, and victories of a Chosen People. It is also a resolutely middlebrow version of a Poundian "poem including history," an epic whose protagonists are multiple and whose significant episodes are related by means of juxtaposed extracts from original documents. Beston serves Waldrop as an occasion to renew the historiographical critique so vigorously asserted in *A Form / of Taking / It All*. Her abridgement and radical revision of *American Memory* uses collage to expose the violence—wreaked on people *and* history—when nationalist-prophets dictate how documents and facts are ordered within an official, shared narrative. When a plurality of memories becomes one *American Memory*.[18]

"Shorter American Memory of Salem" corresponds to chapter 4 of *American Memory*, titled "Geneva and New England," which offers a selection of documents illustrative of Puritan religiosity. Waldrop boils its fourteen pages down to a scant seventeen lines that serve as a quiet but moving meditation on women's place in colonial American society:

> where a great stone
> where unaccountably gone
> where caused soreness and swelling
> where the tail of
> where no body to join them   5
> where in the chimney
> where she was scratched
> where no cattle seen there
> where with apparitions
> where teeth on her breast   10
> where how many fathom
> where no damage

where the mysterious
where a blow on her eye
where there was no body   15
where knowing her own
where pious considerations

Waldrop here concentrates her attention on the first four documents in "Geneva and New England," all of which have been taken either from Cotton Mather's *Magnalia Christi Americana* or from Salem's surviving seventeenth-century court and civic records. She borrows most heavily from a paragraph by Mather (I have emphasized the relevant phrases and indicated where in the poem they occur):

> In June 1682, Mary the wife of Antonio Hortado, dwelling near the Salmon-Falls, heard a voice at the door of her house, calling, "What do you here?" and about an hour after had *a blow on her eye* [14], that almost spoiled her. Two or three days after, *a great stone* [1] was thrown along the house; which the people going to take up, was *unaccountably gone* [2]. A frying pan then *in the chimney* [6] rang so loud, that the people at an hundred rods distance heard it; and the said Mary with her husband, going over the river in a canoe, they saw the head of a man, and, about three foot off, *the tail of* [4] a cat, swimming before the canoe, but *no body to join them* [5] and the same apparition again followed the canoe when they returned: but at their landing it first disappeared. A stone thrown by an invisible hand after this, *caused a swelling and a soreness* [3] in her head; and *she was* [7] bitten on both arms black and blue, and *her breast* [10] *scratched* [7] the impression of *the teeth* [10] which were like a man's teeth, being seen by many. (72–73)

Like *A Form / of Taking / It All*, "Shorter American Memory of Salem" freely alters the order and character of the phrases lifted from its source texts. Waldrop changes "caused a swelling and a soreness" to "caused soreness and swelling"; she omits a run of ten words to produce "she was scratched"; and she decides to associate "the teeth" and "her breast," despite the fact that, as we see in the original, "she was bitten" not on her breast but "on both arms." Furthermore, in "Shorter American Memory of Salem" she changes the sequence in which the phrases appear. She may preserve a trace of that ordering—observable in the run [1], [2], [6], [4], [5], [3], [7] in which only two elements, [6] and [3], are out of place—but the first phrase chosen from this paragraph ends up in the next-to-last line of the poem. Again we see that Waldrop's form of collage is unapologetically interventionist and revisionist.

The most dramatic alteration occurs at the level of historical referent. There is no legible trace of Mary, Antonio Hortado, or Cotton Mather in Waldrop's poem; there are none of the impedimenta of citation, marginal annotation, and bibliographic description that litter Pound's *Cantos* and buttress Beston's authority. She treats all her sources for this lyric just as cavalierly. Despite the fact that they span several decades and describe many events, including the discovery of sunken Spanish treasure, she distills from them a continuous commentary on a single historical episode, the infamous Salem witch trials of 1692. She insures that the poem will be read in that light by offering us no other proper name than "Salem" itself, a town indelibly associated in American popular culture with the likes of the dastardly Justice Hathorne, the unjustly accused John Proctor, the slave fortune-teller Tituba, and the "afflicted" teenagers Mary Warren and Abigail Williams. In her oblique retelling, however, Waldrop offers not Arthur Miller–style realism but an impressionistic, vaguely Gothic ("mysterious," "apparitions") catalog of observations. She culls from Beston phrases that evoke, even invoke, a specter that his inclusion of "The Penitence of the Jurors of Salem" cannot lay fully to rest: the American proclivity to use civic and religious zeal as pretexts for killing innocent men and women.

The poem's opening lines introduce the paradoxical imbrication of absence and presence that dominate the piece. The "great stone" in the first line suggests the heavy stones famously used to crush to death Giles Corey, an accused witch who refused to enter a plea. The "great stone" also hints at the weightiness, the imponderability, of the witch trials for subsequent generations of Americans. The poem's second line—"where unaccountably gone"—suddenly reverses the first line's assertion of presence, a fact emphasized by the slant rhyme "stone" / "gone." Has the stone vanished before it could be "counted," that is, weighed and measured? Or does Waldrop call our attention to "Salem" as a location that combines or juxtaposes the all-too-present (the stone) and the irrevocably lost (that which is "gone")? The remainder of the poem restates but does not resolve this tension. Suggestions of absence or erasure ("no damage," "no body," "no cattle") jostle with vivid statements about all-too-present, injured female flesh ("a blow to her eye," "she was scratched," "teeth on her breast").

One could read this dynamic as an oblique commentary on the people involved in the witch trials: the young girls who based their accusations of witchcraft on mysterious blows from ghostly assailants, the blameless women and men executed for nonexistent injuries to others, the witches' familiars presumed but never seen, etc. One could also read into the poem a subterranean narrative of domestic abuse. A woman is repeatedly harmed without that harm ever being publicly acknowledged or the perpetrator called to account. She knows her pain intimately ("knowing her own") but "pious considerations"—whether hers, her abuser's, or the community's—prevent that pain from ever becoming fully real, in the sense that it would then become a problem demanding response or recognition from others. In "Shorter American Memory of Salem," by selectively excerpting, rearranging, and revising the language used by seventeenth century Puritans to talk about their world and their experiences, Waldrop dramatizes the vulnerability, the violence, and the fear that run just beneath its surface. Moreover, she intimates that the "pious considerations" that they espouse not merely oppress but *damage* women crushed beneath their "great stone." The anaphora here ("where . . . where . . . where") distantly but appropriately echoes the use of another interrogative, "who," as the backbone for the first part of Allen Ginsberg's *Howl* ("I have seen the best minds of my generation . . . who . . . who . . . who"). Like Ginsberg, Waldrop laments the wastefulness of history, bringing suffering and loss to the very people a just or civilized society would liberate and celebrate.

This message is not new. We saw Waldrop making much the same point in *A Form / of Taking / It All*. But in the few years between that work and *Shorter American Memory* Waldrop learned to employ collage with much greater craft. She ceased to rely upon repetition and variation as a principle of construction. The phrases that appear in "Shorter American Memory of Salem" appear nowhere else in *Shorter American Memory*. The abrupt jolts and transitions in *A Form* that lend it the feel of Surrealist *cadavre exquis* have been replaced by a surface that is simultaneously smoother *and* more disorienting, insofar as one cannot guess where Waldrop's contributions end and the found texts in their rawness begin. "Shorter American Memory of Salem" also absorbs, abridges and revises Beston's anthology with an assurance that permits a greater latitude of tone than *A Form*. Finally, *Shorter American Memory* eschews any traces of Poundian parataxis. In place of that giddy form of artifice—dependent on sharp edges and bold transitions, hence a technique well suited to delivering punch lines and epiphanies—she embraces collage within hypotaxis ("where . . . where . . . where"), an art of relationality that explores nuances of subordination and insubordination, both grammatical and political.

And Sometimes

In 1912 Picasso bequeathed to the avant-garde a mode of collage designed to defeat illusionism in painting. At the turn of the twenty-first century Waldrop provides us with a version capable of exposing a different illusionism, the false authority arrogated when prophets have recourse to "history" to justify their visionary dreams. Again, not a new message. It is one we have heard often in the last hundred years. But the last hundred years have also taught that some messages bear repeating. Waldrop has crafted a form adequate to this content.

> She had said that . . . the wonders of a language game. Splice of life . . . . Connected. Weigh your words, heft, live them. Writing and walking, the form already there, in the space, a matter of finding rather than making. No parking. Not transparent. Not making the words disappear into their reference.

> And the sting of the incomplete in each word, insufficient, the work never done, finger to the bone, not enough. Pointing beyond, leaning into between, each word a vector, a versification of estrange. Sometimes a sentence in wishes. (*A Form / of Taking / It All* 227–28)

11

John Ashbery after
All These Years

John Ashbery has been blessed with longevity and high productivity. Literary critics, though, have sometimes seemed less than jubilant over the writer's good fortune. What do you do when a laurelled poet refuses to petrify into a well-wrought urn? It causes all sorts of complications. Much less troublesome are hard-living die-young geniuses who leave behind smaller, more manageable *oeuvres*.

Ashbery's career was launched over half a century ago when W. H. Auden awarded his debut volume *Some Trees* (1956) the Yale Younger Poets Prize. Two decades and six collections later, *Self-Portrait in a Convex Mirror* (1975) won the Pulitzer Prize, the National Book Award, and the National Book Critics Circle Award, firmly establishing him as one of the country's highest profile (and most controversial) poets. During the subsequent remarkable run of books from *Houseboat Days* (1977) to *A Wave* (1984), his reputation only grew. By the time that his *Selected Poems* (1985) appeared, Ashbery had become, like T. S. Eliot before him, not simply a well-known poet but a canonical and defining example of a period sensibility. Ashbery, love him or hate him, was, without a doubt, through-and-through "postmodern."

Then a curious thing happened. Having spent nearly a generation in the public spotlight, he began to be nudged offstage. Critics began to talk about his "late" style. Indeed, John Shoptaw completed a dissertation subtitled "An Introduction to the Later Poetry of John Ashbery" back in 1988. This tendency accelerated after the publication of the long poem *Flow Chart* (1991), an ambitious autobiographical epic that seemed an apt capstone to a life in letters. Why go on writing after such a crowning achievement? Joshua Clover accordingly described Ashbery's next outing, the volume *Hotel Lautréamont* (1992), as "dangerously close to the self-parody and self-reflexive pastiche of someone who has been famously brilliant—and then brilliantly famous—for too long" (177). Andrew DuBois's *Ashbery's Forms of Attention* (2006) is the latest and most extreme version of this heckle-the-spotlight-hog argument. It goes so far as to characterize all of Ashbery's post-*Flow Chart* verse—which, to date, includes eleven volumes—as one long slide into "dotage." He is engaged, DuBois argues, in "an elderly poet's confidence game," a "performance of senility, which is sometimes obviously a performance (he tells us so) and at other times is more *really* realistic, that is, he seems actually to have lost control" (114; emphasis in the original).

Yes, in 2007 Ashbery turned eighty, and, yes, he has been unusually prolific in the years since reaching the minimum age to start receiving Social Security benefits. Moreover, one could hardly deny that decline and death have become increasingly prominent topics in his verse in recent years. But senile? Such a generalization cannot survive a sustained, sympathetic reading of his last fifteen years of work. Individual lyrics such as "And the Stars Were Shining," "Tuesday Morning," and "As Umbrellas Follow Rain" surely rank among the most complex, moving pieces he has ever written, and *Girls on the Run* (1999) is the edgiest, funniest, and most peculiar Ashbery book since *The Tennis Court Oath* (1962). Whenever critics have stopped bemoaning belatedness and instead addressed their attention to specific texts—as Marjorie Perloff does in her review of *Your Name Here* (2001), which discusses "Sonatine Mélancolique," "Redeemed Area," and "Monday's at Seven"—the consequence has been a reawakened sense of the undiminished range, ingenuity, and vitality of the poet's imagination.

Although Perloff rightly cautions that it is "probably too soon to assess the overall trajectory of Ashbery's poetic career," it is not too soon to begin assembling and clarifying the data that will someday enable such a process of assessment to proceed. This chapter concentrates on analyzing one poem from one of Ashbery's recent collections to demonstrate that his understudied "late" work is every bit as demanding and rewarding as his more famous "early" verse. Instead of hurrying one of the premier writers of the last half-century off the stage, it is time to listen to what he is saying.

Let It Snow

To return to Andrew Dubois for just a moment: he claims that Ashbery's publications from 1995 to 2002 leave one "with the impression that the production sector of Ashbery Inc. [is] strong but that quality control might need an evaluation" (114). The "elements that characterize them—randomness peppered with certain persistent repetitions, lost trains of thought, a reversion to childhood, false histories, and boring, fanciful stories" are not new in his writing, but their presence is accentuated and their frequency of appearance is increased (112). The resulting verse is just plain "incoherent," any and all rational adult (as opposed to senile) thinking submerged beneath "rapid, random shifts in language and subject matter" (114).

One could selectively quote from Ashbery's *Where Shall I Wander* (2005) to support this idea of a slow slide into (simulated) dementia. But the collection doesn't really lend itself to such a survey. Its contents are too artful. One extended poem, "Hölderlin Marginalia," wickedly parodies many big names in contemporary American poetry, including everything from a *faux*-Susan Howe title to moments of eccentrically punctuated Jorie Graham-ish precious impressionism:

> Our hero arrives just in time
> in "take charge" mode
>   (feather that falls)
>   (a silk stocking) (peed on) (in the autumn)
>   of bright nights
>   of favorable returns (18)

Other lyrics, such as "Interesting People of Newfoundland," "Composition," and "Novelty Love Trot," seem explicitly calculated to preempt any charges of sphinxdom-without-secrets. Such poems display what one might call a disconcertingly un-Ashberyan coherency, an argument that can be followed, point by point, beginning to end. "Novelty Love Trot" in particular is a conventional *vanitas* piece that features a speaker who, if not identical to the poet, is quite close:

> In the end it matters little what things we enjoy.
> We list them, and barely have we begun
> when the listener's attention has turned to something else.
> "Did you *see* that? The way that guy cut him off?"
> Darlings, we'll all be known for some detail,
> some nick in the chiseled brow, but it won't weigh much
> in the scale's careening pan. (50)

Heady stuff, this: a life's work, the lyric declares, proves reducible to a mere "detail," or worse, to nothing more than a stray mark, a "nick," that defaces the world-as-we-found-it rather than beautifying it. Ashbery, too, reimagines the scales of judgment not as soberly and carefully weighing our actions unto the utmost grain but rather as wildly "careening," in other words, moving rapidly and chaotically like a car out of control. In such an unstable world, all that's left to us, all that we can hold onto, is human intimacy, manifested rhetorically ("Darlings") if not substantively: "You are stuffing squash blossoms / with porcini mushrooms," the poem ends. "I am somewhere else, alone as usual. // I must get back to my elegy" (51).

The best case for the value of Ashbery's recent writings, though, does not lie with this lyrical mode, which, like Gertrude Stein's *Autobiography of Alice B. Toklas* (1933), could be construed as a bad-faith retreat from the experimentalism of earlier work in the name of reaching a wider audience. The most interesting poetry in *Where Shall I Wander* continues, not repudiates, the vanguardism of previous decades. "Coma Berenices" is an ideal example. One of seven prose poems in the collection, it is five pages long and consists of twelve paragraphs of unequal length. Its language tends toward the prosaic: "The satin roof of our Colonial Revival house looked fine from the street, but when you were under it you felt crushed by the weight of the old twentieth century" (9). The connections between ideas and events are often attenuated, inappropriate, or inscrutable: "Some of us, quite a few, were fettered, many were not. The topiary Trojan horse stood outside the gate, not wanting to be let in. The freelance were blue; the staff yellow" (10). The mangled clichés—"No beating about the bed of roses here!" (7)—and yuck-yuck jokes—"Be careful, you'll disturb the pests, er, pets" (10)—become at times groan-a-minute. Read quickly and inattentively, "Coma Berenices" might very well appear to conform to DuBois's account of Ashbery's dotage, offering no more than "boring, fanciful stories" interspersed with "rapid, random shifts in language and subject matter" (112–14).

A hasty dismissal of this kind represents one of the two lapses all-too-common in Ashbery criticism, namely, discontinuing analysis when things begin to get weird. If a given poem or part of a poem doesn't happen to fall within a particular critic's comfort zone, she or he has more often than not resorted to words such as "chaos," "formless," "haphazard," or any number of other adjectives implying lack of design or pattern. For this reason, *The Tennis Court Oath* (1962) remains a semicanonical innovative text more often cited for its failure to gel than patiently probed to determine any deeper formal or stylistic logic. "Coma Berenices," a poem published a generation later, likewise deserves to be lingered over before being dropkicked into a drawer labeled "incoherent." On closer inspection, it in fact possesses a rather elegant structure. It falls readily into two halves. The first six paragraphs tell wry refracted anecdotes concerning an unhappily married suburban couple, Edie and Carl, and their servants.

Paragraph 2, for example, begins with a moment of domestic noir that could have been lifted from any number of TV melodramas, from *Scarecrow and Mrs. King* to *Desperate Housewives*: "Edie had felt vaguely apprehensive since the afternoon a dark-hatted man had called while she was out. He had said something about testing the water, her maid Maria told her. There had never been a problem with the water before. Maybe it was part of some ruse to get inside the house and rummage around in Carl's papers" (7). There are, however, moments when this more-or-less realistic veneer is punctured by mystery or oddity. For instance, while paragraph 4 stays partly in a quotidian register—it informs us that the maid Maria suffers from a "backache"—it also mentions an "arcane arousing" that "had taken place on schedule," "an arraignment" that "was ascendant," and an unnamed unspecified "work of art" that portentously fails to arrive (8). Especially peculiar are two discussions of an intangible, even mystical, snowball that travels through "the dangerous dreams of housewives" (7) and later becomes a "model for the soul" (9). Appearing both in the first and sixth paragraphs, this snowball provides a kind of narrative parentheses around the poem's first half, encapsulating the Edie-Carl story and setting it apart from what follows.

The second six paragraphs are loosely structured by the conventions of the end-of-the-year letter, the sort of chatty superficial epistle that many Americans print out *en masse*, stick in holiday cards, and distribute to one-time friends and distant relatives as a substitute for more regular meaningful communication. First we learn that Stu and the unnamed letter-writer have moved from "Moscow (Idaho!)" to "a large university town" in Illinois, and then we hear about a cavalcade of friends and visitors, among them Jarvis and April, Marnie and Val, Fran and Don, Mary and her little boy Lance, and Casper and his wife's two aunts. After a stray mention in paragraph 9 of a visit by Merle in August, we are treated to a chronological description of the year, from February to its close.

The penultimate paragraph reads in its telegraphic entirety: "November. Grief over Nancy Smith." The sparseness here, after so much volubility, underlines the sudden unexpected convergence between the proximate subject matter (what happened over the course of a year), the poem's form (eleventh month/eleventh paragraph), and a deeper stratum of significance (lives draw to an end, like years do, and we grieve). The final paragraph musters a string of clichés behind which one can detect fear of the future, or more specifically, both fear of possible eventual incapacity and fear of what might follow death: "All in all this has been a fairly active and satisfying year, and I'm looking forward to the next one. Where it will take me I do not know. I just hang on and try to enjoy the ride." After a brief statement that continues the seasonal motif while also referring obliquely back to the snowball in the poem's first half—"Snow brings winter memories"—Ashbery concludes by breaking the frame: "There is a warning somewhere in this but I do not know if it will be transmitted" (11). The poem is not a letter after all, not an intimate exchange between two people; it is closer to something broadcast, or "transmitted," to an unknown invisible audience, one, moreover, which is entirely capable of missing (or, more precisely, not receiving) the message of the poem, its implied "warning."

From "The Grapevine" in *Some Trees* to the title poem in *Chinese Whispers* (2002), Ashbery has repeatedly restated his fascination with the many ways that information can be mishandled, misread, or misplaced. The long poem "Europe" from *The Tennis Court Oath*, for example, ends with enemy spies flashing the letters "N.F." into the sky (*Mooring* 150). What do the initials stand for? What context, what code could lend them significance? In part, this aspect of his poetics is theological (or deconstructive, if you prefer). We live in a fallen world in which one can discern no more than shadows, embers, and scattered maddeningly elusive traces of the full light of the divine. Ashbery also believes in the inability of language to convey subjective experience accurately or adequately. Our interior, what "Coma Berenices" calls "our core of enigma," stubbornly remains privately ours (*Where Shall I Wander* 9). Other people can do little more than guess what goes on inside our skulls. Even when one most fervently wishes to communicate—for example, to say "I am in love"—the results are so partial, so askew, that they might as well be stuttered fragments, as in this passage from "Rain" (1962):

> The missing letter—the crumb of confidence
> His love boiling up to me
> Forever will I be the only
> In sofa I know
> The darkness on his back . . . .
> Spring mounts in me
> of dandelions—lots of it (*Mooring* 85)

The ambivalent close of "Coma Berenices," a "warning" that might be "transmitted" but never understood, is a familiar gesture of completion in Ashbery's work, a concession that no structure, no rhetoric, is capable of disclosing the ultimate truths that we most ardently wish to learn. "[L]ife holds us," he sighs in *Three Poems* (1972), "and is unknowable" (*Mooring* 314).

Dance Fever

Okay then, granted: Ashbery's "Coma Berenices" is too carefully wrought, too thought out, to serve as a document of senility. While true, the argument cannot stop there. Certifying a lyric dementia-free is not the same as making a case for its aesthetic value. Nothing prevents readers such as the critic Stephen Burt from judging it to be an unpalatable extra helping of Ashbery-as-usual delivered long after they had tired of his "almost already intelligible tangle of verities":

> Have
> you, too, been trying to keep up with John Ashbery?
> Every time I check there's another new book,
> another new entry—entrée—on the menu
> from which I seem to have ordered my whole life,
> and been served somebody else's. (*Parallel* 64)

What, if anything, makes "Coma Berenices" an important addition to the Ashbery canon? The title certainly hints at authorial ambition. It is Latin for "Berenice's Hair," and its source is a poem of the same name by Catullus. Catullus tells the story of Queen Berenice II, wife of Ptolemy III Euergetes, who cuts off her luxuriant long hair as an offering to Aphrodite in thanks for her husband's safe return from a military campaign. Her shorn locks then mysteriously disappear from the goddess's temple and, according to the poem, ascend into the heavens and become a constellation. Does Ashbery, too, aspire to celestial immortality?

Perhaps. The second major problem in Ashbery criticism is a failure to understand how tone functions in his verse. Relevant is the French idiom *il y a de jeux*, which literally means "there is play" but refers to a mismatch between container and thing contained. *Il y a de jeux* when, say, a shoe is a tad too large, or a peg doesn't exactly fit a hole. There's enough room that a person can wiggle, rotate, or otherwise "play" with things that ought to dovetail perfectly. Almost every statement in an Ashbery poem looks as if it ought to mean something definite, but when poked or prodded, the fit is imperfect, and there is room for slippage. The resulting "play" allows for a range of effects, from broad humor to arch irony to deflating skepticism.

"Coma Berenices," for instance, on first glance seems like a most serious sort of label. Aureate and erudite, it attaches the poem to the Grand Tradition. Catullus's "Coma Berenices" is in fact an imitation of a Greek original by Callimachus. In book 6 of the *Aeneid*, Virgil has his hero allude to Catullus's lyric while addressing Dido in the underworld. Alexander Pope reprises Catullus to conclude "The Rape of Lock" in appropriately neoclassical fashion. While Ashbery's subject matter might be contemporary and commonplace—"housewives, their hands at rest in the dishwater of a kitchen sink, or retirees and empty nesters wishing to refinance the mortgage on their home" (7)—the title, one could argue, establishes a solid literary-historical genealogy that makes it possible to put the present day into context, that is, to comprehend the here-and-now as a period of decadence and venality incapable of living up to the aesthetic and moral standards of yesteryear. As Ambrose Bierce explains in *The Devil's Dictionary* (1906), while a Classical paragon such as Berenice might have been willing to sacrifice "Her locks . . . Her loving husband to save," "our modern married fair" are unworthy of comparable "stellar recognition." They would cheerfully "give their lords to save their hair" (26).

Are things as clear as all this, however? Ashbery's Edie is not exactly T. S. Eliot's Lil or young man carbuncular, yardsticks for measuring lo how far we have fallen:

> At five she mixed cocktails—for herself and Carl, should he show up—in the shaker old Mrs. Lavergne had left her. Bombay Sapphire martinis. Carl had fallen in love with them in Bangalore where he had been posted on assignment. Somehow it was always a disappointment when they came out of the shaker colorless instead of blue. The sapphire color was in the bottle. She wondered if Carl had noticed this, or, more important, whether it bothered him. He had been so tight-lipped lately—though always the affectionate dear he had been on the day they first met at the Cayuga Country Club. Well, he'd had a lot on his mind. The refinancing hadn't been going too well. (8)

Yes, Edie's life is utterly stereotypical. Her uncommunicative husband, oppressed by business affairs, is "in love" with gin, not with her. She responds like Nora Charles deprived of Nick and downs martinis, except, unlike Nora, she has no wit to speak of. She skips from cliché to cliché as, like Barbara Eden in *I Dream of Jeanie*, she ponders how better to please her master ("whether it bothered him," "so tight-lipped lately," "affectionate dear," "a lot on his mind," "hadn't been going too well"). She is vacuous enough to belabor the observation that Bombay Sapphire comes in a blue bottle but, like all gin, is clear. Yet Ashbery does not appear to condemn Edie. If anything, he seems sympathetic, permitting the vignette to linger and allowing the chatty speaker, reminiscent of a sitcom voice over, to prolong its chirpy free-indirect-discourse presentation of Edie's thoughts. One could dismiss the entire passage as a found text lifted from a bad novel of suburban angst circa 1962—except for the aside that Carl began his romance with Bombay Sapphire in Bangalore. Bombay Sapphire, of course, has nothing to do with India beyond its name. It is a UK-produced premium gin, first introduced in 1987, that is distributed worldwide by the Bermuda-based Bacardi corporation. Nonetheless, it is uncannily apt that salary man Carl, while "on assignment" in Bangalore, a city synonymous these days with high-tech outsourcing, discovers a "love" for a brand of alcohol whose marketing depends on faked warm fuzzy feelings toward the British Raj (Queen Victoria even appears on its label). Ashbery is clearly having fun here—but not exactly of the Ciceronian *o tempora, o mores* sort.

In search of a work with an analogous tone, one might turn, not to "The Waste Land" or even "The Rape of the Lock," but to a contemporary spectacle such as Mark Morris's *The Hard Nut* (1991), a modern dance performed to the music of Tchaikovsky's *Nutcracker* (1892). Its opening act "follows the traditional Christmas party scenario," albeit updated and "transformed into a more carnal and spontaneous gathering." The characters wear "loud Christmas outfits from the 1960s and 1970s," and they socialize in a suburban home with tin-and-tinsel décor. (A black maid, the only dancer *en pointe*, discretely pushes around a cocktail cart and pushes cocktails.) What amazes about the scene is its combination of vim, nostalgia, and devastating critique. Key is the pervasive emphasis on artifice. "Op-art bellbottoms and mini-skirts, one realizes quickly, do as much to produce a role as any Rat costume—or for that matter as any of the 'realistic' Victorian suits and gowns which have paraded through *Nutcrackers* in the past eighty years." Morris exposes daily American middle-class living as a peculiar performance that follows laughable scripts and involves outrageous outfits. Moreover, this is not a horrifying problem, an existential inauthenticity to be lamented à la John Updike. Rather, as the tangled remainder of *The Hard Nut* shows, it is liberating. Morris's Marie Stahlbaum (as he rechristens Clara) experiences a much wider latitude in choosing her future than does her counterpart in Tchaikovsky's ballet:

> While Morris'[s] story re-enacts the focus upon love between the girl . . . and the Nutcracker-become-young man, he rearranges and elaborates its themes and possibilities, so that the union of Marie and her lover appears more as a choice whose process we watch than as an immutable destiny. (Cohen 490)

The Hard Nut is also in-your-face queer. It features more men in tutus than a New Orleans Mardi Gras. Its *Brady Bunch*-meets-*A Charlie Brown Christmas* vision of suburbia is high camp. That is, it exhibits an aesthetic sensibility long identified with gay subcultures: a loving exaggerated superficial imitation that, through selective repetition, reveals that the target of its ambiguous homage is also a thoroughgoing creation of artifice and improvisation. A drag Judy or Barbra or Brittany or Gaga is not so much a parody as a funhouse mirror, one that plays up so as to attract audience attention to the theater involved in maintaining a diva persona (the makeup! the hair! the tiffs! the meltdowns! the comebacks!). The drag queen code maintains not only that all the world is a stage—

that old Shakespearean chestnut—but more specifically that it is a movie set and we are all potential superstars, if, like Anne Baxter in *All About Eve* (1950), we study intently the leading ladies and steal their best material (and their wardrobe).

The Hard Nut is more, however, than a predictable wish-fulfillment illustration of this doctrine. Yes, Morris's piece is campy—never more so than during the Dance of the Snowflakes, when a crowd of men *en travesti* prance around tossing bursts of silvery confetti into the air—but its tone is variable, encompassing dark as well as light, violence as well as joy. At times it becomes downright sinister, including intimations of incest and pedophilia (Cohen 493). Marie might learn that she is a performer, just like everyone else, but, over the course of the work, she also discovers that there are inequalities between roles, limitations placed on which roles people can choose, and serious consequences stemming from what they decide.

Significantly, this insight is, in its own way, as queer as anything else in *The Hard Nut*. As Morris (and Ashbery) know well, life as a bourgeois gay man in the United States requires constant improvisation in response to social situations and power structures beyond one's control. How will you—will you—relate to the family of birth that never quite knows what to do with you or where you fit in the kinship network? Will you define the good life the same way as many heterosexuals: monogamous marriage, children, and a single-family home in a good neighborhood? If you do, given the federal government's inveterate opposition to letting you imitate breeders, what simulacrum of hetero-happiness will you settle for? If you reject assimilation, what will you strive for? Regardless, what do you call your beloved? The questions intensify as you grow older and your childhood straight friends go through the hetero-approved rituals of engagement, wedding, childbirth, and divorce, typically becoming more and more like their (and your) parents in the process. (Few things make a gay man feel gayer than an interminable obligatory dinner where straight folk who used to be the life of the party now seem lost to a religious cult, speaking vacantly at length about which local schools are best and about the dangers of mercury in tuna fish sandwiches.) In short, you face on a daily basis the lack of fit between yourself and the hetero-hegemonic society around you: *il y a de jeux*. That *jeux* can be liberating. It can be tragedy.

Let's return to Edie, whom we left pensively contemplating cocktails a few pages back. Ashbery's sexual orientation often enters discussions of his poetry in regards to occulted subject matter. Aha! a critic declares, here at last we find him talking openly about queer life. The more sophisticated version of this argument locates his "homotextuality" in his poetry's formal characteristics, such as its discontinuity and resistance to closure (Vincent 155–59). Where sexuality most palpably becomes pertinent, though, is via tone, that is, the stance taken toward his subject matter. Edie appears in a poem titled "Coma Berenices." What happens to that title when viewed not "straight" but as *jeux*? Berenice is a name rich in drag potential, up there with Ophelia and Tawanda. Indeed, it shows up as a nickname for one of the main characters in the men-in-frocks extravaganza *Priscilla, Queen of the Desert* (1994). Moreover, the original story-line has "drama queen" scrawled across it in pink cursive. A queen—for real, Mary!—begs the Goddess of Love to Save Her Man. In thanks, she does the unthinkable. She gets a bob cut. Venus is so touched that she put Berenice's curls in heaven to remind all future would-be princesses that a smidge of public martyrdom (plus a good stylist) is the route to stellification. Most things that end up as constellations are blandly butch—dead heroes, dead monsters, the occasional ship or wagon—but OMFG, a hairdo? A *queen's* do? Snap.

Ashbery very rarely employs ink this lavender, of course. Nevertheless, the point still stands. In his verse the myths, history, and platitudes that circulate in the (heterosexual) public sphere are liable to be seen not as real or natural or inevitable but as theatricalized performances that one can appraise, imitate, esteem, or skewer as one might an actress's efforts in *Cats* or *Hair*. Edie is an exercise in ventriloquy. Ashbery imaginatively inhabits—with a sliver of difference, *il y a de jeux*—the role of a stereotypical upper-middle-class bored suburban wife. He does so in full knowledge of, likely because of, its superficiality and typicality. The poet writes *as if* it were possible for him to participate in this scenario lifted from the American pop culture unconscious. He can poetically relish its privileges and pleasures while never being in danger of suffering its suffocating constraints. The revenge of the queer, in other words, is to play at being straight, in full awareness that he or she is not condemned to remain so. Hence, in part, the eruptions of mystery, the strange discontinuities in a lyric such as "Coma Berenices": an "arcane arousing" is forever liable to interrupt one's sojourn among "housewives . . . retirees and empty-nesters" (7–8). Life not only can be otherwise, it is, or soon will be.

Son et Lumière

Drag isn't to everyone's taste. Some people find it unnerving, incomprehensible, or insulting. And some of these disapproving folk have numbered among Ashbery's critics. Michael Leddy, for instance, simply will not countenance Ashbery's assertion that his attraction to the art of Henry Darger—and his consequent book length meditation on it, *Girls on the Run*—originated in "his boyhood fascination with girl culture and the beauty of girls' dresses." The girls in Darger's drawings, Leddy quotes Ashbery as saying:

are constantly under attack by violent enemy forces and being saved and surviving storms and evil armies. I was fascinated by little girls when I was a little boy, and their clothes and their games and their dolls appealed to me much more than what little boys are doing. Therefore I was sort of ostracized.

Leddy's rejoinder: "Ashbery's explanation defies plausibility and is, I think, meant to be recognized as doing so." Why?

> It acknowledges only indirectly the most obvious feature of Darger's work— the gruesome violence done unto the (often naked) bodies of girl chil- dren, focusing instead on the averting of that violence ("being saved and surviving") and offering a remarkable non sequitur in the recollection of childhood interest in what American boys once called "girl-stuff."

This argument is tone-deaf. It misses the force of the poet's identification with the Vivian Girls (the girls "constantly under attack by enemy forces"). Ashbery was born in 1927. He is reminiscing about a lonely queer childhood during the Depression. Far from engaging in a "remarkable non sequitur," he is quite de- liberately connecting the "gruesome violence" in Darger's work to the painful experience of growing up sissy. We do not hear about, say, bullying, parental dis- cipline, gym-class shame, or any other autobiographical details about the ostra- cism that he suffered—that's not Ashbery's way—but connecting the dots is easy. Leddy's complaint that the poet focuses on "averting . . . that violence" ought to be flipped one hundred and eighty degrees. Thanks are due to Aphrodite when- ever a queer kid eludes the dangers of peer pressure, self-hatred, and competi- tive machismo and survives into adulthood. *Girls on the Run* might be a horror story but hallelujah! it has a happy ending.

There have also been subtler but equally revealing misreadings. Again con- cerning *Girls on the Run*, the fine poet Forrest Gander proposes precisely the wrong metaphor: "Just as in our lives, where we aren't conclusive, where we change our minds and tell our kids one thing and then take it back as they argue and we speed along trying to make out the street signs to wherever it is we are driving them, in Ashbery's poems our focus never quite settles, but careens along, taking in this and that, the relevant and the extraneous, juggling it all at once." The "our" here ("tell our kids one thing") is not universal. It includes Gan- der, his wife C. D. Wright, and their son Brecht, presumably, but it does not au- tomatically include the writer whom he is discussing, nor any other queers who might read Gander's review. Some gays would find this passage coercive. How dare he assume that his audience will identify with a scene so patently Soccer

Daddish! Others, more sympathetic, might rearrange things and, to make visceral sense out of it, cast themselves in a child's, not the parent's, role. Still others would pass over Gander's simile without a second thought, either because they are so used to being excluded from hetero-speak that it no longer registers as a problem or because they have become so accustomed to legal progress that they no longer feel excluded from traditional parenthood. (The latter sort should sit down with Rosie O'Donnell for a chat. She'd give them an earful.)

Regardless, one can imagine Ashbery reading this sort of comment and immediately perceiving its lack of fit. Even better, one can imagine Ashbery writing such a statement and delighting in *il y a de jeux*. His verse is full of portentous generalities that might or might not be serious, that might or might not include the poet and his readers in their reach: "We see us as we truly behave" (*Mooring* 3); "the avatars / Of our conforming to the rules and living / Around the home have made—well, in a sense, 'good citizens' of us" (233); "we must learn to live in others, no matter how abortive or unfriendly their cold, piecemeal renderings of us: they create us" (315). He frequently arrogates the voice of putative universalism and revels in its rhetorical resonance while also dropping a hairpin now and then, as they used to say, reminding readers that he is offering anything but unvarnished all-inclusive truth. Toto pulls back the curtain and reveals to Dorothy that the Great Oz is actually a fabulous sound and light show.

One could call this sensibility the higher drag. Over its imperial court presides not buzz cut Berenice but Scheherazade, the Persian queen who earned her crown by dint of the fecundity, variety, and careful pacing of her word-witchery. ("Scheherazade" [1975] is in fact the title of one of Ashbery's profoundest lyrics, in many ways a better lyric than the more famous title poem from the same collection, "Self-Portrait in a Convex Mirror.") In his ongoing avant-garde staging of *One Thousand and One Nights* Ashbery sequentially rehearses different discourses, showing each to be incomplete or provisional, in need of discarding so as to move on, at least momentarily, to a more promising alternative. Admittedly, this incessant one-man-show might appear nihilistic or self-defeating—but only to readers in search of candor, certainty, or veracity. It can, though, be positively invigorating if, throughout your entire life, the self-styled purveyors of truth—civic leaders, organized religion, educational institutions—have consistently pretended that you don't exist, treated you as a problem to be solved, or advocated your non-existence. (If you think things are nowadays hunky-dory in re: sexual orientation, at least in Blue States, go count how many public school districts in the United States include any discussion of homosexuality whatsoever in their approved sex ed curriculum.)

If *Girls on the Run* addresses queer childhood, poems such as "Coma Berenices" are responses to the later stages in a gay man's life. There are few maps of this *terrain vague*. There are fewer still that date from recent years. From 1982 to 1992 HIV/AIDS killed off almost an entire population cohort of gay men. The next generation, the one currently coming into its prime, has few elders to share wisdom or to warn of what lies ahead. How do you handle an aging body in a subculture that fetishizes youth? If you can't count on blood relations to support you, who will be there for you in advanced years? How do you navigate a medical system that tends to treat everyone the same (a.k.a heterosexual)? What are just and beneficial ways to settle an estate when *posterity* might not mean grandchildren and great-grandchildren?

Poetry cannot answer the practical side to such questions, but it can convey the thoughts, desires, and dreams that follow from being put into such a position. Allen Ginsberg, for one, responds in *Death and Fame* (1997) with nakedly melodramatic personal revelation. He places the spotlight squarely on his unpleasant struggles with his leaky cranky abject elderly body:

> tender Hemorrhoids
> High Blood
> Sugar, low
> leaden limbs
> lassitude
> bed rest
> shit factory
> this corpse (*Collected* 1139)

"Coma Berenices"—like Ashbery in the 1990s and 2000s more generally—takes a dramatically different approach. It could hardly be otherwise, of course, given his long-term belief that confession is a fundamentally misleading kind of performance, misleading, that is, because readers mistakenly expect it to provide special access to an author's interior life. As stated earlier, for Ashbery that "core of enigma" cannot be brought to light, no more than poetry can make God tangibly intelligibly manifest (*Where* 9). Accordingly, he places emphasis not on who he *is* but on what he can *do*, which is gallantly to take the stage once more. The show must go on, even if the parts must change somewhat to suit the performer's age. (Only Mary Pickford can eternally play the ingénue.) He tries different culturally sanctioned ways of growing old: settling into suburban discomfort, wrestling with monogamy's long-term downsides, and discovering that one's life can be summarized by annual letters detailing who visited whom and whether "the new fish place" is worth a special trip (10). His verse seems to take comfort in its ability to mimic the utterly flatly quotidian:

> Casper took me and his wife's two aunts on a leaf-peeping trip in north-
> ern Vermont. We were near Canada but didn't actually cross the border.
> You can get the same souvenir junk on this side for less money Max said.
> He is such a card. (11)

The poem also, however, finds such quiet interludes unsustainable. The basic narrative line in each of its two halves is again and again interrupted via digression, quick costume changes, relocations, and one-liners. "Then one day a remarkable change occurred," the lyric characteristically announces at one point, pulling off a quick switcheroo of scenes (10). Throughout, the tone, despite the occasional note of grief or longing, is generally upbeat and comic: "we, we all, are the stuff of legends" (11). The title might hint at hubristic aspirations toward canonical greatness, but the poem itself proves content with smaller scale happiness and what amounts to a succession of Vaudevillian skits. It informs the "younger generation" that while fear might be in the future—and likewise boredom ("Many's the time we'd stare at each other across the living room and wonder, 'So what?'")—there will nevertheless, too, be joy in scads ("I am benison, it sang") (10).

In his forties Ashbery famously advised "learning to accept / The charity of the hard moments as they are doled out" (*Mooring* 233). Who would ever have guessed that, in his late seventies, he would adopt an altogether sunnier outlook? A life lived otherwise, he teaches, doesn't have to fall into conformity in its final third, nor does it have to become thinned to the coat-on-a-stick version of old age that W. B. Yeats despised. He suggests, on the contrary, that daily living can remain fluidly improvisatory. It can jump from track to track, path to path. The thespian pleasures of *il y a de jeux*, too, maintain their allure. To judge such wickedly satisfying transgressive play senile is to foreclose possibility. It singles out one life course among many as normative. Yet if Ashbery can be Edie for a while, and then become someone else, why must the Edies of the world stay fixedly Edie, or Carls Carl? One must never confuse dementia with a willed, willful refusal to be "reasonable" like "normal" people. The alternative is much more entertaining. Has John Ashbery gone on and on? Yes. All hail Aphrodite!

12

The ABCs of
Substitutional Poetics

In his essay "Sestina! or, The Fate of the Idea of Form" (2008), Stephen Burt ponders the runaway popularity of the sestina among contemporary North American poets, many of whom otherwise display no consistent commitment to rhyme, meter, or other aspects of traditional poetic form. How can one explain the frequent recourse to the sestina's "six-word seven-times structure," a verse form so "artificial," so detached from "conversation" or "the logic of discursive prose," that it registers chiefly as a kind of verbal "game" (222)? The form's arbitrariness is its message, Burt concludes. "The sestina is a favored form now . . . because it allows poets to emphasize technique and disavow at once tradition, organicism, and social and spiritual efficacy." In other words, they tacitly but legibly confess their political impotence post-9/11 and promise to pursue the only public role still left open to them: to provide "entertainment" through a demonstration of their virtuosic "craft." (221). They are thereby able to circumvent (and sometimes comment wryly on) nebulous, vexing, lingering audience expectations that they fulfill a "public mission for artists that no actual artist can fulfill, a demand for poetic value of kinds never specified, and a substitute for religion that does not save" (241).

Burt connects the sestina renaissance to other aspects of contemporary verse, such as the widespread use of anagrams, lipograms, and "other poems in numerically and alphabetically constrained forms" (237). His list could be extended considerably. Burt's own collection *Parallel Play* (2006) contains, in addition to the sestinas "Our History" and "Six Kinds of Noodles," a remarkable exercise in monorhyme entitled "Paysage Moralisé" whose thirty lines all end in the word "place" or a near variant (e.g., "displays," "plac- / ate," "complac- / ently" and "sewn-up lace") (11). Today's poets do appear apt to employ any form at hand or to improvise new ones on the fly. Especially favored are patterns dependent less on rhyme schemes than permutation, repetition, or other preconceived algorithms. Natasha Trethewey's *Native Guard* (2006), winner of the 2007 Pulitzer Prize, is representative. It includes familiar Western forms—a villanelle ("King Cotton, 1907") and a crown of free verse sonnets ("Native Guard")—as well as non-Western forms—a ghazal ("Miscegenation") and a pantoum ("Incident")—and, finally, a palindromic poem whose second stanza repeats the twelve lines from the first in reverse order ("Myth"). Few books could be further from the conversational, phrasally lineated free verse that predominated in American verse during the closing decades of the twentieth century.[1]

Burt is surely correct that the current popularity of predetermined forms—inherited, borrowed, or invented—frequently coincides with a skepticism toward poetry's ability to advance revolutionary causes. (Indeed, as Christopher Nealon has argued in another context, the belief that global capitalism's ills cannot be wholly or rapidly cured in our time could be considered a distinguishing trait of much North American verse published in recent years.[2]) Significantly, though, in the poetries that Burt singles out for attention, a distaste for utopian grandstanding is not generally accompanied by an atmosphere of despair, doom, or desuetude. One of the books that he cites, Christian Bök's *Eunoia* (2001), is in fact notable for its mood of Tom Sawyer–like boisterous glee. "Look at me! Look at me!" the implied author seems to say as he creates witty-weird scenarios within the harsh constraints governing word selection. In the following example, for instance, Bök uses no vowel but *e:*

> Whenever Helen dresses herself *en fête,* her sewn vestments reflect her resplendence. Whenever she needs new ensembles, her sempstresses sew her ten, velveteen dresses, then hem her red, checkered sleeves. Her jewelers bevel the best gems, then bejewel her sceptre *(l'emblème des régences célestes).* Her eldest helpers preen her tresses; then her effete servers serve her dessert. The empress prefers sweetened preserves; hence, her serfs get her the best gels ever jelled: *les pêches gelées*—blended sherbet, served fresh. The scented dessert smells even sweeter, when served, ere the sweetness melts. (35)

The interjected arch French phrases in this passage are like the "blended sherbet" and the "best gems" that the poet mentions, that is, pleasurable rich *divertissements.* There are many other clever writerly touches worth lingering over, too, such as the sly substitution of the archaic "sempstresses" for the impermissible "seamstresses" and the hyperbolic use of "empress" to refer to Helen of Troy ("Chapter E" in *Eunoia* retells the whole of the *Iliad* from her viewpoint).

Is there a moral here? Bök seems squarely on the side of his heroine. His "serfs," "servers," and "jewelers" go unnamed. Lacking all interiority, their sole purpose seems the fulfillment of an aristocrat's idle wishes. One could say that Bök has given up on justice for the working class, or that he betrays the sanctity of his art by hinting that it, too, is a bauble fashioned for the entertainment of the leisured set. Such comments, though, recall Marjorie Levinson's infamous complaint that William Wordsworth's "Tintern Abbey" omits any mention of the smokestacks visible in the Wye Valley.[3] That is, while undeniably focusing one's attention on genuine and important political issues, criticism of this kind also reads poems against their grain. The unalloyed joy with which contemporary poets such as Bök deploy predetermined modes of composition suggests that they are successfully achieving ambitions other than the pursuit of regime change. Before summarily dismissing *Eunoia* or similar recent works for failing to advance a transformative political agenda, it is worth pausing to ask: What explains their buoyant affect in a time of war, curtailed civil rights, and economic insecurity?

The present-day vogue for inorganic poetic forms, this chapter argues, largely stems from their value as spurs to and road maps for composition. Writers creatively demonstrate their capacity to navigate complex situations involving both immutable systemic rules (formal constraints) and chaotic freedom (permission to fill in the blanks however desired). As Burt suggests, this scenario provides a euphoric alternative to feeling overwhelmed in an era when poetry all-too-often fails to grant poets visible, viable authority within the public sphere whether as prophets, revolutionaries, or voices of conscience. There is more to it, however. Today's poets are obeying what Alan Liu has christened the logic of cool, a self-conception associated with "knowledge work" in the twenty-first-century globalized information economy (316). Contemporary writers, like any other content providers, cannot permit themselves to be tied down by respect for or duties toward tradition. Ideally, they should be mobile, flexible, and inexhaustibly creative, ready to write brilliantly on any topic any time. Under such circumstances, poets are liable to express a giddy self-satisfaction in excess of the occasion. A successfully executed poem momentarily distracts attention from the arbitrary cruelty of the labor market, a swiftly eroding social safety net, and the disruptive boom-and-bust economic cycles of the last decade.

Recent writing on avant-garde literature has drawn attention to procedural poetry, that is, poetry "predetermined to allow into the act of composition such things as chance, found text, limited vocabularies, and real-time events" so as to challenge the "emphasis" in "mainstream free verse" on "intention, mimesis, organicism, spontaneity, and expression" (Watkin 499).[4] The phenomenon that this essay describes is distinct albeit at times overlapping or intersecting. The pages that follow focus on one contemporary form—the *abecedary*, a poem in which most or all the letters of the alphabet appear prominently in alphabetic order—that has proved fashionable among both procedure-savvy experimentalists and write-from-the-heart populists.[5] One discovers that the so-called mainstream—the default mode of writing in a particular era—is a moving target. The abecedaries of the twenty-first century might not be organic or confessional, but they hardly eschew spontaneity or mimesis. And while they might not exhibit the radical depersonalization, technophilia, and performative bent associated with such notable proceduralists as Jackson Mac Low and John Cage, they do illustrate that some varieties of page-based procedurality have become standard stock in trade across the entire profession. Avant-gardes, as always, are subject to co-optation; in this case, devices first used in a Marxist, anarchist, and other politically radical contexts are susceptible to being recycled in the service of a chastened, qualified humanism. This chapter ends with speculations concerning what a vanguard poetics might look like after ingenuity and technical skill have displaced confessional self-exposure as the preferred (hegemonic) means of affirming a poet's (imaginary, bourgeois) independence and agency.

A to Z an Altar an Arch[6]

In *Jersey Rain* (2000), the American Poet Laureate Robert Pinsky brought renewed attention to the venerable poetic form of the abecedary.[7] The best-known early examples are biblical. In Psalm 119, for instance, the verses in each of the twenty-two strophes begin with the appropriate Hebrew letters, from *aleph* to *tav*.[8] Abecedaries continued to be used for other religious and mystical ends well into the Middle Ages, as Geoffrey Chaucer's "An A.B.C." (also known as "La prière de nostre dame") demonstrates. Its stanzas' opening lines make an alphabetical acrostic:

> Almighty and al merciable quene . . . .
> Bountee so fix hath in thyn herte his tente . . . .
> Comfort is noon, but in yow, lady dere . . . .
> Doute is ther noon, thou queen of misericorde . . . .
> Ever hath myn hope of refut [refuge] been in thee . . . .
> Fleeing, I flee for socour to thy tente . . . . (261–63)

After the invention of the printing press the abecedary became an important tool for teaching novice readers. *The New England Primer* (ca. 1688) helped generations of students in the American Colonies learn to associate letters and sounds:

In *Adam's* Fall
We Sinned All.
Thy Life to Mend
This *Book* Attend.
The *Cat* doth play
And after slay.
A *Dog* will bite
A Thief at night.
An *Eagles* flight
Is out of sight.
The Idle *Fool*
Is whipt at School.[9]

Pinsky's version of the abecedary, titled "ABC," is much terser, although it retains the impersonality and moralizing tone of its antecedents:

Any body can die, evidently. Few
Go happily, irradiating joy,

Knowledge, love. Most
Need oblivion, painkillers,
Quickest respite.

Sweet time unafflicted,
Various world:

X = your zenith. (10)

Pinsky takes twenty-five words that each begin with a different letter and puts
them into alphabetical order. To this bare armature, he adds punctuation, capitalization, lineation, stanza breaks, and mathematical notation. His subject matter is traditional, a meditation on mortality. Echoing Emily Dickinson's "The
Heart asks Pleasure—first" (1862), Pinsky asserts that most people, instead of
passing "happily, irradiating joy," long for a quick, painless transition. "Knowledge" of the moment of death—being conscious of one's own dissolution—is
such a terrifying prospect that most people would prefer the "oblivion" brought
on by sleep or "painkillers."

The poem's most original touch is its closing line. *X* is a troublesome letter
in modern English: it begins only a small assortment of words, few of which
would be useful in the present context (xebec? xenia? xenon? xylem? *The New*

England Primer's choice, "Xerxes," would look entirely out of place in a poem that otherwise eschews proper nouns. Chaucer's cheat, to hybridize the Greek Χριστος [Christos] and the English "Christ" to create "Xristus," would look even stranger [271]). To handle this awkwardness, Pinsky chooses to switch sign systems, from alphabetical to algebraic. *X* becomes a variable. "X = your zenith" (10)—the opening of the line suggests "X = Y," the equation for a line with a slope of one, and the word "zenith," drawn from astronomy, feels part of the same rationalist discourse-radius. "X," we are told, is shorthand for whatever represents the highest point in the arc of "your" (a.k.a. "any body's") life. The moral here is somewhat vague, but a paraphrase is possible. While "any body" is still alive and hale, that is, "unafflicted," the "[v]arious world" awaits exploration. Though one will eventually die, during the "[s]weet time" this side of death one will attain an "X," an achievement one can be proud of. The precise nature of that "X" might vary from person to person, and it might differ in degree, but it nonetheless exists. There has to be some kind of "zenith," a high point, in everyone's lifespan. Of course, Pinsky could have concluded differently, by highlighting instead the inevitable lows—if there is a zenith, there must be a nadir, too—but he opts for optimism. However grim the endgame, he teaches, humanity can find consolation somewhere *in medias res*.

While not as popular as the sestina, in the wake of Pinsky's "ABC," abecedaries have also proliferated.[10] And poets have tended to share his association between the swift linear march of the form from A to Z and the inevitability of fate. In "Star Chart" (2005)—a double abecedary, that is, a poem that is both an acrostic (the first letters of each line spell out *A* to *Z*) and a telestich (the last letters of each line spell out *Z* to *A*)—Catherine Wing recounts the ill-starred story of a "heartbreaker":

> As if she had no alibi, no razz
> backing up her dazz, no pitty-patty
> carrying her tune in the world's jukebox.
> Don Juan once beat her down. Who knew
> electricity came in such a pretty packet? The entire V
> FD (Unit 36, Company 3) out of Kathmandu,
> Georgia, fell for her while watching *What's Up Kitty Cat?* (60)

As the poem proceeds, things go from bad to worse, until "the queenpin / nose-dive[s] into the gutter" and turns murderess ("It was she, shot J. / R."). After a brief rally—she stars as herself in a "mini- / series" about "her fall from heaven"—clouds gather:

The candle twice as bright burns only half as long
until it gutters out and dies from disbelief.
Venus to verboten in a single sentence.
What gives? How are we so easily misled?
X marks the spot, we're told, but it's at the bottom of the Pacific
—you're in cement shoes. And life, a hard heart throb,
zephyr-like, fails. Her last words were "Abracadabra." (60)

The protagonist's *Sopranos*-like drowning-by-"cement shoes" is curiously gener-
alized. Wing twice uses "we" and once "you" before she again mentions "[h]er,"
and meanwhile the language tends toward the pithily abstract. She moralizes
about a "candle twice as bright," recalling Edna St. Vincent Millay's "First Fig"
(1920), and she resorts to Robert Lowell–like lapidary portentousness in describing the death "sentence" that turns the attractive "Venus" at the poem's
center into *persona non grata*, someone who is "verboten." Wing's abecedary,
unlike Pinsky's, might be full of manic energy and Gen-X irony, but hers, too,
ultimately turns out to be a *memento mori*. "We," she hints, like the one-time
star of the fictional film *What's Up Kitty Cat?*, have been "misled" by the assumption that our adventures could last forever, and our antics, instead of leading us
to glorious treasures, will likewise eventually lead us to a different kind of "X"
in the proverbial "X marks the spot"—a grave—and the "hard heart throb" that
sustains "life" will cease. Wing's protagonist greets this destiny with a word, abracadabra, that is both a magical charm and, in terms of the poem's structure,
a peculiar return to origins. The final line might begin with a Z ("zephyr-like")
but it ends in a sequence of A's. The character dreams of a do-over, but her bra-
vado and witchery do nothing to prevent her death. "Abracadabra," after all, is
her "last" word.

Andrew Feld's three-part lyric "Best and Only" (2004) ends in an abecedary
titled "19—: An Elegy" that represents an illuminating variation on the tale-of-
a-life plotline found in Pinsky's and Wing's poems. He purports to tell the story
not of an everyperson but of the twentieth century as a whole:

Apollo. Bebe Rebozo. Beatniks.
The Car. Counting backwards.
Cold Warriors. The century
I was born in. Disney. The Great
Depression and Anti-Depressants.
Everest. The Evil Empire. (59)

What could have been a monotonous list of dates and names turns out to be much more subjective and playful. The details that Feld mentions range from the vague and general ("The Car") to the precise ("Bebe Rebozo," a Florida businessman implicated in Watergate). He engages in word play ("Depression" / "Depressant"); employs repetition with variation (first "Apollo," the space craft, then "Counting backwards" to its launch); and occasionally throws in a reference so telegraphic that its import remains private and hermetic ("Everest"? The mountain has been there for millennia. Is Feld thinking about its first successful ascent in 1953? The late century vogue among "extreme" sports enthusiasts for scaling it? The high-profile ecological efforts to prevent its degradation?) By allowing himself the latitude to include one or more entries for any given letter, Feld also varies the pace of delivery. "Apollo," for example, is the only *A*, whereas the lyric serves up four *C*'s: "Car," "Counting," "Cold," and "century." Similarly, a single entry can range in size from a single word to a baggy multi-line list-within-a-list. *J* is represented by:

> Joke: how many right-wing
> neo-conservative, conspiracy theory,
> survivalist, NRA, MIA, VFW,
> free-market, anti-establishment
> radio-talk-show-host-loving loners
> does it take to screw in a lightbulb? (59)

Finally, Feld exploits unexpected juxtapositions for powerful effect. His "Joke," for instance, is followed immediately by a reference to the genocide committed by the Khmer Rouge regime in Cambodia: "The Killing Fields" (59). Alphabetically ordering terms in a series normally results in arbitrary relations of proximity, but there is nothing accidental about Feld's placing an act of mass murder in apposition to traits conventionally associated with far-right-wing politics in the United States. He gives an overview of the twentieth century, A to Z, as filtered through one person's openly biased point of view.

In fact, as one reads "19—: An Elegy," it becomes increasingly clear that there is less distance between Feld's tale-of-an-era and Pinsky's and Wing's stories-of-a-life than one might at first assume. The historical references are heavily weighted toward the postmodern era:

> Love Beads.
> Love-Ins. Love Canal. The Mall
> of America. Medical waste. Richard
> Nixon . . . *People*. Peaceniks.

Plutonium. Post-. Pop-. Plastic-wrapped
bundles of cocaine washing up
on Florida beaches. Queer theory. (59)

Over the course of the poem, we hear nothing about the Scopes Trial, the Lind-
bergh Baby, Sacco and Vanzetti, *Gone with the Wind* (1939), or, it turns out, any
other comparable historical landmarks from the decades before Feld was born
in 1961. (Significantly, the "Apollo" program, this poem's *A*, was announced by
John F. Kennedy in the summer of 1961, and the first test of the Saturn booster
rocket had occurred by year's end. In a sense, "Elegy 19—" is "born" at the same
time as its author.) This truly is *Feld's* century, the one that he remembers and
whose culture he has imbibed first hand. Or more accurately, this is American
history as he has absorbed it via movie and television screens. The poem ends:

Televangelists. Uncut. Unadulterated.
Vietnam. Watergate. World Wars. The X ray.
Yeah Yeah Yeah. Zen Koan. Ground Zero. (60)

As matters move toward completion (and *Z* nears), Feld's range of reference nar-
rows. First, we hear about TV ("Televangelists," obviously, but likewise "Yeah Yeah
Yeah," a tag line associated with the fast-talking New Yorkers in the blockbuster
sitcom *Seinfeld* [1989–98]).[11] We also encounter history in its most splashy epic
Oliver Stonesque guise ("Vietnam. Watergate. World Wars."). In this company,
the words "Uncut" and "Unadulterated" seem self-reflexive, that is, a way of
implying that this poetic unreeling of American cultural history has itself become a kind of film, one worthy of being described in the hyped language of
the movie trailer. The gnomic, penultimate statement "Zen Koan" proposes that
there is no clear moral or message that one can draw from this spectacle. In its
totality, it remains more of a puzzle than an object lesson. And then the climax:
"Ground Zero." The twentieth century's culmination turns out to be an act of
televised mass death, terrorist-flown airplanes crashing into the World Trade
Center. For decades people had feared that the century might end in an atomic
apocalypse, but this "Ground Zero" event is of a different order and kind. Its
shockwaves and fall out spread via the mass media further and faster than ever
possible via wind, water, and earth.

Feld's elegy is not a memorial to a neutral slice of time. It commemorates an
extended period of on-again off-again intimacy between a writer and popular
culture—a romance, the poem implies, perhaps on the rocks since the War on
Terror and the Iraq War took over the airwaves. Regardless, as presented here,
individuality seems to be achieved, as Henry Jenkins has argued about con-

temporary sociality more generally, through "selective" forays into "vast media culture whose treasures . . . can be mined and refined" (27). A person decides which images to watch, which events to recollect, and which virtual communities to join (Feld's sympathies appear inclined toward "Beatniks" and "Peaceniks" [60]). His poem arranges raw materials plucked from the incessant, engulfing global infostream into an implied narrative that might at first glance look objective but on further inspection proves to be highly personal, a litany that reshapes a "century" according to lived experience.[12]

What, though, is the point of partly occulting his lively interventionist mediaplay through recourse to an impersonal form, an alphabetized list of noun phrases? Shouldn't he write differently if he wants to critique broadcasting and the corporate monopoly over most mass media? This oblique variety of autobiography deliberately downplays autonomy in favor of noting (*sans* explanation, *sans* causality) the Parade of Great Events, in this case from the launch of Sputnik to 9/11. Feld's abecedary would appear to confirm Burt's argument that today's inorganic closed forms often serve as vehicles for dramatizing a poet's feelings of remove from the public sphere. Wing's does, too, insofar as she presents a picaresque life whose successes and then eventual decline and fall occur for no apparent reason. Could such an Edie Sedgwick-like self-destructive spiral be prevented? Is it just fate, what her "Star Chart" dictates? How can one build a plan for revolutionary action on the basis of such a superstitious outlook? Pinsky, finally, in pondering the human life cycle, provides little more than the language of empty proverbial wisdom ("any body can die") and aggregate description (math and science). He connects his reflections to no evaluative system, whether philosophical, theological, or ideological. Instead, he relies on a quickstep stride from *A* to *Z* to grant aptness and inevitability to a poem that might otherwise strike a reader as underdeveloped and insufficiently appreciative of the full diversity of possible life courses.

Burt's argument about the poet's exclusion from the *res publica* does not, however, fully account for the irreverent rowdy delight in formal ingenuity detectable in many contemporary abecedaries. Harryette Mullen's "Blah-Blah" (2002), for example, is a rambunctious celebration of what linguists call *reduplicative compounding*, a basic, early-learned means of word-coinage (Dienhart 3):

Ack-ack, aye-aye.
Baa baa, Baba, Bambam, Bebe, Berber, Bibi, blah-blah, Bobo, bonbon, booboo, Bora Bora, Boutros Boutros, bye-bye.
Caca, cancan, Cece, cha-cha, chichi, choo-choo, chop chop, chow chow, Coco, cocoa,

come come, cuckoo.
Dada, Dee Dee, Didi, dindin, dodo, doodoo, dumdum, Duran Duran.
Fifi, fifty-fifty, foofoo, froufrou. (12)

Mullen's poem shows that the same linguistic principles are at work across languages, not only in standard English but also in pidgin English ("chop chop"),
in Spanish ("Bebe"), French ("bonbon," "froufrou"), and non-Indo-European
tongues ("Berber," "Bora Bora"). It occurs in baby talk ("booboo," "Caca," "doodoo"), high art ("Dada," "Coco" Chanel), and pop culture ("Bambam" the son
of Barney Rubble, Bill the Cat's tag line "Ack-ack" from the comic strip *Bloom
County* [1980–89], and "Duran Duran" the British pop band, named for Jane
Fonda's nemesis in the film *Barbarella* [1968]). "Blah-Blah" exults in the jangling
variegated miscellany of words that a single generative device can produce. The
A-to-Z framing locates this fecundity in the *combinatoire* that is the alphabet,
that is, the primal units of written language. Crucially, this revelry in word-
smithery is detectable, too, in the earlier-discussed abecedaries, albeit in a more
subdued fashion, when, for instance, Pinsky evades the problem of "X," when
Wing splits apart the acronym "VFD" with a line break to satisfy the formal demands of both telestich and acrostic, and when Feld uses the word "Joke" as an
occasion for a humorous catalogue-within-a-catalogue.

Another recently published lyric, "The Wife of Bath's Tale" (2002) by Steve
McCaffery, suggests a way of reconciling the strict linearity of the abecedary
with the whimsy and ingenuity characteristic of its contemporary practitioners.[13] McCaffery's Chaucerian subject matter might superficially connect his
poem back to "La priere de nostre dame," but he evokes not Marian devotion
but more earthly love:

Because his name was Brian
I married him first, after Arthur, but before
Charles
Then Dave and Eric. (3)

The poem continues to itemize the speaker's husbands ("Harvey, Ian, John" are
"mere harbingers" of "Ken, Len, Mike," e.g.) until "Victor arrive[s] . . . announcing /
Walter's back and you should marry him":

I did
and then divorced him for Xerxes
(strange name for an Yvonne and that too
a pseudonym for Zelda). (3)

X again proves tricky. McCaffery repeats the "strange name" of "Xerxes" from *The New England Primer*. The last two lines are confusing, though. Is Xerxes supposed to be a peculiar name for a woman like the speaker—"an Yvonne," that is, a woman with a French name—to choose for a lover? Most of her earlier partners do have blandly British monikers. Alternatively, "Yvonne" and "Zelda" could refer not to the speaker but to her latest (and unprecedented) amour, a woman who also has the "strange name" (drag king name?) "Xerxes." In this retelling, does the Wife of Bath end up swearing off men for a lesbian beloved? It depends on how one chooses to interpret the "for" in the interjection "strange name for."

This dilemma is only one of many that the poem presents. Its title refers to the Wife of Bath's tale, yet it clearly draws inspiration not from the revisionist fairytale full of knights, ladies, and magic that the Wife of Bath recites but instead from the tale's egregiously inflated prologue. In that prologue, the Wife—whose name, by the way, is Alisoun (or Alys), certainly not "Yvonne" or "Zelda"—recounts her five marriages, dwelling especially on the most recent, to a man named Jankyn (not "John"). When we meet her, she is actively looking for husband number six, a quest that already puts her into an elite group, among such wedding-addicts as Henry VIII, Norman Mailer, and Elizabeth Taylor. Chaucer doesn't dare, despite making her a figure of verbal and physical excess, go on, as McCaffery does, to assign Alisoun twenty plus husbands. He hopes, after all, to maintain some degree of verisimilitude. McCaffery, in contrast, implies that the true tale that the Wife of Bath tells is her prologue's narrative of serial monogamy. A to Z, she goes from lover to lover, until there are no more, and only then the story ceases. She is almost more process than persona: a Lacanian would say that her husbands "all play substitutive roles in displacing the lost object(s) along a signifying chain of Desire" (Ragland-Sullivan 8). In other words, McCaffery is giving us a model for how desire functions psychologically. It impels people always onward, no act or accomplishment capable of fully and forever sating their cravings.

Significantly, McCaffery links this demonstration of mental processes to alphabetical order. Again as in Lacan, linguistic structure proves homologous to unconscious drives. One does not have to be steeped in French poststructuralism, however, to appreciate that the speaker's zest for marrying is tacitly compared to a poet's delight in word play. After mentioning "George," for example, the speaker interjects the perplexing statement "a mirrored disjunction" (3). She is tersely noting that the word *George* can be broken down into three parts, *GE - OR - GE*. The two *GE*'s mirror each other, and they are linked by the disjunctive conjunction *OR*. Words and letters are objects every bit as fascinating, and

worthy of close scrutiny, as objects of sexual desire. They are also equally dis-
cardable. On to the next!

McCaffery usefully poses the problem of the abecedary as involving language, poetic form, pleasure, and psychology. Moreover, what appears to be a
focus on mortality in other lyrics here takes the form of narrative closure. The
writer avidly fills in a predetermined form until the assigned end. The content
might veer toward the defeatist, especially as *Z* looms, but on another level of
meaning—that is, insofar as a text calls attention to itself as a work of artifice—
joy bubbles up. The poem, as it progresses, seems to be fulfilling, at least provisionally, desire in and for language.

Approached via "The Wife of Bath's Tale," the contemporary abecedary begins to seem a means of achieving a particular (and particularly energizing)
conjunction between language, temporality, form, and subject formation. It remains to be seen, of course, what that relationship is and how it is achieved.
McCaffery himself, in his essays on poetics collected in *North of Intention* (1986)
and *Prior to Meaning* (2001), tends to prefer Continental philosophy as a departure point, but there is no need to follow his lead here. There happens to be
a remarkably rigorous and self-reflexive meditation on the art of the abecedary
that can better serve our purposes: Hollis Frampton's experimental film *Zorns
Lemma* (1970).[14] Although *Zorns Lemma* is not a poem, its director did display
a life-long interest in verse. (In 1957 he moved to Washington, D.C., specifically
to study with Ezra Pound. For much of the year he was a near-daily visitor to
St. Elizabeth's Hospital, where the modernist was incarcerated at the time, and
he had a ringside seat as the poet wrote *Thrones* [1959], the next-to-last installment of the *Cantos* [1917–69]. Although Frampton eventually decided that his
talents were better suited to photography and cinema, Pound always remained
among his supreme touchstones for artistic accomplishment.) Moreover, as we
shall see, *Zorns Lemma* is itself an abecedary, if a rather odd, hybrid, and multimedia one. In trying to understand the appeal of the form, we have the luxury
of learning from one of its most inventive, visionary practitioners.

So Much Depends on X[15]

During the first part of *Zorns Lemma,* the screen remains black. Meanwhile,
the Canadian filmmaker Joyce Wieland reads aloud a text that we have already
encountered, the alphabet poem from *The New England Primer*. For a contemporary audience, this recitation can sound incomplete, since it skips the letters
I and *V*. (The seventeenth-century textbook valiantly if perversely tries to respect classical Latin precedent, in which *I* and *J* were represented by one letter, as

were *U* and *V*. One can only imagine how teachers explained this orthographical peculiarity to students.) In case anyone misses this fact, the film then runs silently through the abridged twenty-four-letter alphabet, one Roman square capital at a time, each held for a second. This run-through sets the pattern for what now ensues. Words start appearing in alphabetical order. Most are filmed somewhere in lower Manhattan using a hand-held camera, usually as they appear on a sign or advertisement. The opening cycle begins:

a
baby
cabinet
daily
each
fabric
gain
hack
I
kangaroo
labor[16]

Although the first three words here—"a baby cabinet"—could conceivably begin a sentence—as could the next three, "daily each fabric"—outwardly unrelated words nonetheless continue to arrive at precise short intervals, and it quickly becomes impossible to discern any ordering principle beyond the alphabet itself. After reaching *Z*, a second of blackness ensues, and then the procession of words starts over, back at *A*. "[A]bbey back cable dairy eagle." For the next forty-seven minutes, *Zorns Lemma* continues in this vein. "[A]ble bag calf . . . about baggage calorie . . . abuse bail camel . . . accent baker camp."

The manner of proceeding does gradually alter. During the fourth iteration, Frampton begins to substitute short film segments for particular letters. *X* is the first to go. It is replaced by a shot of a blazing bonfire. This twist is both unexpected and apt. Frampton had already tried "X," "x-ray," and "xylene"; instead of resorting to "Xerxes," "xanthum," or other clunky options, he, like Pinsky and Wing, treats *X* as a variable, a placeholder to which one can assign an entirely new value. After several further cycles to accustom viewers to "bonfire" instead of *X*, *Z* is next to fall away. In its place one starts seeing waves break on a beach. *Y* later gives way to a tracking shot of a field of waving grasses; then steam pouring from a vent replaces *Q*.

Taken individually, these first substitutions appear arbitrary. Nothing intrinsically links *Z* with the ocean or *Y* with plants. Frampton pointedly avoids devices such as sound-linkage (*Z* could have become a man snoring) and puns (*Y* could be a woman scratching her head) that would suggest connections between the images and the letters. True, in the manner of Arthur Rimbaud's "Voyelles" (1870–71) or Paul Valéry's *Alphabet* (1999), he could be sharing with the audience associations or symbols that are purely private and subjective. "When I think of the letter *Q*, I imagine white clouds billowing from a tenement's roof!" That option loses plausibility, though, when, after the fourth substitution, a viewer realizes that there has been a covert motivating principle at work. Into one list of fundamental terms—the alphabet—Frampton has introduced a second comparably primal set—the four Empedoclean elements of fire, water, earth, and air (Weiss 125–26). The only relationship that the film proposes between, say, *X* and flame is accidental and procedural. Frampton dumps four letters rarely used in English in initial position and replaces them with a four-element (literally!) substitution set.

In the process, of course, the film also implicitly suggests an analogy between the letters of the alphabet and the building blocks of creation. The emphasis, though, falls less on the sacredness of the poet's (or a divinity's) imagination than, as in Mullen, on the alphabet's infinite combinatory potential. In the film, one runs through all the letters (or their designated substitutes), beginning to end, over and over, as if there was something marvelously gratifying in that ambit, akin to hitting home run after home run. In part, this circuit is rewarding because the alphabet contains *in posse* the basis for any and all texts that one might choose to write, from, say, *Gorboduc* (1565) to *Valley of the Dolls* (1966). This alphabet-game also provides the pleasures of what Allen Weiss has called *enumeration*, the serial listing of all elements in a set. Enumeration, Weiss argues, is a conservative operation. It reconfirms the existence of "a central term" by establishing the presence of its "ancillary terms" (121). *A* to *Z*, every letter touched in turn, every element in order: once that's verified, God's in his heaven, all's right with the world. Unsurprisingly, at least two authors—Louis Aragon and Kurt Schwitters—have composed poems that consist solely of a list of the letters of the alphabet.[17] They dare anyone else to find a more concise summary statement of a poet's vocational resources.

Zorns Lemma, though, does not wholly endorse enumeration. As Weiss points out, in the film enumeration exists in tension with a second dynamic, *accumulation*. The process of substitution does not cease after fire, water, earth, and air have been introduced. At regular intervals, new substitutions occur. Some of these function as meta-commentary. *A*, for example, is replaced by a close up of hands interacting with a book. Others appear utterly random, that is, lacking in "any necessary formal or material connection" between themselves (Weiss 121). *E* becomes a woman speaking silently, *F* a single tree seen at a distance, *H* a man walking through city streets, *I-J* meat falling from a meat grinder, *K* a man painting a wall, *O* a man dribbling a basketball, *U-V* hands peeling an orange, *W* a wobbly urban night scene, and so forth. Such a chance accumulation of associations is "disjunctive," according to Weiss. It tends toward the "de-totalizing destruction of taxonomia" (121). In other words, it resists any efforts to discover generally shared qualities or any other organizational principles underlying the entire list.

Once events, images, and vignettes have replaced the twenty-four letters, the second part of *Zorns Lemma* comes to an end. In a final twelve-minute sequence, a man, woman, and dog walk deeper and deeper into a landscape until they become lost to view. Meanwhile, six women read aloud an English translation of a mystical text by Robert Grosseteste, Bishop of Lincoln (1168–1253), that "celebrate[s] light as the shaping agent of form" (Michelson, "About Snow" 116). The reading is oddly difficult to understand, however. Each of the six women reads only a single word. They do so in a designated order, and they each are allotted precisely one second. Sometimes they have to rush to fit long words into that interval. Other times they leave a slight but awkward pause before the next person speaks. As a consequence of these rules, the choral reading entirely lacks intonational curves, measured pauses, changes in pacing, and other cues that conventionally signal divisions between clauses, sentences, or items within catalogues. One tends to hear not complete thoughts but individual words that are frequently repeated such as "light," "form," "matter." If the film begins with a reminder of the expulsion from Eden—"In *Adam's* Fall / We Sinned All"—and an invitation to overcome sin through diligent reading—"Thy Life to Mend / This *Book* Attend"—it now ends with a modern-day couple, a new Adam and new Eve, vanishing into a flood of white light, accompanied by a spoken rondo strangely reminiscent of Gertrude Stein's *Lucy Church Amiably* (1930) and *Four Saints in Three Acts* (1934). Not only is alphabet-study associated with erotic coupling, as in McCaffery's "The Wife of Bath's Tale," but it also proves to be the route back to paradise.

What explains—or better yet, justifies—this conclusion? How might alphabetizing found texts and playing substitution-games grant access to heaven-on-earth? Annette Michelson has argued that what makes Frampton's work unique is a contradiction between his "analytic" impulses, derived from such "modernist" precursors as Pound, Stein, and Charles Olson, and a "lyric," even "idealist," side that can find the "scientific method" and "theor[ies] of knowledge" constraining to the point of suffocation ("About Snow" 116). He tries to resolve this contradiction by drawing on two sources. First, he looks to the Second Viennese School of musical composition (Alban Berg, Arnold Schönberg, Anton Webern), men whose "constraints of serial composition" satisfy his need for art that proceeds logically and that rewards patient sustained analysis.[18] Paradoxically, he also feels attracted to the "aesthetic of chance" associated with John Cage, Yoko Ono, and Fluxus, figures whose compositional methods promise liberation from tradition and escape from the ossification of any set of rules, even self-imposed ones ("Frampton's Sieve" 160). In other words, Frampton dreams of combining enumeration (serial procedures) and accumulation (random accretion).

Zorns Lemma fulfills this ambition brilliantly, Michelson contends, because of Frampton's decision to focus on the alphabet. It provides an order that is "unmotivated but not arbitrary." That is, no absolute law governs why C must follow B and precede D. The only explanation is "general agreement and acceptance" (162). Hence, the words Frampton chooses to represent each letter can appear in any sequence, random or intentional, without broken taboos offending a viewer. (Undergraduates might laugh mid-way through the film when L turns up as "limp" and M as "member," but they do not show anger at "lee massage," "lime mead," "loud moderate," or "lotus model." The same students, though, typically react negatively when confronted by similarly peculiar juxtapositions in syntactically adventurous works such as Gertrude Stein's "Pink Melon Joy": "Leaning. / Maintaining maintaining checkers. / I left a leaf and I meant it" [*Stein Reader* 281].) Frampton maximizes his opportunities for arbitrary word-selection while nonetheless also clearly adhering to rigorous compositional rules. Indeed, he shows that, as long as it happens gradually and predictably, viewers will not resist if the slots occupied by the letters in alphabetical order are entirely given over to nonlexical material. The wheels still turn, the cogs still mesh, whether an image of the ocean or the word *zest* is doing the work of Z. Anything can follow anything, as long as the materials continue to loop predictably, over and over, and as long as the number of elements in the set does not change.

The third and final part of *Zorns Lemma* generalizes this compositional principle by changing the number of elements from twenty-four (the letters of the Latin alphabet) to six (the number of voices intoning the text by Grosseteste). Frampton also shows how an uninflected reading of one word at time, each occupying uniform time intervals, can render those words strangely interchangeable. An auditor easily loses track of the syntax that links the words. The linguist Roman Jakobson would describe this phenomenon as a weakening of the axis of combination, that is, the rules governing how words ought to be assembled. There is a corresponding increase of emphasis on what he calls the axis of selection, the "repository of all possible constituent parts" for a "given utterance" (61). By attenuating the ties between terms in a series one perceptibly increases the scope and diversity of what can be included in that series.

Maximal freedom of choice and strict adherence to order: the abecedary provides Frampton with a neat formal solution to his paradoxical wish to embrace both restraint and freedom simultaneously. It is no wonder, then, as Michelson comments, that the mood of *Zorns Lemma* goes beyond ludic to positively "euphoric." Not only does "Frampton's adoption of the alphabet as an ordering form" participate in the "more generally installed predilection for the systemic" discernible in minimalist sculpture, structural cinema, conceptual art, and a range of other artistic practices in the 1960s and '70s. He demonstrates, at the height of the anti–Vietnam War movement, that an artist's "confidence in the . . . generative power of the system" did not also automatically imply admiration for soulless totalities, socioeconomic or otherwise ("Frampton's Sieve" 162). One could take a stand both for rule-governed art and for untrammeled personal liberty. The ecstatic and religious rhetoric in *Zorns Lemma* indexes the bliss of finding an imaginative resolution to an urgent art-historical dilemma.

The film, however, should not be seen as providing a window only on a narrow slice of time. Today's abecedaries exhibit a comparable intoxicated self-satisfaction as the conclusion of *Zorns Lemma*; moreover, the recurrence of the form linked with a similar tone suggests that recent abecedaries might also be attempting to harmonize impulses toward both constraint and liberty. Finally, Frampton's film helps one appreciate abecedaries as a paradigm for other substitutional forms that provide occasion for both enumeration and accumulation. Here is an orderly predictable procession of containers: fill them as you will.

There have been some changes, of course. Contemporary poets appear to be more concerned than Frampton with narrating lives, whether actual or fictional, whether one's own or someone else's. In particular, self-fashioning seems to be a newly urgent concern. The lyric has, of course, long been a privileged genre for asserting, exploring, and critiquing self-expression. Today, though, expression is less a problem than what one might call the interface between person and world, more specifically, between twenty-first century individuals and the media-saturated, hybrid real-and-virtual spaces they must navigate on a daily basis. What patterns, what structures, what rules, if any, can guide one through this swiftly changing labyrinth? In *Globalization* (1998), Zygmunt Bauman has written eloquently about the loss of ontological security that the present-day global economy has induced. Money and credit travel with quicksilver alacrity around the world. States can do little more than impede the restless mass movement of jobs, corporations, technology, and information that occur in response to the demands of international capital.

An abecedary offers an imaginary solution to this situation. On the one hand, it provides a clear invariable structure. Moreover, it reassuringly derives that structure from alphabetic order, something literate English speakers have known since their earliest years of education. Thank goodness: the building blocks of language have not changed! On the other hand, the abecedary accommodates unbounded possibility. Almost anything whatsoever can be chosen to fill in the blanks. The fact that the form does not prescribe a rhyme scheme or a meter is a plus, too. The model of subjectivity it proposes is not that of the rhetor, storyteller, or bard. Writers do not have to recite the tale of a tribe, channel shamanic energies, or genuflect to the Mind of Europe. Success requires balancing fixity and flows. Allusions to Scripture? Echoes of Chaucer? Permissible, laudable even, but unnecessary. The fact is—to round back to Pinsky—"any body can die" any time, and the proper measure of a life is how creatively and persuasively one fills the X between the A of birth and the Z of death.

Other popular contemporary fixed forms work similarly. The sestina, too, prescribes an itinerary that is strict and invariable (a permutational blueprint called *retrogradatio cruciata* that determines the order of the end words in a given stanza) while also permitting a poet a remarkable degree of latitude in penning the rest of the poem. Ghazals, pantoums, and palindromes are exercises in endurance. How long can a poet sustain the necessary repetitions while also continuing to come up with new material? (The answer is: a long time. Peter Gizzi's palindrome "Vincent, Homesick for the Land of Pictures" [2007] contains one hundred fifty four lines [*Outernationale* 47–53].) The model of the self that this species of writing proposes is not exactly the monadic, autonomous bourgeois ego, as critiqued by Theodor Adorno and other Frankfurt School thinkers. Instead, these poems envision a protean self that thrives despite limited agency. Moreover, instead of irritably grasping after totality—to misquote Keats—these poets work on a smaller scale by productively working with and against the proximate manifestations of global capitalism. Back in 1991, Fredric Jameson argued that postmodern poetry is characterized by "a peculiar kind of euphoria" that is "free-floating and impersonal" (*Postmodernism* 16), and he explained it as a new modality of the sublime, a recognition of the impossibility of ever representing "the whole world system of a present-day multinational capitalism" (37). Today's writing, less abject and benumbed, exhibits a different, more personalized bliss that stems from an affirmation of one's own creative capacities. That stance has been won at a cost. When favoring abecedaries and related closed forms, poets no longer confront totality directly; they substitute for that unmasterable whole an enumerable immutable set of rules that provide a pretext for solacing virtuosic displays of craft.

Stephen Burt claims that today's writers feel cut off from politics. It would be more accurate to say that they appear cut off from a living tradition. Alan Liu has described this situation as the loss of "the history that makes us *us*." He argues that the "late-capitalist and democratic world system" has changed the "ethos—the generalizeable character, posture, or attitude—of the individuals" in the United States and other first-world nations who work directly with the "technologies and media produced by postindustrialism." In the past, such individuals defined themselves via "folk, class, gender, racial, ethnic, religious, and other historical identities," that is, via categories that connected them with past communities and (sub)cultures. In the present, however, corporations (including the ever-more-corporatized American university system) preach the obsolescence of these categories. People are progressive and hip, we are told, if they participate in a multimedia, technophilic youth culture that is untroubled in its full-spectrum diversity. We "become the people of the cutting-edge new," an amorphous identity that requires a constant search for novelty as a replacement for the rootedness that we have lost. In this manner, global corporations defuse old conflicts and create a harmonious, malleable work force. History ceases to be "foundational" and becomes no more than a resource for further inventive cultural production (4–5).

Like the therapeutic model of the self that informs much 1960s and '70s confessional poetry, this "cool" authorial self-presentation is likely to find few intellectual defenders. Instead of laying bare or seeking redress for economic injustice, poets who prefer to write ghazals, palindromes, sestinas, and other preset forms offer a dream of graceful mastery of the given world. Nevertheless, whatever its limitations, this mode of self-fashioning has served any number of poets, especially young poets, as a founding fiction. A balance between order and chaos has been struck that *feels* new to them and that consequently serves as the occasion for new writing. Will such verse age well? As with any perceived period style, its prominence is easily overestimated, so too its value. It is surely significant, though, that abecedaries and comparable poetic genres are currently being written across poetic camps, by everyone from Language Poets to Poets Laureate. And this was not the case twenty years ago.

Furthermore, knowing the emotions and assumptions often associated with predetermined forms enables a critic to identify and appreciate significant deviations within today's poetry world. Kenneth Goldsmith, for instance, is a writer with close ties to Christian Bök, a poet whose *Eunoia*, as we saw at the beginning of this chapter, typifies the buoyancy that suffuses much contemporary writing that obeys strict generative constraints. Altogether different, however, is Goldsmith's *Day* (2003), which reproduces in book form the complete text of the late edition of the *New York Times* from Friday, 1 September 2000. (A few changes have been made: the book employs one uniform font throughout and omits all photographs, drawings, and other visual effects.) Opening *Day*, one witnesses the uncanny return of a long ago day's news under a new, malapropos heading, verse. The text's effects derive from this category error, that is, the gap between readers' expectations regarding "poetry" and the outlandish oddities served up instead.

A number of scholars have explored the ramifications of Goldsmith's appropriation and recontextualization of a very large block of data.[19] For present purposes, it is sufficient to note that, if a reader is familiar with the abecedary-vogue of the past decade, parts of *Day* read like demonic undoings of what the form elsewhere achieves. Instead of late capitalism remaining off stage, too amorphous, immense, and all encompassing to confront directly, here it is bureaucratically subdivided and itemized:

Advertising Column C6
American Stock Exch. C15
Company News C4
Currency Markets C4
Dividend News C9
Foreign Exchange C12
Foreign Stocks C12
Futures Markets C6
Highs and Lows C9
International News C4 (196)

Instead of the actions of corporations remaining secretive and offstage, they are blandly overt. A "COMPANY INDEX" helpfully informs readers where to look in *Day* to locate them:

A&E E23
Advanced Micro Devices C6
AES C4
Aliani C17
Amazon.com C2 . . . .
B Com3 Group C6
Bayer C6 . . . .
Carrefour C4
CD Warehouse C2 . . . .
Dell Computer C6 (208)

Then come the interminable but oh-so-carefully alphabetized stock quotes, options prices, and other numerical tabulations, which begin with the NYSE's AAR and end hundreds of pages later with the mutual fund Yacktman (239–430). If these abecedaries *manqué* convey any affect, it is tedium, or perhaps an intermittent amazement that anyone would devote precious time and labor to preserving such ephemera. Goldsmith, after all, retypes a mass of text—over many, many days—that a laser could etch onto a CD-R in seconds. The truth of the computer age, as *Day* reveals it, concerns the near-instantaneous storage, transmission, and manipulation of huge amounts of raw information. In contrast, merely human activity can look meager, marginal, and anachronistic. Goldsmith excludes creativity from the execution of art in an impossible quest to mimic the efficiency, thoroughness, and versatility of a machine. If other poets seek empowering ways of living *with* computers, Goldsmith aspires to *become* one. Is such a desire utopian? Dystopian? Is it even practical? Regardless, it is somehow both stirring and sad to imagine his attempting to reproduce, via his own fingers and sweat, simple word processor functions such as "cut and paste," "change font," and "print to printer."

Judged against the backdrop of today's substitutional poetics, *Day* can look like a perverse outlier. It provokes—even infuriates—by conflating data entry and writing a poem. This boundary blurring is disconcerting, since poets generally want to see their work as culturally privileged. But both versecraft and data entry are forms of knowledge work. Both generate texts that validate and advance an individual's vocation. The care and rigor with which Goldsmith produced *Day* approximates the rule-bound aspect of an abecedary, but the text utterly declines to fulfill the *rest* of the abecedary-agenda. It does not mystify craft, creativity, and technique. As a consequence, it courts dismissal as antipoetry. Since its publication, I've had everyone from students to peer reviewers react with horror on finding Goldsmith discussed alongside "real" poets—ones, that is, whose more "authentic" writings showcase what they "ought," namely, satisfying (and marketable) virtues such as inventiveness and technical accomplishment.

In comparison, many self-styled avant-garde works of the last half-century have lost shock value and have instead begun to look prescient. When, for instance, Lyn Hejinian published the second edition of *My Life* in 1987, the idea of writing forty-five chapters, each forty-five sentences long, still sounded like a bold, defiant gesture. Instead of employing variable-count organic free verse in the manner of prize-winning high-profile poets such as Louise Glück and Jorie Graham, she chose to write an *autobiographia literaria* in an estranging mechanistic form. Two decades later, her modular structure appears commonsensical. Forty-five is as good a number to pick as twenty-six or twelve or six. That decision made, the fun of blank filling can begin.

As critics come to understand what kinds of verse are being written across the full spectrum of American poetries in the first decade of the twenty first century, they will have to modify their assumptions about what constitutes a central poet who counts as oppositional and what an average lyric looks like. When I entered graduate school in the mid-1990s, *workshop poem* was a dismissive term for short, free verse, first-person lyrics centering on moments of epiphanic insight. In the last few years, I have begun hearing the same label, accompanied by the same sneer, directed instead at sestinas, ghazals, and abecedaries. The essentials of the art form, the rudiments a novice poet is presumed to have mastered, are rapidly shifting. Scholars will have to keep up. *X* marks the spot. How to fill it in?

Notes

Preface

1. See Sara Ahmed, *Queer Phenomenology: Orientations, Objects, Others* (Durham, NC: Duke UP, 2006); Rita Felski, *The Uses of Literature* (Oxford, UK: Blackwell, 2008); Mark B. N. Hansen, *New Philosophy for New Media* (Cambridge, MA: MIT P, 2006); Caroline A. Jones, *Eyesight Alone: Clement Greenberg and the Bureaucratization of the Senses* (Chicago: U of Chicago P, 2008); Erin Manning, *Relationscapes: Movement, Art, Philosophy* (Cambridge, MA: MIT P, 2009); and Malin Wahlberg, *Documentary Time: Film and Phenomenology* (Minneapolis: U of Minnesota P, 2008).

2. See, e.g., Couser, Kleege, and Finger. They discuss specifically the value of life writing as a means of communicating the lived experience of "somatic variation" (Couser 604).

Chapter 1

1. Readers familiar only with MacLeish's high modernist writings of the 1920s—especially his best known poem, "Ars Poetica" (1926), with its epigrammatic conclusion "A poem should not mean / But be"—might find this review rather baffling. For MacLeish's drastic changes of opinion in the 1930s, see Harrington 35–36, 50, and 84. See also Kalaidjian 160–61. Only in December 1935 did the *New Masses* and the *Daily Worker* consent to begin publishing his work (Nelson, *Repression* 163).

2. For particularly forceful examples, see Marjorie Perloff's articles "Janus-Faced Blockbuster" (esp. 206 and 208–10) and "Barbed Wire Entanglements" (esp. 165–71).

3. For Nelson on Hughes's "Christ in Alabama," see *Revolutionary* 68–75. For Thurston on Rolfe's "First Love," see 82–85, esp. 85 for an extended discussion of both metrics and intertextual allusions (to W. B. Yeats).

4. For Sandburg's appearance on the cover of the 21 February 1938 issue of *Life*, see Niven 519. For his appearance on the cover of the 4 December 1939 cover of *Time*, see 533. For Bette Davis and the Broadway production *The World of Carl Sandburg*, see 681 and 685. For Roosevelt, see 495. For Truman, see 562. For Stevenson, see 621–22. For Kennedy, see 687.

5. These statistics are taken from the National Park Service web site "Carl Sandburg Home National Historic Site (NPS)—Park Facts" <http://www.nps.gov/carl/pphtml/facts.hmtl>. Last accessed 28 Dec. 2002.

6. For samples of the few substantial articles on Sandburg published in the last twenty years, see Kurt Dittmar, "Carl Sandburg: Chicago," *Amerikanische Lyrik: Perspektiven und Interpretationen* (Berlin: Schmidt, 1987), 223–39; C. K. Doreski, "From News to History: Robert Abbott and Carl Sandburg Read the 1919 Chicago Riot," *African-American Review* 26.4 (Winter 1992): 637–50; Charles Kostelnick, "Sandburg, Futurism, and the Aesthetics of Urban Dynamism," *American Poetry* no. 8 (Fall 1990): 46–56; John Marsh, "A Lost Work of Art: The Arts and Crafts Movement in Carl Sandburg's Chicago Poems," *American Literature* 79.3 (Sept. 2007): 527–551; Charles Molesworth, "Moore's 'New York' and Sandburg's 'Chicago': How Modern Can a City Be?" *William Carlos Williams Review* 14.1 (Spring 1988): 33–38; Adrian Oktenberg, "From the Bottom Up: Three Radicals of the Thirties," *A Gift of Tongues: Critical Challenges in Contemporary American Poetry*, eds. Marie Harris and Kathleen Aguero (Athens: U of Georgia P, 1987): 83–111; and Mark Van Wienen, "Taming the Socialist: Carl Sandburg's *Chicago Poems* and Its Critics," *American Literature* 63.1 (March 1991): 89–103.

7. See Thurston 7–9 for an account of the "refrain that political poetry equals bad poetry" in American criticism from the later 1930s onward.

8. See Harrington 36–40 for a concise statement of Tate's and Ransom's arguments against politicized verse.

9. See Shulman 305n1 for a list of representative examples of Cold War attacks on propaganda masquerading as art, including texts by Clement Greenberg, Philip Rahv, Alfred Kazin, Lionel Trilling, and Leslie Fiedler.

10. Between 1990 and his death in 2008 Hatlen wrote articles on such poets as H.D., Edward Dorn, Robert Duncan, Rachel Blau DuPlessis, Denise Levertov, Charles Olson, George Oppen, Ezra Pound, Joan Retallack, Charles Reznikoff, Wallace Stevens, William Carlos Williams, and Louis Zukofsky.

11. See Perkins 330ff for an overview of the history of the Imagist movement from its founding in 1912 through Amy Lowell's stewardship in the late 1910s and 1920s. He gives the Three Principles of Imagism—of which this was the second—together with their first printed form as well as their initial publication history.

12. My personal copy is dated February 1937 and listed as the third printing. *The People, Yes* was sent to reviewers in August 1936 (*Letters* 342).

13. When reading excerpts from *The People, Yes*, he used "Proverbs" as a collective title for passages written in freestanding, *non sequitur* sentences. See, for example, the recording *The People, Yes!* (Caedmon DL 5135, c.1949).

14. In making this assertion, I am thinking of Georg Lukács's essay "What Is Orthodox Marxism?" Lukács argues that the proletariat will only become conscious of its "class situation" once "the whole of society is understood" (*History* 20). That understanding takes the form of "that *relation to totality* (to the whole of society seen as a process), through which every aspect of the struggle acquires its revolutionary significance." This "relation to totality," once brought to consciousness, raises to the level of the "real" the proletariat's unique role as both object and subject of history, that is, as at once a product of economic development *and* the engine driving that development (22; his emphasis). Sandburg would have had no access to Lukács's writings, and he would never have expressed himself in these terms, but I would argue that his depiction of United States society is, in several fundamentals, consonant with Lukács's "orthodox Marxism." Sandburg portrays a proletariat ("the people") both shaped by and shaping a capitalist order (a totality) that has arisen in recent centuries and that, should the people act, will also pass away in the future (in short, Sandburg does not reify the totality).

15. Although there is not space to go into it here, there are other important aspects of *The People, Yes* that are characteristic of the Popular Front. Sandburg's exaltation of "the people" instead of "the proletariat," as well as his focus on the United States instead of the Soviet Union, run directly counter to official CPUSA doctrine during the preceding, so-called "Third Phase" years (1928–1934). See Shulman 4–6, 14–15. See also Kalaidjian 125–26.

16. Compare Thurston's argument here to Cary Nelson's brief comments on Sandburg's *Chicago Poems*: "he aimed in part to articulate and humanize certain socially constituted subject positions, to depict types not individuals. In so doing, he would make these types available to a popular audience, not so they could be regarded with self-congratulatory empathy but so they could be reoccupied with a newly politicized self-awareness" (*Repression* 68–69).

17. See Solomon 404–12 for an analysis of Dahlberg's use of "abjection" in *From Flushing to Calvary* to counter the encroachment of the culture industry on (white) male subjectivity in the 1930s. See Pérez 159–63 for an argument that *Lawd Today!* anticipates contemporary cultural criticism in its insistence that "media culture pervade[s] the lives of urban Americans at every level" (159). See Barnard 139ff for an investigation of Nathanael West's "(potentially) parodic citation" (142), "ironic shiftiness" (155), and other strategic responses to the commodification of mass culture. For *Day of the Locust* in particular, see chapter 7 (166–87).

18. See Shulman 12–22 for a quick overview of the role of the Communist Party in American intellectual life on the left during the 1930s, as well as for its depen-

dency on Moscow. Shulman rightly emphasizes the diversity, dissension, and vitality in this milieu, but he also illustrates the preeminence of the Soviet influence over any possible Western Marxist alternative, such as the Frankfurt School.

Chapter 2

The two drawings from "West Wind" are reproduced here from *Collected Poems* (2003), by Tom Raworth, by permission of the publisher, Carcanet Press Limited.

1. By labeling Raworth's early verse "the purest product of sixties culture to appear in Britain," Middleton does not intend to group it with the "peripheral symptoms" of the sixties such as "Eastern styles," "anti-utilitarianism of dress and hair," and "the use of drugs for visions." Raworth's early writing, he argues, remains valuable because it undertakes "one of the most intensive questionings of what might constitute an English poetry produced since the brief ascendancy of high modernism" ("Silent Critique" 14–15).

2. In this essay, solely for convenience's sake, I use "British" to refer to England, Wales, Scotland, and Northern Ireland. I do not intend to include the Republic of Ireland. This definition is arbitrary, and I recognize that at times my usage of "British" will elide differences among the United Kingdom's constituent nations.

3. There are, of course, exceptions to these generalizations. See Tuma, *Fishing* 33ff for the more detailed, cautious version of this argument, which takes into account such poet-critics as Donald Davie and Eric Mottram. It is worth noting that avant-garde leaning periodicals such as *Angel Exhaust, fragmente* [sic], *Jacket*, and *Parataxis* have provided venues for poets and critics to challenge the old consensus about postwar verse. Anthologies, too, have proved a useful vehicle in calling attention to alternative verse practices. See *Floating Capital: New Poets from London*, ed. Adrian Clarke and Robert Sheppard (Elmwood, CT: Potes and Poets P, 1991); *New British Poetries*, ed. Robert Hampson and Peter Barry (Manchester: Manchester UP, 1993); *Conductors of Chaos: A Poetry Anthology*, ed. Iain Sinclair (London: Picador, 1996); *Out of Everywhere: Linguistically Innovative Poetry by Women in North America & the UK*, ed. Maggie O'Sullivan (London: Reality Street, 1996); and *Other: British and Irish Poetry Since 1970*, ed. Richard Caddell and Peter Quartermain (Hanover, NH: Wesleyan UP, 1999).

4. For a few of the partial academic overviews of the expanded canon of contemporary British poetry that were available when this essay was written, see Acheson and Huk; Tuma, *Fishing*; the "Pocket Epics" special issue of *The Yale Journal of Criticism* 13.1 (2000); and the two-issue spotlight on contemporary British poetry in the *Cambridge Quarterly* 31.1–2 (2002). Things are changing swiftly, however. One recent publication—*A Concise Companion to Postwar British and Irish Poetry*, ed. Nigel Alderman and C. D. Blaton (Oxford, UK: Blackwell, 2009)—attempts precisely the kind of synthetic survey heretofore lacking.

5. Despite Raworth's reputation as one of the most important avant-gardists

in postwar Britain, the secondary literature on his work remains meager. See Dorward, "Tom" 270–75 for a recent, detailed, comprehensive bibliography. The few readily available academic studies include Barrell; Dietz; Sheppard, "Poetics"; and Ward. The May 2003 special issue of the Canadian journal *The Gig* titled "Removed for Further Study: The Poetry of Tom Raworth" has decisively advanced Raworth criticism. In this special issue see esp. Perril and Sheppard, "Whose," for the two preliminary statements on Raworth and British political history that inspired this chapter in my book.

6. The decline of the British welfare state is only one of many possible, relevant historical narratives. Others—decolonization, devolution, immigration, little englandism, and transatlanticism—should also be (and in many cases have been) taken into account. See Acheson and Huk; Craig; Hitchcock; Huk, "In AnOther's Pocket"; Huk, *Assembling Alternatives*; McHale; Ramazani; and Tuma, *Fishing*.

7. There is also the odd manner in which "blackness" is an attribute projected on Thatcher in a poem written so soon after the Brixton and Toxtheth Riots (1981). This is probably not a case of oversight. "West Wind" is aware of British racial politics. At one point, it satirizes the market logic by which racial difference loses its socio-historical specificities (its diverse narratives of colonization and immigration) and becomes instead a selling point, a vague but glowing promise of community despite and across boundaries: "an advertisement / of how happy they are / showed / 'a west indian or asian'" (*CP* 369–70). Associating Thatcher with "blackness," Raworth might intend to invert British racial rhetoric and ascribe to the Conservatives precisely the racist stereotypes that they covertly or overtly ascribed to black British subjects in the era of the infamous "sus laws," that is, laws that permitted the Metropolitan Police to stop and search people (all too often young men of color) based on suspicion alone.

8. For important but partial exceptions, see Barrell 391–92; Dietz 7 and 9; and Sheppard, "Poetics" 86. See, too, Dorward, "On Raworth's Sonnets," for an article that, while not taking up the topic of coherence *per se*, nonetheless concentrates on presenting recurrent formal devices and unifying themes in Raworth's long poem "Sentenced to Death" (1987).

9. See Barrell 398–99 and 401; Davidson 217; Dietz 13; Munton 249; Perloff 137; Retallack 255; Skinner 175–76; Tuma, "Collaborating" 210; Tuma, *Fishing* 238; and Wilkinson 157.

10. See Tuma, *Fishing* 48–50 for an overview of NAP influence on British poetry, especially its value as an "alternative to the withered canons of the neo-Georgian lyric as they were being extended and ironized by the Movement." See also 52–59 for an overview of the so-called "British Poetry Revival" (1960–1975), that is, the institutions, publication outlets, and literary politics that provide the immediate historical background to the NAP's British reception.

11. For more information about these schools of poetry, see Michael Davidson,

The San Francisco Renaissance: Poetics and Community at Mid-Century (New York: Cambridge UP, 1989); Martin Duberman, *Black Mountain: An Exploration in Community* (New York: Dutton, 1972); Alan Golding, "The New American Poetry Revisited, Again," *Contemporary Literature* 39.2 (Summer 1998): 180–211; Daniel Kane, *All Poets Welcome: The Lower East Side Poetry Scene in the 1960s* (Berkeley: U of California P, 2003); Libbie Rifkin, *Career Moves: Olson, Creeley, Zukofsky, Berrigan, and the American Avant-Garde* (Madison: U of Wisconsin P, 2000); and Geoff Ward, *Statutes of Liberty: The New York School of Poets* (Basingstoke: Macmillan, 1993). Also useful as introductions are the following studies of individual figures: Tom Clark, *Charles Olson: The Allegory of a Poet's Life* (New York: Norton, 1991); Lew Ellingham and Kevin Killian, *Poet Be Like God: Jack Spicer and the San Francisco Renaissance* (Hanover, NH: Wesleyan UP, 1998); and Marjorie Perloff, *Frank O'Hara: Poet Among Painters* (Chicago: U of Chicago P, 1998).

12. A clarification is in order: "unapologetically" indebted to NAP models does not mean exclusively indebted to them. He was also, for example, deeply invested in the work of selected British contemporaries. See *CP* 38 ("Going Away Poem for Lee Harwood") and *CP* 103 (the poem "7/8 of the Real," dedicated to Christopher Middleton). While at Goliard Press Raworth accepted for publication two landmark volumes of postwar British verse, J.H. Prynne's *Kitchen Poems* (1968) and Elaine Feinstein's *In a Green Eye* (1966).

13. For Berrigan, see *CP* 79 and 195–96; Ward 19 and 24–25; Edwards 42–43; and Sheppard, 202n1. For Creeley, see Middleton, "Silent Critique" 11–12 and 24–27. For O'Hara, see *CP* 76–77; Middleton, "Silent Critique" 20. For Koch, see *CP* 76 and 89; Middleton, "Silent Critique" 11, 24–25 and 27. For Padgett, see *CP* 36.

14. See Dietz 14 for an important elaboration of this argument. Dietz diagnoses "explainers" as suffering from an excessive self-consciousness that can only be remedied by "un grado aún mayor de consciencia, debidamente aplicado," that is, an even greater degree of consciousness, properly applied. Dietz also discusses "explanation" as an "infidelidad . . . a las premisas olsonias," a betrayal of Charles Olson's poetic principles.

15. The two quotations in this paragraph beginning "the constant flowage from meaning to meaning" and "We are free now to delight" are taken from an extended passage credited to Clark Coolidge that constitutes the whole of the entry for 18 February 1971.

16. See Dietz 15 for an illuminating discussion of Raworth's dissatisfaction with haiku as a "closed form."

17. One might wonder, since Raworth had been in touch with Creeley since the early 1960s, whether the direction of indebtedness could have traveled the other direction. In other words, could *Pieces* imitate Raworth instead of Raworth imitating *Pieces*? I do not deny that Creeley's book might show Raworth's influence in any

number of respects; nevertheless, I would assert that the specific form that the verse takes in *Pieces*—a long poem that consists of a radically paratactic, serial aggregate of minimalist compositions—does not appear to have a precise parallel in Raworth's writing before "Perpetual Motion." (Creeley, by the way, could have shared his poetic innovations with Raworth during a visit to England in 1970: see the "In London" section of Creeley's *A Day Book*, written during that trip, which not only repeats the form of *Pieces* but also mentions both Raworth and his wife Val [unpaginated].)

18. In this paragraph I am paraphrasing Robert Sheppard's Levinasian argument in "Poetics and Ethics." Elsewhere Sheppard states that his argument applies chiefly to verse written after "West Wind," but I believe that in its rudiments it applies equally to pre-"West Wind" long-skinnies such as *Writing*, *Ace*, and *Bolivia*. See "Whose" 202.

19. See Yve-Alain Bois and Rosalind Krauss, *Formless: A User's Guide* (New York: Zone, 1997); Dworkin, *Reading the Illegible* 79–81; McCaffery, *North of Intention* 201–21 and *Prior to Meaning* 3–14.

Chapter 3

1. This table, compiled from the thirteenth printing of the *Cantos*, is, it must be confessed, inexact. The editorial history of the *Cantos* is complex, and the frequency and distribution of the Chinese characters in the present volume does not precisely reflect either what Pound intended or what his first readers would have encountered. For instance, Ronald Bush recounts Pound's fight to include more Chinese characters in the *Pisan Cantos* against the wishes of James Laughlin (84n3). Nevertheless, the general trend that the table indicates is undeniable.

2. For a fuller explication of this passage, see Kearns 199–208.

3. For the purposes of this paper "ideogram," "ideograph," and "Chinese character" are used interchangeably, as in most Pound scholarship. I recognize, though, that "ideogram" is a contentious term. See Cayley 227.

4. Scholars of Chinese literature such as Shih-Hsiang Chen (260) and James J. Y. Liu (18–19) offer typical, thorough criticisms of Fenollosa's and Pound's Chinese reading practices. Hugh Kenner summarizes the debate well, and, although a staunch defender of Pound, he nonetheless feels compelled to itemize the "canonical" list of Pound's mistranslations from the Chinese (203ff). I have borrowed the term "etymosinology" from Angela Jung Palandri, who derives it from Achilles Fang (280). Since this essay was first published in 1997, the bibliography on Pound's approach to the Chinese language has grown enormously. See, e.g., the second chapter of Yunte Huang, *Transpacific Displacements: Ethnography, Translation and Intertextual Travel in Twentieth-Century American Literature* (Berkeley: U of California P, 2002); the first chapter of Josephine Park, *Apparitions of Asia: Modernist Form and Asian American Poetics* (New York: Oxford UP, 2008); and the first chapter of

Steven Yao, *Foreign Accents: Chinese American Verse from Exclusion to Post-Ethnicity* (New York: Oxford UP, 2010).

5. Another alternative to calling Pound a bad translator would of course be to declare his translation methods "good," either because the result is truer to the spirit of the original or because it expands our definitions of translation and forces us to rethink our understanding of language and communication. For a summary and critique of the positions on Pound's merits as a translator, see Chang 113–32. This essay shifts the emphasis away from translation so that discussion of Pound's use of Chinese characters might at last escape this intellectual sand trap.

6. See also Paul Wellen's "An Analytic Dictionary of Ezra Pound's Chinese Characters," which provides a handy compilation of the source materials for Pound's idiosyncratic readings of individual characters.

7. See, e.g., Jiewei Cheng's "Derrida and Ideographic Poetics," which presupposes that Pound ignores the "phonetic element" in Chinese writing (135). See also Cayley, who contends that ideograms work as "purely visual signifiers" (232); Géfin, who contends that Pound follows Fenollosa in disparaging the "phonetic word" (188); and Froula, who speaks ominously about the "obscure and silent presence" of the characters in the *Cantos* (144).

8. Pound's reading of Canto 99 in Washington, D.C., in 1958 supports this argument. He ignores many of the visual games in the text yet occasionally tries to compensate. For instance, he stops and explains how the words he is reading ("Man by negation") pair with a Chinese character only visible on the page.

9. See Géfin 187ff for an analysis of the importance of the "iconic" in Pound's ideogrammic poetics.

Chapter 4

1. Unfortunately, the Caedmon LP includes no specific information about the origin of these recordings. They could have been recorded during the "broadcast" that Stein reports making on first arriving in New York (*Everybody's* 290); more plausibly, they date to a somewhat later point, when she was filmed reading from *Four Saints in Three Acts* (288). That occasion was a confusing whirl, and it could easily have included further readings that failed to make it into the completed newsreel: "more came and more and more and then it was decided that I would be cinemaed [sic] and read to them, and we rehearsed that . . . our things were everywhere and perhaps some things disappeared and there was a great deal of apparatus" (177).

2. See <http://writing.upenn.edu/pennsound/x/Stein.html>, <http://www.ubu.com/sound/stein.html>, and <http://www.salon.com/audio/2000/10/05/stein/>. Last accessed 19 Dec. 2007.

3. See Meyer for an exemplary version of this issue. Although his remains by far the best discussion of Stein's intonation, he does rely on the recordings to in-

terpret much earlier work (302). For example, he concludes that intonation and word play are "equally balanced" in "If I Told Him," an assertion that treats the performative decisions of 1934–1935 as already fully present and legible in the 1924 text.

4. I have written out these lines as they appear in Stein, *A Stein Reader* 463.

5. I have transcribed this passage from the relevant sound file, which can be found at <http://writing.upenn.edu/pennsound/x/Stein.html> Last accessed 30 May 2011.

6. When transcribing passages from the recorded version of "If I Told Him," I have used a virgule to represent a short but audible pause in Stein's delivery.

Chapter 6

1. There is also a so-called forty-eighth translation—an electronic manipulation of Bergvall's voice—that runs continually in the background. See Piers Hugill, "Love and Grammar." He comments that this "produces sometimes a quite eerie undertone to the reading, a subvocalization of the text, that draws a concrete analogy with the transformations of text occurring at its 'surface.'" Unfortunately, I own audio equipment too primitive to distinguish this "undertone" from static and background noise. One can listen to this 2000 version of "Via" on the PennSound web site. See <http://writing.upenn.edu/pennsound/x/Bergvall.php> Last accessed 30 May 2011.

2. Compare this account to the one given in Perloff, "The Oulipo Factor." She analyzes the written text, whereas this article deliberately limits itself to discussing only the 2000 recording of "Via."

3. Since 2003, "Via" has appeared in at least two more versions. It can be found in a 2005 volume titled *Fig* from Salt Publishers, and it is the title track on the 2005 CD *Via: Poems 1994–2004* from Carcanet Press. (One can listen to the version of "Via" that appears on the 2005 CD on the PennSound web site, available at <http://writing.upenn.edu/pennsound/x/Bergvall.php> Last accessed 30 May 2011.)

4. Bergvall describes her composition process in a note reproduced in Perloff, "The Oulipo Factor": "Faced with the seemingly inexhaustible pool of translations into English of Dante's *Inferno*, I decided to collate all translations archived at the British Library up until May 2000."

5. The relevant sound files, along with many others, can be found on PennSound's Gertrude Stein page: <http://writing.upenn.edu/pennsound/x/Stein.html> Last accessed 30 May 2011.

6. For González-Torres, see Bergvall, "ex / Creme / ental / eaT / ing" 125.

7. Following these directions would create a version of González-Torres's *Untitled (Public Opinion)* (1991), an artwork owned by the Solomon R. Guggenheim Museum, New York. A photograph of this installation is available at <http://www .guggenheim.org/new-york/collections/collection-online/show-full/piece/?search=

%22Untitled%22%20%28Public%20Opinion%29&page=&f=Title&object=91.3969>
Last accessed 30 May 2011.

8. For Creed, see Bergvall, "ex / Creme / ental / eaT / ing" 132.

Chapter 7

1. These population statistics have been taken from Table 22 ("Nativity of the Population for Urban Places Ever Among the 50 Largest Urban Places Since 1870: 1850 to 1990") in Campbell J. Gibson and Emily Lennon's report "Historical Census Statistics on the Foreign-Born Population of the United States: 1850–1990." Available at <http://www.census.gov/population/ www/documentation/twps0029/ twps0029.html> Last accessed 30 May 2011.

2. These lyrics have been taken from the Lied and Art Song Text Page, available at <http://www.recmusic.org/lieder/> Last accessed 13 December 2007. Translation mine.

Chapter 8

I would like to thank Robert Bertholf, Stephen Fredman, Albert Gelpi, and Jeanne Heuving for their advice concerning earlier drafts of this chapter.

1. This broadside can be found in The Poetry Collection at the State University of New York at Buffalo.

2. See Hamilton, "*Letters*" 248–49 and Walker.

3. "Grtde" is of course short for Gertrude. Duncan often experiments with orthography and spelling; to reduce clutter, I have avoided using "[sic]" in this essay. One should assume that any peculiarities in quotations from Duncan appear in the original. The same is true of Stein.

4. Duncan's copy of the 1933 Plain Edition version of *GMP* is now part of The Poetry Collection at the State University of New York at Buffalo.

5. This passage is taken from Stein's "Many Many Women," one of the two "shorter stories" mentioned in *GMP*'s subtitle.

6. See the "Reading Stein" symposium in *L=A=N=G=U=A=G=E* no. 6 (Dec. 1978): 1–13. See also Hejinian 83–130 and Bernstein, *A Poetics* 142–49.

7. In "From a Notebook," Duncan claims he first read Stein when he was eighteen (*Fictive* 66). See Duncan and Levertov 819 for more about how Haas, Kraus, and Stein served as his guides to modernism.

8. See Duncan's 28 August 1955 letter to Charles Olson ("Ten Letters").

9. For *How to Write,* see Duncan and Levertov 14 and 24. For *The World Is Round,* see 11, 16, and 28. For *A First Reader,* see 28. For *Bee Time Vine,* see 29.

10. Jeff Hamilton contends that Duncan's turn to Stein is an outcome of a prior engagement with another female modernist, Laura Riding. See "*Letters*" 248–49 and "Wrath Moves in the Music."

11. See, e.g., Bernstein's essay "Thought's Measure," which insists that the more opaque a text's referential meaning becomes the more intensely a reader can "experience" it. At the extremes, "the text [becomes] viscerally present to you, [and] the 'content' and the 'experience of reading' are collapsed onto each other, the content being the experience of reading, the consciousness of the language and its movement and sound" (*Content's* 69).

12. For the chronology here, see Duncan and Levertov 52, 131, 140, and 806.

13. See n.2 of Hamilton, "Wrath Moves in the Music" (unpaginated).

14. I learned this fact in conversation with Robert J. Bertholf.

Chapter 9

1. For Shepherd's 2008 blog posts, see <http://www.poetryfoundation.org/harriet/author/rshepherd/> Last accessed 30 May 2011.

2. See, e.g., Archambeau; Bergman 80; Gilbert 258–59; Martin 261–79; and Thomas.

3. See <http://reginaldshepherd.blogspot.com/2008/04/narcissus-as-narcissus.html> Last accessed 30 May 2011.

4. In his "Editor's Note," Rowell does not explicitly label Shepherd a "third wave" poet, but later in the same issue of *Callaloo*, the poet Terrance Hayes, questioned by Rowell about third-wave writing, does mention him by name (1080).

5. Rowell's arguments are consonant with recent discussions of a "post-Soul" aesthetic discernible in African American culture from the mid-1980s onwards. See Reed, "Dark Room" 729 and 732–33. (Common alternatives to "post-Soul" include "post-black," coined by the visual artist Glenn Ligon, and "post-Negritude," proposed by the cultural critic Mark Reid. See Shaw 68 and 158n9.)

6. For Tolson's *Libretto of the Republic of Liberia* (1953) and Crane's *Bridge*, see Nielsen, *Writing* 55. For Crane's presence in Wright's *Soothsayers and Omens* (1976) see Doreski 186, 187, 189, 191, and 199. For Kaufman, see chapter 8 in Reed, *Hart*.

7. Philip Horton's 1937 biography represents a turning point in Crane scholarship. It made a grand show of outing the poet, and it proffered a "psychoanalytic explanation" of the "causes of his homosexuality" (60). Thereafter, Crane's homosexuality became a frequent, explicit topic in the secondary literature. See Spiller et al. 1344–45 and Tate 324–28.

8. For recent discussions of Crane's sexuality, see Merrill Cole, *The Other Orpheus: A Poetics of Modern Homosexuality* (New York: Routledge, 2003); chapter 1 of Christopher Nealon, *Foundlings: Lesbian and Gay Historical Emotion Before Stonewall* (Durham: Duke UP, 2001); Ernest Smith, "Spending out the Self: Homosexuality and the Poetry of Hart Crane," *Literature and Homosexuality*, ed. Michael J. Meyer (Amsterdam: Rhodopi, 2000): 161–81; Gordon Tapper, "Morton Minsky

Reads *The Bridge*: Hart Crane and the Meaning of Burlesque," *Arizona Quarterly* 56.4 (Winter 2000): 83–117; Michael Trask, *Cruising Modernism: Class and Sexuality in American Literature and Social Thought* (Ithaca: Cornell UP, 2003); and chapters 4 and 6 of John Vincent, *Queer Lyrics: Difficulty and Closure in American Poetry* (New York: Palgrave Macmillan, 2002).

9. "Snow queen" is slang for a black man whose preferred sex partners are white men.

10. See Vickery 21–36 for a concise history of Language writing.

11. See Vickery 120–28 for a series of examples of this problem.

12. See Stefans 48–50 for an overview of Berssenbrugge's importance within the history of experimentalism in "Asian North American poetry."

13. For Lacan, see Shepherd, "Coloring" 134 and *Otherhood* 96. For Fanon, see Shepherd, "Coloring" 134. For Bhabha, see 140.

14. See Burt, "The Elliptical Poets," for a series of examples and explanation.

15. The Lacanian "triad" of "imaginary, symbolic, real" is difficult to define clearly, in part because they are not separate qualities but rather intertwined, mobius-strip fashion (Shepherdson paragraphs 5–7). To roughly explain: The "imaginary" is the phantasmatic self that arises at the so-called mirror stage when an infant recognizes itself as a body apart from other bodies. The "symbolic" is the self that arises through accession to language and, by extension, through participation in society. The "real" is a lack excluded from but inaugural to the symbolic and imaginary. For a more complete account, see Zizek 96–97. For a Lacanian account of racialization arising from "the Real of epidermilization," see Sedinger 46–48.

16. For the masochistic erotics of Crane's "Voyages," see Reed, *Hart* 111–21.

17. For the term "propositional will" see Stewart 116; for "lyric possession" see 124.

18. For Lacan's use of the term "imaginary," see note 15 above.

19. For a suggestive overview of the range of scholarly material that appeared in response to Hemphill, Julien, and Riggs during the second half of the 1990s, consult Boggs.

20. See Shepherd, "Coloring" 140 for his agreement with Riggs's account of the positionality of being black and gay in American society but his disagreement regarding the political and ethical consequences of this.

21. See Cutrone 249–55 for a summary of (and preliminary responses to) objections against art and literature celebrating homoerotic interracial intimacy.

22. See DuPlessis and Nielsen, *Writing,* and North, chapters 6–7.

Chapter 10

1. Vickery freely and frequently acknowledges Waldrop's stature and accomplishments—see 9, 17, 42–43, 50, 64, 73, and 108–9—but, constrained by length limitations, she simply cannot provide extended treatment of every worthy, eligible

woman writer in a single book-length study. In the end, she is able to devote only two pages to discussing one of Waldrop's works in detail, the prose poem *Differences in Four Hand* (240–41).

2. See Freitag, "Rosmarie Waldrop's Language Games" 176–88. See also Retallack 339–40.

3. For Waldrop's earlier foray into collage—the collection *When They Have Senses* (1980)—see Freitag, "Rosmarie Waldrop's Language Games" 188–96.

4. The chief exception is Retallack's "A Conversation with Rosmarie Waldrop." Retallack states that she conducted the interview because she wished to bring greater exposure to Waldrop's novels (329–30), and, although the bulk of the interview focuses on *The Hanky of Pippin's Daughter,* its last six pages do concentrate almost exclusively on *A Form / of Taking / It All* (372–78). The topics treated include: the relationship between Waldrop, her fictionalized alter ego in the book, and the character Amy Lowell (371–72); the novel's thematics of exploration, conquest, and sexual dominion (372–73); and the anomalous, versified fourth section of the book, especially the parallels asserted between Columbus and Heisenburg (373–75). For another perspective on *A Form,* see Freitag, "Rosmarie Waldrop's Language Games" 256–58.

5. For accounts of Waldrop's engagement with Wittgenstein, see Perloff, *Wittgenstein's Ladder* 205–11; Kornelia Freitag, "Rosmarie Waldrop's Language Games" 151–269, esp. 196–226, in which she treats *Reproduction of Profiles;* and Keller 380–97, esp. 387–91, in which she investigates Waldrop's borrowings from Wittgenstein in *Lawn of the Excluded Middle.*

6. The lyric "Between" appeared in the volume *The Aggressive Ways of the Casual Stranger* (1972) and was reprinted in *Another Language: Selected Poems* (1997). For an acute reading of "Between," see Freitag, "Rosmarie Waldrop's Language Games" 157–60.

7. For the source of the title, see Creeley, *Collected Poems* 589 ("Mind's a form / of taking / it all," which appears, slightly revised, as an epigraph to Waldrop's novel, "mind is a form / of taking / it all" [155]). Waldrop has indicated that she used the title to refer specifically to the disjunctive juxtapositions in the novel's second section, "an enactment of 'taking it all'" (Retallack 375).

8. Translation mine. The original sentence reads, "trotzdem ist die wahl der figur vitus bering nur als standort zu werten, von dem aus beziehungen hergestellt werden, wie der fischer ein netz wirft, in der hoffnung, etwas zu fangen" (168).

9. Compare her earlier version of this argument in Retallack 347.

10. Compare what she tells Joan Retallack: "There is an immensity of data around us, and to choose the ones that are relevant and to connect them is my sense of life" (370).

11. Compare Waldrop's argument that "No text has a single author" in the course of elucidating her theory of the "palimpsest" in "Form and Discontent" 61.

12. See Kenner 360–81 for Pound's evolution from "vortex" to "subject rhyme" as the *Cantos* got underway. See esp. 365 and 376 for practical instances of the structuring device.

13. See Perloff, *Poetics* 180–89 for an analysis of Pound's habitual "linguistic deformation" of his source materials in the *Cantos*. The idea of the "*directio voluntatis*" comes to the fore in the later *Cantos,* from the *Pisan Cantos* onward. For explicit invocations, see Pound 467 and 576.

14. See Bürger 22–23 for a concise statement of his thesis that the "aim" of the avant-garde is to "reintegrate art into the praxis of life."

15. See "The Circulation of the Sign," the first chapter of Krauss's *The Picasso Papers.* Her primary purpose is to explain how the incorporation of newspaper into Cubist collages extends this visual gaming by fostering a "polyphonic space" in which signs cross and crisscross transgressively (85).

16. A friend who lives in Key West reports that urine will indeed cure the sting of a stingray—though Calamine lotion is preferable.

17. Waldrop recalls that her initial intent in placing "A Form of Memory" second was to set it up as "a fever vision" that Amy Lowell endures while "sick in Mexico." In other words, Waldrop sought to "normalize" the collage welter of part II by framing it with part I's "interior monologue" (Retallack 375). The particular echo-effect that I detail here may be a trace of this plan. In the book's final published form, though, the lack of any transition coupled with the drastic shift in style between parts I and II render it highly unlikely that a reader will consistently read "A Form of Memory" as akin to a medieval dream vision. As I proceed to explain, the interplay between the first two sections is less stable, more variable—in short, designedly disorienting.

18. For a fuller account of *Shorter American Memory* and its historiographical significance, see Freitag, "Decomposing American History."

Chapter 12

1. See Perloff, *Poetry* 146–54 for an overview of the origins and characteristics of this variety of free verse.

2. Nealon's "Camp Messianism" argues that today's poets in their thirties and forties do not exhibit a "depoliticized humanism," as some have argued (599); rather, their writing adopts a stance of "waiting" (597). They knowingly embrace "obsolete, misguided, or trivial" ideas and strategies, not because they believe that they will accomplish anything in the here and now, but because they might someday have their suffering redeemed or their visions fulfilled under different historical circumstances (581). Compare Spahr and Young, who argue that the contemporary vogue for "[r]est[r]ictive, numbe[r]-based p[r]ocesses and const[r]aints," while "avoid[ing] emotional and pe[r]sonal exp[r]essiveness," nonetheless in themselves do not guarantee the creation of "feminist, anti[r]acist self-investigation" (n.p.).

3. See the first chapter of Levinson's *Wordsworth's Great Period Poems*. She argues that Wordsworth's erasures of local traces of the Industrial Revolution are integral to the lyric's portrait of mental processes at work.

4. In addition to Watkin, for recent discussions of what could be called "procedural poetics" (although the term is not always used) see Dworkin, "The Imaginary Solution"; Harryman; Osman; Prevallet; Perloff, "The Oulipo Factor"; and Spahr and Young. See also David Huntsperger, "Tactical Reading: The Ideology of Form in David Antin's 'Novel Poem,'" *Textual Practice* 22.4 (2008) 705–32.

5. There is no unanimity among critics concerning the proper term for this poetic form. Alternatives to *abecedary* include *abecedarian* and *abecediary* as well as the Latin *abecedarium* and the French *abécédaire*. I have chosen to employ the shortest English derivative of the original Latin term.

6. Merrill 252. The original appears all in caps.

7. I make no claims for the originality of Pinsky's "ABC." Its publication simply coincided with and partly inspired a vogue for the form. Contemporary English-language abecedaries that predate *Jersey Rain* include Ciaran Carson's "The Letters of the Alphabet" (1996), Joshua Clover's "Zealous" (1997), Daniel Hoffman's "Essay on Style" (1986), Denise Levertov's "Relearning the Alphabet" (1970), and James Merrill's "Book of Ephraim" (1976). Lyn Hejinian's *Writing Is an Aid to Memory* (1978), while not strictly an abecedary, does obey alphabetic constraints in its layout; its opening word is "apple," echoing the "A is for apple" opening line common in abecedaries used as a schoolroom mnemonic. "Abecedarian" prose works include Walter Abish's *Alphabetical Africa* (New York: New Directions, 1974); Eve Rhymer's (Karen Reimer's) *Legendary, Loquacious, Lexical Love* (Chicago: Sarah Ranchouse, 1996); and Gilbert Sorrentino's *Splendide-Hôtel* (New York: New Directions, 1973).

8. I have followed the King James numbering. The same psalm appears as 118 in the Douay translation.

9. I have reproduced the opening lines of the alphabet poem as they appear in Ford (n.p.). I have retained the lineation, spelling, capitalization, and punctuation of the original, but I have omitted the accompanying pictures and the oversized letters that serve as rubrics for each couplet.

10. In addition to traditional acrostic abecedaries such as Carolyn Forché's "On Earth" (2003) and Harryette Mullen's "Jingle Jangle" (2002) and double abecedaries such as Mike Dockins's "Dead Critics Society" (2007) and Julie Larios's "Double Abecedarian: 1963" (2005), new variations have begun to proliferate such as the "found text" abecedary—Dan Farrell's *The Inkblot Record* (2000)—the partial abecedary—Thomas Sayers Ellis, "Marcus Garvey Vitamins" (2005)—the animated abecedary—Brian Kim Stefans, "The Dreamlife of Letters" (2000)—and the scrambled abecedary—Joel Bettridge, "potted" (2006). Campbell McGrath's *Pax Atomica* (2004) contains a conventional acrostic abecedary ("Xena, Warrior Prin-

cess"), an acrostic abecedary divided into irregular stanzas ("Of Pure Forms"), an acrostic abecedary with one to four entries per letter ("The Glann Road"), and a reverse abecedary ("Zeugma"). Karl Elder's *Mead* (2005) wins the prize for perseverance. It contains twenty-six blank verse abecedaries. In 2001 New Directions made available in the United States for the first time an English translation of Inger Christensen's *alfabet* (1981), a book-length abecedary that is also based on the Fibonacci series.

11. A friend points out that "Yeah Yeah Yeah" could also be a quotation from the Beatles song "She Loves You" (1963).

12. I concede that this reading of Feld's "Elegy: 19—" is incomplete. For the purposes of concision, it entirely ignores the first two parts of the poem sequence "Best and Only" of which it is part.

13. McCaffery's "The Wife of Bath's Tale" appears in a volume with the subtitle "Shorter Poems 1974–2002," so it could in fact have been written in the mid 1970s, but no date is provided, and the book credits no previous publication for any of its contents. It seems to have first appeared in print in 2002.

14. *Zorns Lemma* has been digitized and can be viewed online at Ubu.com as a streaming video. Available at <http://www.ubu.com/film/frampton.html> Last accessed 30 May 2011.

15. Gizzi 93.

16. I have reproduced the words from *Zorns Lemma* in all lower-case letters. In the original they employ different fonts, font sizes, and mixtures of majuscules and minuscules.

17. Louis Aragon's "Suicide" (1920) consists of the letters *A* to *Z* arranged into five lines. Kurt Schwitters's "Alphabet von hinten" (1921) is a sound poem that involves the recitation of the alphabet *Z* to *A*. He later reused this piece as a coda to his *Ursonate* (1922–32).

18. In the twelve-tone variety of serialism identified with the Second Viennese School, a score makes use of all pitches in the chromatic scale before repeating any of them. Examples include Alban Berg's Violin Concerto (1935), Schönberg's Piano Concerto, op. 42 (1942), and Webern's String Trio, op. 20 (1927).

19. See, e.g., Christie, who compares Goldsmith to a DJ (79–81); Schuster, who claims that Goldsmith's "uncreative writing" provokes the height of "creative reading" in annoyed audiences (112–13); and Schwartzburg, who emphasizes the weariness and exhaustion conveyed by the text (22–25).

Works Cited

Acheson, James, and Romana Huk, eds. *Contemporary British Poetry: Essays in Theory and Criticism*. Albany: SU New York P, 1996.

Archambeau, Robert. "A Portrait of Reginald Shepherd as Philoctetes." *Pleiades* 28.1 (2008): 159–71.

Ashbery, John. *The Mooring of Starting Out: The First Five Books of Poetry*. Hopewell, NJ: Ecco, 1997.

———. *Where Shall I Wander*. New York: Ecco, 2005.

Attridge, Derek. *The Singularity of Literature*. New York: Routledge, 2004.

Barnard, Rita. *The Great Depression and the Culture of Abundance: Kenneth Fearing, Nathanael West, and Mass Culture in the 1930s*. New York: Cambridge UP, 1995.

Barrell, John. "Subject and Sentence: The Poetry of Tom Raworth." *Critical Inquiry* 17 (Winter 1991): 386–409.

Barthes, Roland. *Fragments d'un discours amoureux*. Paris: Éditions du Seuil, 1977.

Bauman, Zygmunt. *Globalization: The Human Consequences*. New York: Columbia UP, 1998.

Bayer, Konrad. *Sämtliche Werke*. Ed. Gerhard Rühm. Stuttgart, Germany: Klett-Cotta, 1985.

Beach, Christopher. *Contemporary American Poetry Between Community and Institution*. Evanston, IL: Northwestern UP, 1999.

Bergman, David. "Race and the Violet Quill." *American Literary History* 9.1 (1997): 79–102.

Bergvall, Caroline. "ex / Creme / ental / eaT / ing: An Interview." *Sources* no. 12 (Spr. 2002): 123–35.

———. *Via: Poems 1994–2004*. Manchester: Carcanet, 2005. Media CD.

Bernstein, Charles. *Content's Dream*. Los Angeles: Sun & Moon P, 1986.

———. *A Poetics*. Cambridge, MA: Harvard UP, 1992.

Best, Stephen, and Sharon Marcus. "Surface Reading: An Introduction." *Representations* no. 108 (Fall 2009): 1–21.

Beston, Henry. *American Memory: Being a Mirror of the Stirring and Picturesque Past of Americans and the American Nation*. New York: Farrar and Rinehart, 1937.

Bettridge, Joel. "potted [sic]." *Drunken Boat* no. 8 (2006). <http://drunkenboat.com/db8/oulipo/feature-oulipo/toward/bettridge/potted.html> Last accessed 3 April 2008.

Bierce, Ambrose. *The Unabridged Devil's Dictionary*. Eds. David E. Schulz and S. T. Joshi. Athens: U of Georgia P, 2000.

Boggs, Nicholas. "Queer Black Studies: An Annotated Bibliography, 1994–1999." *Callaloo* 23.1 (2000): 479–94.

Bök, Christian. *Eunoia*. Toronto: Coach House Books, 2001.

Bürger, Peter. *The Theory of the Avant-Garde*. Minneapolis: U of Minnesota P, 1984.

Burt, Stephen. "The Elliptical Poets." *American Letters & Commentary* no. 11 (1999): 45–55.

———. *Parallel Play*. Saint Paul, MN: Graywolf Press, 2006.

———. "Sestina! or, The Fate of the Idea of Form." *Modern Language Philology* 105.1 (Aug. 2007): 218–41.

Bush, Ronald. "Modernism, Fascism and the Composition of Ezra Pound's *Pisan Cantos*." *Modernism/modernity* 2 (1995): 69–88.

Carson, Ciaran. "Letters from the Alphabet." *Opera et Cetera*. Newcastle: Bloodaxe, 1996.

Cayley, John. "The Literal Image: Illustrations in the *Cantos*." *Paideuma* 14 (1985): 227–51.

Chang, Yao-Xin. "Pound's Chinese Translations." *Paideuma* 17 (1988): 113–32.

Chaucer, Geoffrey. "An A.B.C." *The Complete Works*, vol. 1: *Romaunt of the Rose and Minor Poems*. Ed. Walter W. Skeat. Oxford: Clarendon Press, 1899. 261–71.

Chen, Shih-Hsiang. "Re-Creation of the Chinese Image." *The World of Translation*. New York: PEN American Center, 1987. 253–66.

Cheng, Jiewei. "Derrida and Ideographic Poetics." *British Journal of Aesthetics* 35 (1955): 134–44.

Christie, Jason. "Sampling the Culture: 4 Notes toward a Poetics of Plundergraphia and on Kenneth Goldsmith's *Day*." *Open Letter* 12.7 (Fall 2005): 69–74.

Clark, T. J. "El Lissitzky in Vitebsk." *Situating El Lissitzky: Vitebsk, Berlin, Moscow*. Eds. Nancy Perloff and Brian Reed. Los Angeles: Getty Research Institute, 2003. 199–210.

Clover, Joshua. "In the Act: John Ashbery's *And the Stars Were Shining*." *Iowa Review* 25.1 (Winter 1995): 177–82.

———. "Zealous." *Madonna anno domini*. Baton Rouge: Louisiana State UP, 1997. 62.

Cohen, Sarah. "Performing Identity in *The Hard Nut*: Stereotype, Modeling and the Inventive Body." *Yale Journal of Criticism* 11.2 (1998): 485–505.

Couser, G. Thomas. "Disability, Life Narrative, and Representation." *PMLA* 120.2 (March 2005): 602–05.

Craig, Cairns. "'Where Is the Nation You Promised?': American Voice in Modern Scottish and Irish Poetry." *Poetry and Contemporary Culture: The Question of*

Value. Eds. Andrew Michael Roberts and Jonathan Allison. Edinburg: Edinburg UP, 2002. 185–207.

Crane, Hart. *The Complete Poems.* Ed. Marc Simon. New York: Liveright, 1986.

———. *Complete Poems and Selected Letters.* Ed. Langdon Hammer. New York: Library of America, 2006.

———. *O My Land, My Friends: The Selected Letters.* Eds. Langdon Hammer and Brom Weber. New York: Four Walls Eight Windows, 1997.

Creeley, Robert. *Collected Poems.* Berkeley: U of California P, 1982.

———. *A Day Book.* New York: Scribner, 1972.

———. *Pieces.* New York: Scribner, 1969.

Cutrone, Christopher. "The Child with a Lion: The Utopia of Interracial Intimacy." *Gay and Lesbian Quarterly* 6.2 (2000): 249–85.

Davidson, Ian. "On 'All Fours'." *The Gig* no. 13/14 (May 2003): 217–222.

Derrida, Jacques. *Of Grammatology.* Baltimore: Johns Hopkins UP, 1976.

Dienhart, John M. "Stress in Reduplicative Compounds: Mish-Mash or Hocus-Pocus?" *American Speech* 74.1 (Spring 1999): 3–37.

Dietz, Bernd. "Inteligencia que no sustituye a la intuición: La poesía de Tom Raworth." *Revista Canaria de Estudios Ingleses* 11 (Nov. 1985): 1–23.

Dockins, Mike. "Dead Critics Society." *Best American Poetry 2007.* Ed. Heather McHugh. New York: Scribner, 2007. 27–28.

Doreski, C.K. "Decolonizing the Spirits: History and Storytelling in Jay Wright's *Soothsayers and Omens*." Nielsen, *Reading Race* 183–208.

Dorward, Nate. "On Raworth's Sonnets." *Chicago Review* 47.1 (Spr. 2001): 17–35.

———. "Tom Raworth: A Selected Bibliography." *The Gig* no. 13/14 (May 2003): 260–75.

DuBois, Andrew. *Ashbery's Forms of Attention.* Tuscaloosa: U of Alabama P, 2006.

Duncan, Robert. *Ground Work: Before the War/In the Dark.* Eds. Robert J. Berthoff and James Maynard. New York: New Directions, 2006.

———. *Fictive Certainties.* New York: New Directions, 1985.

———. Introduction. *Bending the Bow.* New York: New Directions Press, 1968. i–x.

———. *Letters: Poems 1953–1956.* Ed. Robert J. Bertholf. Chicago: Flood Editions, 2003.

———. *Play Time Pseudo Stein.* New York: The Tenth Muse, 1969. Unpaginated.

———. *Selected Poems.* New York: New Directions, 1993.

———. "Ten Letters." Eds. Robert J. Bertholf and James Maynard. *Jacket* no. 28 (Oct. 2005). n.p.

———. "Ten Prose Pieces, 1945 to 1978." Eds. Robert J. Bertholf and James Maynard. *Jacket* no. 28 (Oct. 2005). n.p.

Duncan, Robert, and Denise Levertov. *The Letters.* Eds. Robert J. Berthoff and Albert Gelpi. Stanford, CA: Stanford UP, 2004.

DuPlessis, Rachel Blau. "'Darken Your Speech': Racialized Cultural Work of Modernist Poets." Nielsen, *Reading Race* 43–83.

———. *Genders, Races and Religious Cultures in Modern American Poetry 1908–1934.* New York: Cambridge UP, 2001.

——. "Propounding Modernist Maleness: How Pound Managed a Muse." *Modernism/ modernity* 9.3 (Sept. 2002): 389–405.

Dworkin, Craig. "The Imaginary Solution." *Contemporary Literature* 48.1 (Spr. 2007): 28–60.

——. *Reading the Illegible.* Evanston: Northwestern UP, 2003.

——. "Seja Marginal." *Consequences of Innovation: 21st Century Poetics.* Ed. Craig Dworkin. New York: Roof, 2008. 7–24.

Dydo, Ulla. *Gertrude Stein: The Language That Rises: 1923–1934.* Evanston, IL: Northwestern UP, 2003.

Eagleton, Terry. *How to Read a Poem.* Oxford: Blackwell, 2007.

——. *Literary Theory: An Introduction.* Rev. ed. Minneapolis: U of Minnesota P, 1996.

Elder, Karl. *Mead: Twenty-Six Abecedariums.* Marshfield, WI: Marsh River Editions, 2005.

Eliot, T. S. *The Complete Poems and Plays 1909–1950.* New York: Harcourt, 1971.

Ellis, Thomas Sayers. "Marcus Garvey Vitamins." *The Maverick Room.* Saint Paul: Graywolf, 2005. 4.

Farrell, Dan. *The Inkblot Record.* Toronto: Coach House, 2000.

Feld, Andrew. *Citizen: Poems.* New York: Perennial, 2004.

Finger, Anne. "Writing Disabled Lives: Beyond the Singular." *PMLA* 120.2 (March 2005): 609–14.

Finkelstein, Norman. "Late Duncan: From Poetry to Scripture." *Twentieth Century Literature* 51.3 (Fall 2005): 341–72.

Forché, Carolyn. "On Earth." *Blue Hour: Poems.* New York: HarperCollins, 2003. 23–68.

Ford, Paul Leicester, ed. *The New England Primer: A Reprint of the Earliest Known Edition.* New York: Dodd, Mead, and Co., 1899.

Francese, Joseph. "On Homoerotic Tension in Michelangelo's Poetry." *MLN* 117.1 (2002): 17–47.

Freccero, Carla. *Queer/Early/Modern.* Durham, NC: Duke UP, 2006.

Freitag, Kornelia. "Decomposing American History." *Construction and Contestation of American Cultures and Identities in the Early National Period.* Ed. Udo J. Hebel. Heidelberg, Germany: Carl Winter Universitatsverlag, 1999. 443–59.

——. "Rosmarie Waldrop's Language Games," *Cultural Criticism in Contemporary Women's Experimental Writing in the U.S.A.* Unpublished Dissertation. University of Potsdam (Germany), 2000. 151–269.

Fried, Michael. "*Hover* by Kenneth Noland." *Acquisitions (Fogg Art Museum)* no. 1964 (1964): 60–63.

Froula, Christine. "The Pound Error: The Limits of Authority in the Modern Epic." *Ezra Pound: Modern Critical Views.* Ed. Harold Bloom. New York: Chelsea House, 1987. 141–76.

Gander, Forrest. "Often a Strange Desire." Rev. of *Girls on the Run* by John Ashbery. *Jacket* no. 8 (July 1999): n.p.

Gardner, Jared. "'Our Native Clay': Racial and Sexual Identity and the Making of Americans in *The Bridge*." *American Quarterly* 44.1 (March 1992): 24–50.

Géfin, Laszlo K. "So-shu and Picasso: Semiotic / Semantic Aspects of the Poundian Ideogram." *Papers on Language and Literature* 28 (1992): 185–205.

Gilbert, Roger. "Awash with Angels: The Religious Turn in Nineties Poetry." *Contemporary Literature* 42.2 (Summer 2001): 238–69.

Ginsberg, Allen. *Collected Poems 1947–1997.* New York: HarperCollins, 2006.

Gizzi, Peter. *The Outernationale.* Middletown, CT: Wesleyan UP, 2007.

———. *Periplum.* Penngrove, CA: Avec, 1992.

Goble, Mark. "Cameo Appearances; or, When Gertrude Stein Checks into Grand Hotel." *Modern Language Quarterly* 62.2 (2001): 117–63.

Goldsmith, Kenneth. *Day.* Great Barrington, MA: The Figures, 2003.

Greenberg, Clement. *Collected Essays and Writings,* vol. 4. Ed. John O'Brian. Chicago: U of Chicago P, 1995.

Greene, Sally. "'Things Money Cannot Buy': Carl Sandburg's Tribute to Virginia Woolf." *Journal of Modern Literature* 24.2 (Winter 2001): 291–308.

Grenier, Robert. *for Larry Eigner. The Dust and Light Mobile Anthology of Poetry.* Ed. Karl Young. <http://www.concentric.net/ ~lndb/greneier/lgl00.htm> Last accessed 20 Aug. 2000.

———. "ON THE EMPTY / SUBLIME." *non* [sic] no. 2 (Feb. 1998). <http://socrates .berkeley.edu/~moriarty/2/grenier.htm> Last accessed 17 Aug. 2000.

———. "A Packet for Robert Creeley." *Boundary 2* 6.3/7.1 (Spring-Fall 1978): 421–41.

Hamilton, Jeff. "*Letters,* Abroad and Back." Rev. of 2003 ed. of *Letters* by Robert Duncan. *Chicago Review* 51 (Spr. 2005): 242–49.

———. "Wrath Moves in the Music: Robert Duncan, Laura Riding, Craft and Force in Cold War Poetics." *Jacket* no. 26 (Oct. 2004): n.p.

Harrington, Joseph. *Poetry and the Public: The Social Form of Modern U.S. Poetics.* Middletown, CT: Wesleyan UP, 2002.

Harryman, Carla. "Rules and Restraints in Women's Experimental Writings." *We Who Love to Be Astonished: Experimental Women's Writing and Performance Poetics.* Eds. Laura Hinton, Cynthia Hogue, and Rachel Blau DuPlessis. Tuscaloosa, U of Alabama P, 2002. 116–24.

Haselstein, Ulla. "Gertrude Stein's Portraits of Matisse and Picasso." *New Literary History* 34.4 (2003): 723–43.

Hatlen, Burton. "Regionalism and Internationalism in Basil Bunting's *Briggflatts.*" *Yale Journal of Criticism* 13.1 (2000): 49–66.

Hejinian, Lyn. *The Language of Inquiry.* Berkeley: U of California P, 2000.

———. *Writing Is an Aid to Memory.* Berkeley: The Figures, 1978.

Hemphill, Essex. Introduction. Hemphill, *Brother to Brother* xv-xxxi.

Hemphill, Essex, ed. *Brother to Brother: New Writings by Black Gay Men.* Boston: Alyson, 1991.

Hesse, Eva. Introduction. *New Approaches to Ezra Pound.* Ed. Eva Hesse. Berkeley: U of California P, 1969. 13–53.

Hitchcock, Peter. "'It Dread Inna England': Linton Kwesi Johnson, Dread, and Dub Identity." *Postmodern Culture* 4.1 (1993).

Hoffman, Daniel. "Essay on Style." *Hudson Review* 39.3 (Fall 1986): 449–51.

Hollo, Anselm. "A Conversation with Gunnar Harding." *The Gig* no. 13/14 (May 2003): 75–82.

Hugill, Piers. "Love and Grammar." Rev. of *Fig: Goan Atom 2* and *Via: Poems 1994–2004* by Caroline Bergvall. *Jacket* no. 31 (Oct. 2006): n.p.

Huk, Romana. "In AnOther's Pocket: The Address of the 'Pocket Epic' in Postmodern Black British Poetry." *Yale Journal of Criticism* 13.1 (Spr. 2000): 23–47.

Huk, Romana, ed. *Assembling Alternatives: Reading Postmodern Poetries Transnationally*. Middletown, CT: Wesleyan UP, 2003.

Jakobson, Roman. "Two Aspects of Language and Two Types of Aphasic Disturbances." *Fundamentals of Language*. Eds. Roman Jakobson and Morris Halle. The Hague: Mouton, 1956. 52–82.

Jameson, Fredric. *Postmodernism, or the Cultural Logic of Late Capitalism*. Durham, NC: Duke UP, 1991.

———. "The Selves in the Texts: Sartre and Literary Criticism." *Critical Essays on Jean-Paul Sartre*. Ed. Robert Wilcocks. Boston: G. K. Hall, 1988. 97–119.

Jenkins, Henry. *Textual Poachers: Television Fans and Participatory Culture*. New York: Routledge, 1992.

Jung, Hwa Jol. "Misreading the Ideogram: From Fenollosa to Derrida and McLuhan." *Paideuma* 13 (1984): 211–27.

Kalaidjian, Walter. *American Culture Between the Wars: Revisionary Modernism and Postmodern Critique*. New York: Columbia UP, 1993.

Kearns, George. "Reading Pound Writing Chinese: A Page from *Rock-Drill*." *Ezra Pound*. Ed. Harold Bloom. New York: Chelsea House, 1987. 199–208.

Keats, John. *Poems*. Boston: Ginn, 1896.

Keller, Lynn. "'Fields of Pattern-Bounded Unpredictability': Recent Palimptexts by Rosmarie Waldrop and Joan Retallack." *Contemporary Literature* 42.2 (Summer 2001): 376–411.

Kenner, Hugh. *The Pound Era*. Berkeley: U of California P, 1971.

Kleege, Georgina. "Reflections on Writing and Teaching Disability Autobiography." *PMLA* 120.2 (March 2005): 606–09.

Krauss, Rosalind. "Le cours de latin." *Cahiers du Musée d'art moderne* no. 53 (Fall 1995): 5–23.

———. *The Picasso Papers*. New York: Farrar, 1998.

Krauss, Rosalind, and Yve-Alain Bois. *Formless: A User's Guide*. New York: Zone, 1997.

Larios, Julie. "Double Abecedarian: 1963." *Georgia Review* 59.2 (Summer 2005): 231.

Leddy, Michael. "Lives and Art: John Ashbery and Henry Darger." *Jacket* no. 17 (June 2002): n.p.

Levertov, Denise. "Relearning the Alphabet" (1970). *Poems 1968–1972*. New York: New Directions, 1987. 90–100.

Levinson, Marjorie. "What Is New Formalism?" *PMLA* 122.2 (March 2007): 558–69.

———. *Wordsworth's Great Period Poems: Four Essays*. New York: Cambridge UP, 1986.

Liu, James J.Y. *The Art of Chinese Poetry*. Chicago: U of Chicago P, 1962.

Lukács, Georg. *History and Class Consciousness*. Trans. Rodney Livingstone. Cambridge, MA: MIT P, 1971.

McCaffery, Steve. *Bouma Shapes: Shorter Poems 1974–2002*. La Laguna, Canary Islands: Zasterle, 2002.

——. *North of Intention: Critical Writings 1973–1986*. New York: Roof, 1986.

——. *Prior to Meaning: The Protosemantic and Poetics*. Evanston: Northwestern UP, 2001.

McGrath, Campbell. *Pax Atomica*. New York: Ecco, 2004.

McHale, Brian. "Brit-Pop; or, Bringing It All Back Home: On Andrew Greig's *Western Swing*." *Yale Journal of Criticism* 13.1 (Spr. 2000): 195–205.

Mackey, Nathaniel. *Discrepant Engagement: Dissonance, Cross-Culturality, and Experimental Writing*. Tuscaloosa: U of Alabama P, 2000.

MacLeish, Archibald. "The Tradition of the People." Rev. of *The People, Yes* by Carl Sandburg. *New Masses* 1 (Sept 1936): 25–27.

Marin, Louis. "Toward a Theory of Reading in the Visual Arts: Poussin's *The Arcadian Shepherds*." *The Reader in the Text: Essays on Audience and Interpretation*. Princeton: Princeton UP, 1980. 293–324.

Martin, Robert K. *The Homosexual Tradition in American Poetry*. Rev. ed. Iowa City: U of Iowa P, 1998.

Masters, Edgar Lee. *Starved Rock*. New York: Macmillan, 1919.

Merleau-Ponty, Maurice. *The Phenomenology of Perception*. Routledge: New York, 1958.

Merrill, James. *The Changing Light at Sandover*. New York: Knopf, 1982.

Meyer, Steven. *Irresistible Dictation: Gertrude Stein and the Correlations of Writing*. Stanford: Stanford UP, 2001.

Michelson, Annette. "About Snow." *October* no. 8 (Spr. 1979): 111–25.

——. "Frampton's Sieve." *October* no. 32 (Spr. 1985): 151–66.

Middleton, Peter. *Distant Reading: Performance, Readership, and Consumption in Contemporary Poetry*. Tuscaloosa: U of Alabama P, 2005.

——. "Silent Critique: Tom Raworth's Early Books of Poetry." *The Gig* no. 13/14 (May 2003): 7–29.

Moretti, Franco. *Graphs, Maps, Trees: Abstract Models for a Literary History*. London: Verso, 2005.

Mullen, Harryette. *Sleeping with the Dictionary*. Berkeley: U of California P, 2002.

Munton, Alan. "Raworth's Community of Readers: 'Firewall.'" *The Gig* no. 13/14 (May 2003): 242–52.

Nealon, Christopher. "Camp Messianism, or, the Hopes of Poetry in Late-Late Capitalism." *American Literature* 76.3 (Sept. 2004): 579–602.

——. *Foundlings: Lesbian and Gay Historical Emotion Before Stonewall*. Durham: Duke UP, 2001.

Nebeker, Eric. "Broadside Ballads, Miscellanies, and the Lyric in Print." *ELH* 76.4 (Winter 2009): 989–1013.

Nelson, Cary. *Repression and Recovery: Modern American Poetry and the Politics of Cultural Memory, 1910–1945*. Madison: U of Wisconsin P, 1989.

——. *Revolutionary Memory: Recovering the Poetry of the American Left.* New York: Routledge, 2001.

Nielsen, Aldon Lynn. *Integral Music: Languages of African American Innovation.* Tuscaloosa: U of Alabama P, 2004.

——. *Writing Between the Lines: Race and Intertextuality.* Athens: U of Georgia P, 1994.

Nielsen, Aldon Lynn, ed. *Reading Race in American Poetry: An Area of Act.* Urbana U of Illinois P, 2000.

Niven, Penelope. *Carl Sandburg: A Biography.* New York: Scribner's, 1991.

North, Michael. *The Dialect of Modernism: Race, Language, and Twentieth-Century Literature.* New York: Oxford UP, 1994.

O'Hara, Frank. *Collected Poems.* Ed. Donald Allen. Berkeley: U of California P, 1971.

Olson, Charles. "Projective Verse." *Human Universe and Other Essays.* New York: Grove, 1967. 51–61.

Osman, Jena. "'Multiple Functioning': Procedural Actions in the Poetry of Tina Darragh." Wallace and Marks, *Telling It Slant* 255–79.

Palandri, Angela Jung. "'The Stone Is Alive in My Hand'—Ezra Pound's Chinese Translations." *Literature East and West* 10 (1966): 278–91.

Palmer, Michael. Introduction to *Ground Work* by Robert Duncan. ix–xiv.

Pérez, Vincent. "Movies, Marxism, and Jim Crow: Richard Wright's Cultural Criticism." *Texas Studies in Literature and Language* 43.2 (2001): 142–168.

Perkins, David. *A History of Modern Poetry*, vol 1: *From the 1890s to the High Modernist Mode.* Cambridge, MA: Harvard UP, 1976.

Perloff, Marjorie. "'Barbed Wire Entanglements': The 'New American Poetry,' 1930–1932." *Modernism/modernity* 2.1 (1995): 145–175.

——. *The Dance of the Intellect: Studies in the Poetry of the Pound Tradition.* New York: Cambridge UP, 1985.

——. "Filling the Space with Trace: 'Letters from Yaddo.'" *The Gig* no. 13/14 (May 2003): 130–44.

——. "Janus-Faced Blockbuster." *Symplokē* 8.1–2 (2000): 205–213.

——. "The Oulipo Factor: The Procedural Poetics of Christian Bök and Caroline Bergvall." *Jacket* no. 23 (Aug. 2003): n.p.

——. *The Poetics of Indeterminacy: Rimbaud to Cage.* Princeton: Princeton UP, 1981.

——. *Poetry On and Off the Page: Essays on Emergent Occasions.* Evanston, IL: Northwestern UP, 1998.

——. "Still Time for Surprises: John Ashbery's Recent Books." *Thumbscrew* 18 (Spring 2001): 46–48.

——. *Wittgenstein's Ladder: Poetic Language and the Strangeness of the Ordinary.* Chicago: U of Chicago P, 1996.

Perril, Simon. "'What Rhymes with Cow / And Starts with an N': Tom Raworth's Time and Motion Studies." *The Gig* no. 13/14 (May 2003): 108–29.

Pfeiler, Martina. *Contemporary American Performance Poets.* Tübingen: Gunter Narr Verlag, 2003.

Pinsky, Robert. *Jersey Rain: Poems*. New York: Farrar, 2000.

Pound, Ezra. "Canto 99." *Ezra Pound Reading His Poetry*, record 2. Caedmon, TC 1155, 1958.

——. *The Cantos*. Thirteenth printing. New York: New Directions, 1993.

——. "I Gather the Limbs of Osiris." *Selected Prose 1909–65*. New York: New Directions, 1973. 19–43.

——. *Shih-ching: The Classic Anthology Defined by Confucius*. Cambridge, MA: Harvard UP, 1982.

Prevallet, Kristin. "Investigating the Procedure: Poetry and the Source." Wallace and Marks, *Telling It Slant* 115–29.

Ragland-Sullivan, Ellie. "Jacques Lacan: Feminism and the Problem of Gender Identity." *SubStance* 11.3 (1982): 6–20.

Ramazani, Jahan. *The Hybrid Muse: Postcolonial Poetry in English*. Chicago: U Chicago P, 2001.

Raworth, Tom. *Collected Poems*. Manchester: Carcanet, 2003.

——. "Notebook." *The Gig* no. 13/14 (May 2003): 89–101.

Rechy, John. *The Sexual Outlaw*. Rev. ed. New York: Grove, 1990.

Reed, Brian M. "The Darkroom Collective and Post-Soul Poetics." *African American Review* 41.4 (Winter 2007): 727–47.

——. *Hart Crane: After His Lights*. Tuscaloosa: U of Alabama P, 2006.

Retallack, Joan. "A Conversation with Rosmarie Waldrop." *Contemporary Literature* 40.3 (1999): 329–77.

——. "Geometries of a Meadow." *The Gig* no. 13/14 (May 2003): 253–58.

Rexroth, Kenneth. *One Hundred Poems from the Japanese*. Verona, Italy: New Directions, 1955.

Riggs, Marlon. "Tongues untied." Hemphill, *Brother to Brother* 200–205.

Rossetti, Christina. *The Goblin Market, The Prince's Progress, and Other Poems*. London: Macmillan, 1875.

Sandburg, Carl. *The Letters*. Ed. Herbert Mitgang. New York: Harcourt Brace, 1968.

——. *The People, Yes*. New York: Harcourt Brace, 1936.

Schuster, Joshua. "On Kenneth Goldsmith: The Avant-Garde at a Stand-Still." *Open Letter* 12.7 (Fall 2005): 102–09.

Schwartz, K. Robert. "Steve Reich: Music as a Gradual Process: Part I." *Perspectives on New Music* 19.1/2 (Fall 1980/Summer 1981): 373–92.

Schwartzburg, Molly. "Encyclopedic Novelties: On Kenneth Goldsmith's Tomes." *Open Letter* 12.7 (Fall 2005): 21–35.

Sedinger, Tracey. "Nation and Identification: Psychoanalysis, Race, and Sexual Difference." *Cultural Critique* 50 (2002): 40–73.

Serres, Michel. *Hermes*. Baltimore: Johns Hopkins UP, 1982.

Shaw, Gwendolyn Dubois. *Seeing the Unspeakable: The Art of Kara Walker*. Durham, NC: Duke UP, 2004.

Shepherd, Reginald. "Coloring Outside the Lines: An Essay at Definition." *Callaloo* 22.1 (1999): 134–140.

——. Interview with Charles H. Rowell. *Callaloo* 20.2 (1998): 290–307.

——. *Orpheus in the Bronx: Essays on Identity, Politics, and the Freedom of Poetry.* Ann Arbor: U of Michigan P, 2007.

——. *Otherhood.* Pittsburgh: U of Pittsburgh P, 2003.

——. *Wrong.* Pittsburgh: U of Pittsburgh P, 1999.

Shepherdson, Charles. "The Intimate Alterity of the Real." *Postmodern Culture* 6.3 (1996): n.p.

Sheppard, Robert. "Poetics and Ethics: The Saying and the Said in the Linguistically Innovative Poetry of Tom Raworth." *Critical Survey* 14.2 (May 2002): 75–88.

——. "'Whose Lives Does the Government Affect': Looking Back at *West Wind*." *The Gig* no. 13/14 (May 2003): 192–203.

Shulman, Robert. *The Power of Political Art: The 1930s Literary Left Reconsidered.* Chapel Hill: U of North Carolina P, 2000.

Skinner, Jonathan. "Lines that Go Bump in the Night: *Writing*." *The Gig* no. 13/14 (May 2003): 172–76.

Smith, Ernest. "Spending Out the Self: Homosexuality and the Poetry of Hart Crane." *Literature and Homosexuality.* Ed. Michael Meyer. Amsterdam: Rhodopi, 2000. 161–81.

Sole, Kelwyn. "'The Deep Thoughts the One in Need Falls into': Quotidian Experience and the Perspectives of Poetry in Postliberation South Africa." *Postcolonial Studies and Beyond.* Eds. Ania Loomba et al. Durham, NC: Duke UP, 2005. 182–205.

Solomon, William. "Disinterring Edward Dahlberg." *Texas Studies in Literature and Language* 43.4 (2001): 389–417.

Spahr, Juliana, and Stephanie Young. "Foulipo." *Drunken Boat* no. 8 (2006). <http://drunkenboat.com/db8/index.html> Last accessed 15 March 2008.

Spiller, Robert et al., eds. *Literary History of the United States*, vol. 2. New York: Macmillan, 1948.

Stefans, Brian Kim. *The Dreamlife of Letters* (2000). UbuWeb. Available at <http://www.ubu.com/contemp/stefans/dream/index.html> Last accessed 3 April 2008.

——. "Remote Parsee: An Alternative Grammar of Asian North American Poetry." Wallace and Marks, *Telling It Slant* 43–75.

Stein, Gertrude. *Everybody's Autobiography.* Cambridge, MA: Exact Change, 1993.

——. *Geography and Plays.* Boston: Four Seas, 1922.

——. *The Gertrude Stein Reader.* Ed. Richard Kostalenetz. New York: Cooper Square P, 2002.

——. *Gertrude Stein Reads from her Work.* LP. Caedmon, 1956.

——. *How to Write.* New York: Dover, 1975.

——. *Lectures in America.* Boston: Virago, 1988.

——. *The Making of the Americans: Being a History of a Family's Progress.* Normal, IL: Dalkey Archive P, 1995.

——. *A Stein Reader.* Ed. Ulla Dydo. Evanston, IL: Northwestern UP, 1993.

Stewart, Susan. *Poetry and the Fate of the Senses.* Chicago: U of Chicago P, 2002.

Sundquist, Eric. "Bringing Home the Word: Magic, Lies and Silence in Hart Crane." *ELH* 44.2 (Summer 1977): 376–99.

Tapper, Gordon. "Morton Minsky Reads *The Bridge*: Hart Crane and the Meaning of Burlesque." *Arizona Quarterly* 56.4 (Winter 2000): 83–117.

Tate, Allen. *Essays of Four Decades*. Chicago: Swallow, 1968.

Teres, Harvey. "Left and Literary." Rev. of *American Culture Between the Wars: Revisionary Modernism and Postmodern Critique* by Walter Kalaidjian. *Modernism/ modernity* 2.1 (1995): 177–184.

Terrell, Carroll. *A Companion to the Cantos of Ezra Pound*. Berkeley: U of California P, 1984.

Thomas, Max. "Mighty Lines." *Iowa Review* 30.2 (2000): 169–75.

Trethewey, Natasha. *Native Guard*. New York: Houghton Mifflin, 2006.

Thurston, Michael. *Making Something Happen: American Political Poetry Between the World Wars*. Chapel Hill: U of North Carolina P, 2001.

Tucker, Herbert. "Tactical Formalism: A Response to Caroline Levine." *Victorian Studies* 49.1 (Fall 2006): 85–93.

Tuma, Keith. "Collaborating with 'Dark Senses.'" *The Gig* no. 13/14 (May 2003): 207–16.

———. *Fishing by Obstinate Isles: Modern and Postmodern British Poetry and American Readers*. Evanston, IL: Northwestern UP, 1998.

Vadillo, Ana Pareja. *Women Poets and Urban Aestheticism: Passengers of Modernity*. New York: Palgrave, 2005.

Vickery, Ann. *Leaving Lines of Gender: A Feminist Genealogy of Language Writing*. Hanover, NH; Wesleyan UP, 2000.

Vincent, John. "Reports of Looting and Insane Buggery Behind the Altars: John Ashbery's Queer Poetics." *Twentieth Century Literature* 44.2 (Summer 1998): 155–75.

Waldrop, Rosmarie. *Against Language? 'Dissatisfaction with Language' as Theme and Impulse Towards Experiments in Twentieth Century Poetry*. The Hague: Mouton, 1971.

———. "Between, Always." Introduction to *The Hanky of Pippin's Daughter & A Form / of Taking / It All*. vii–xviii.

———. "Form and Discontent." *Diacritics* 26.3–4 (1996): 54–62.

———. *A Form / of Taking / It All*. Barrytown, NY: Station Hill P, 1990. Reprinted in *The Hanky of Pippin's Daughter & A Form / of Taking / It All*. 153–248.

———. *The Hanky of Pippin's Daughter & A Form / of Taking / It All*. Evanston, IL: Northwestern UP, 2001.

———. *Shorter American Memory*. Providence, RI: Paradigm P, 1988.

Walker, Jayne L. "Excercises in Disorder: Duncan's Imitations of Gertrude Stein." *Robert Duncan: Scales of the Marvelous*. Eds. Robert J. Bertholf and Ian W. Reid. New York: New Directions, 1979. 22–35.

Wallace, Mark, and Steven Marks, eds. *Telling It Slant: Avant-Garde Poetics of the 1990s*. Tuscaloosa: U of Alabama P, 2002.

Ward, Geoff. "Tom Raworth and the Invisibles." *Cambridge Quarterly* 31.1 (2002): 17–32.

Watkin, William. "'Systematic Rule-Governed Violations of Convention': The Poetics of Procedural Constraint in Ron Silliman's *BART* and *Chinese Notebook.*" *Contemporary Literature* 48.4 (Winter 2007): 499–529.

Watten, Barrett. "The Secret History of the Equal Sign: *L=A=N=G=U=A=G=E* between Discourse and Text." *Poetics Today* 20.4 (1999): 581–627.

Weiss, Allen. "Frampton's Lemma, Zorn's Dilemma." *October* no. 32 (Spr. 1985): 118–28.

Wellen, Paul. "An Analytical Dictionary of Ezra Pound's Chinese Characters." *Paideuma* 25 (Winter 1996): 59–100.

Wershler-Henry, Darren. *The Tapeworm Foundry, andor [sic], the Dangerous Prevalence of Imagination.* Toronto: Anansi, 2000. Unpaginated.

Whitman, Walt. *Leaves of Grass.* New York: Modern Library, 1921.

Wilkinson, John. "Tripping the Light Fantastic: Tom Raworth's *Ace.*" *The Gig* no. 13/14 (May 2003): 145–60.

Williams, William Carlos. "Carl Sandburg's *Complete Poems.*" *Poetry* 78.6 (Sept. 1951): 345–51.

Wilson, Sarah. "Gertrude Stein and the Radio." *Modernism/modernity* 11.2 (Apr. 2004): 261–78.

Wing, Catherine. *Enter Invisible.* Louisville: Sarabande, 2005.

Woods, Gregory. *Articulate Flesh: Male Homo-Eroticism and Modern Poetry.* New Haven: Yale UP, 1990.

Woolley, Lisa. *American Voices of the Chicago Renaissance.* DeKalb: Northern Illinois UP, 2000.

Yannella, Philip. *The Other Carl Sandburg.* Jackson: U of Mississippi P, 1996.

Yee, Cordell D. K. "Discourse on Ideogrammic Method: Epistemology and Pound's Poetics." *American Literature* 59 (1987): 242–56.

Yingling, Thomas. *Hart Crane and the Homosexual Text: New Thresholds, New Anatomies.* Chicago: U of Chicago P, 1990.

Ziarek, Krzysztof. "The Turn of Art: The Avant-Garde and Power." *New Literary History* 33.1 (2002): 89–107.

Zizek, Slavoj. "The Rhetoric of Power." *Diacritics* 31.1 (2001): 91–104.

Index